WHY ARE THE BRITISH BAD AT MANUFACTURING ?

WHY ARE THE BRITISH BAD AT MANUFACTURING ?

KAREL WILLIAMS, JOHN WILLIAMS AND DENNIS THOMAS

Routledge & Kegan Paul

London, Boston, Melbourne and Henley

First published in 1983
by Routledge & Kegan Paul plc
39 Store Street, London WC1E 7DD,
9 Park Street, Boston, Mass. 02108, USA,
296 Beaconsfield Parade, Middle Park,
Melbourne, 3206, Australia, and
Broadway House, Newtown Road,
Henley-on-Thames, Oxon RG9 1EN
Set in 10pt Baskerville by
Input Typesetting Ltd, London
and printed in Great Britain by
T. J. Press (Padstow) Ltd
Padstow, Cornwall

ISBN 0-7100-9561-9

Contents

Preface ix

Introduction: Why are the British bad at manufacturing? 1
1 The nature and consequences of British manufacturing's
   relative failure 2
2 Explanatory frameworks 16
3 Enterprise control over the labour process 34
4 Market structure and the composition of demand 47
5 Relation to financial institutions (a) external finance from
   banks and stock exchange 58
6 Relation to financial institutions (b) the merger boom and
   stock exchange market in issued securities 76
7 Government economic policies 92
Appendix A British trade in manufactures 111
   Notes to appendix A 120
   Addendum A The CSO and National Institute series on
      import penetration and export/sales ratios 122
   Addendum B Estimation procedures used in calculating UK
      manufacturing sales, 1955–69 125
References 126

Case studies 131

1 GEC – an outstanding success? 133
   1 A flying start 134
   2 The stock market 137
   3 Financial success 140

4 Manufacturing – a growing concern? 143
  (a) Output 143
  (b) Exports 147
  (c) Labour 151
5 The cash reserve and acquisitions 153
6 Innovation and the long view 157
  (a) Innovation and some producer goods 157
  (b) Time horizons in consumer products 162
7 Labour and the workforce 168
8 Government 171
9 Conclusion 175
Notes 176
References 177

2 Shipbuilding – demand linkage and industrial decline 179
1 Relative decline 180
2 Changing patterns of demand 184
3 The British response 187
4 Why so poor? 188
5 The demand linkage 191
6 The contribution of government 196
7 Enterprise calculations 204
  (a) Two miscalculations 204
  (b) Getting it right 207
8 Conclusion 212
Notes 213
References 214

3 BMC/BLMC/BL – a misunderstood failure 217
1 BMC's output expansion and its results, 1952–68 219
2 The 1968 merger and saving the company with new models, 1968–74 225
3 Market limitations at home 229
4 Market limitations abroad 235
5 Product-led decline, 1971–9 239
6 Accounting practices delay a profits crisis, 1971–4 246
7 The workforce as scapegoats 251
8 Profits crises after 1974 259
9 Why did Ryder fail? 263
10 BL under Edwardes, 1977–82 266

Appendix B Production totals for selected BMC/BLMC models,
1958–81 269
  Notes to appendix B 272
Appendix C The UK market for new cars, 1945–80 274
References 281

Index 283

Preface

Alongside the long-running, still-continuing debate on the reasons why Britain emerged as the first industrial nation towards the end of the eighteenth century, there has in recent years been a growing discussion of the reasons for Britain's relative economic decline in the second half of the twentieth century. Our justification for adding one more book to the literature is that we have aimed at an approach that is sufficiently different to open out a useful debate.

Most of the existing investigations of Britain's economic problems focus on the economy as a whole and most of the interpretations emphasise one causal factor or simply list a variety of relevant factors. Our objective in this book is both more modest and more ambitious. It is more modest because we are concerned solely with the problems of one sector of the economy, manufacturing industry. We have restricted our object of investigation in this way because, in Britain's mature industrial economy, poor manufacturing performance is a major determinant of our deepening economic and social crisis. Furthermore, on our analysis, the problems of the manufacturing sector are different from, and not necessarily reducible to, the problems of other sectors. At the same time our objective is ambitious because we aim to construct an explanation which consists of something more than a list of heterogeneous factors. We have tried to do this by developing a coherent argument about the particularly British nature of the problems of our national manufacturing sector; this argument emphasises the conditioning influence of a coherent set of specifically national institutional conditions.

This emphasis on inter-related national institutional conditions is an innovation which represents a departure from the existing literature which is either concerned with broad social factors (like the education system or the class structure) or uses orthodox economic theory to define the problems. The social factors are undoubtedly important but it is extraordinarily difficult to establish the connection between general social factors and particular events or problems which are specific to a given industry or manufacturing firm. As for economic theory, we find that to be constricting. The critique of economic theory which we present does not purport to convey any overall judgment: it is simply that orthodox economic theory is not very pertinent for attacking the particular question which we have set ourselves.

In saying that orthodox economic theory works at an inappropriate level of generalisation for our purposes we are not mainly concerned to repeat the traditional attacks. These have criticised the unreal assumptions of economic theory and its lack of empirical content. We stress instead a more recent line of criticism which has been developed particularly by Cutler et al. (1978). Here orthodox economic theory is identified as a theory which relates to the capitalist economy in general. The results may be interesting but they are not directed towards what happens in specific national economies. Thus orthodox economic theory is not obviously relevant for our concern with the failure of a particular sector of a particular capitalist society at a particular period of time. As Cutler also shows, a great deal of Marxist economic analysis is open to similar objections.

The difficulty with economic theory is not that it is abstract, but what it abstracts from. General theory necessarily pays little attention to particular institutional conditions which can, and quite clearly do, vary considerably from one advanced capitalist economy to another. We are concerned with the relative performance of one sector of a national economy in a specific period of time. In this case, we would argue that attention should be concentrated on the variable national conditions. This book therefore represents an attempt to press beyond Cutler's negative critique of current neoclassical and Marxist orthodoxies by constructing a more positive argument about the linkage between variable national conditions and variable national performance.

Our basic premise is that the institutional environment, or more precisely a specific part of that environment, has important effects on the ways in which enterprises behave within a given economy. We would also argue that the institutional conditions of enterprise calculation tend to vary systematically on a national basis, partly because the relevant institutions tend to be inter-connected. Enterprises within a national manufacturing sector will tend therefore to be influenced in broadly consistent ways in reaching their operational decisions. The demonstration of these points would, of course, require a more comprehensive and systematic comparative study than is offered here. Our argument uses a great deal of comparative material but its main object is, of course, the British experience. It might, however, serve to open up a debate.

Given these broad objectives, the organisation of the book is mostly obvious and straightforward. A general introduction sets out to establish, first, that there is a problem of British manufacturing which is, in several important respects, specific to Britain. It then aims to establish that poor British manufacturing performance becomes intelligible when the national conditions of enterprise calculation are analysed. For this purpose *four* such conditions are identified as being especially relevant in the British context: management control over the labour process; market limitations; the relation of manufacturing industry to financial institutions; and the inter-relationship between manufacturing industry and government.

The primary aim of the introduction is to describe how these conditions fitted together into a coherent pattern which affected the whole of British manufacturing after 1950. But we are also concerned to show how the individual conditions impinged differently on various segments of manufacturing. Here the argument discriminates the conditioning effects on big business and small business, on multi-national companies and on state-owned enterprise. Throughout the general introduction, our aim has been to open up issues: we do not pretend that our schema of four conditions operating on the different segments is exhaustive. We do believe, however, that the general introduction provides a basis for a worthwhile shift in the problems dealt with by 'applied economics'.

The work concludes with three case studies. Since one of our central concerns is to emphasise the importance of calculations made at the enterprise level, the inclusion of some such material seemed essential. None the less, we would emphasise that only limited claims should be made on the basis of the case studies. They do not prove or justify the general argument, which probably cannot be proved in such a way. On the other hand the case studies do fulfil important functions. They illustrate particular problems in specific enterprises and industries and show that these relate to the national institutional conditions. For this reason, the case studies should demonstrate how, on our approach, it is possible to connect the particular and the general in an effective way: this connection must form an important part of any satisfying explanation. At the same time the studies also feed back an awareness of the complexity of industry by qualifying and complementing the general argument.

We would not claim that the enterprises and industries studied are 'representative' or 'characteristic' of British manufacturing; indeed, we would argue that there cannot be one typical enterprise or industry situation if national conditions operate variably on different segments of manufacturing capital. The cases were not, however, chosen at random. In different ways all three case studies cover aspects of engineering, which is technically the core of manufacturing capability in Britain and other advanced capitalist countries. At the same time, it was clearly desirable to cover a variety of enterprise situations and experiences. The cases fulfil this requirement reasonably well given that constraints on resources and time dictated a small number of case studies.

The inclusion of GEC and BLMC gave coverage to the very large firm, but these enterprises were in other respects usefully different. GEC is a firm which produces a remarkable diversity of products, ranging from major capital goods like complete power stations to such basic consumption goods as electric lamp bulbs. In contrast, BLMC was, and BL is, essentially a single-product firm. Shipbuilding represents an attempt to cover a quite different situation. During the period with which the case study is concerned, prior to nationalisation in 1977, shipbuilding was an industry composed of many small firms. This case has been used to demonstrate how the particular national conditions affected first the industry as a whole and then the individual enterprises. Finally, the cases can be said to span a wide spectrum of success and failure. GEC is widely accepted as the outstandingly successful British manufacturing firm of the 1970s, whilst BLMC must be a serious contender for the title of largest failed firm. Shipbuilding provides an instance of spectacular industrial failure; no other British industry declined so rapidly from such a strong position of world leadership in 1950.

As far as possible, we have resisted the temptation to draw policy conclusions from the analysis and description in the general introduction and the case studies. This decision was taken quite deliberately even though our analysis clearly does have policy implications;

for example, it implies that neo-Keynesian or monetarist macro-policies are unlikely to regenerate British manufacturing industry when they do not affect the conditions of enterprise calculation. A sustained discussion of policy solutions would distract from our primary purpose which is to change problem definitions. We expect disagreement. But we shall be well satisfied if we can persuade some readers to share our own conviction that it is necessary to make a problem shift of the kind which this book proposes.

Introduction: Why are the British bad at manufacturing?

Karel Williams

Even if we concentrate on the recent past and focus on the short period from approximately 1950 to 1980, this question is one which orthodox applied economics has not answered successfully. This essay's central argument is that the question about British manufacturing performance can be constructively approached if it is re-posed in a new explanatory framework which emphasises the national conditions of enterprise calculation. An answer is then provided by describing the specifically British institutional conditions which have constrained the performance of different segments of national capital. Four relevant national conditions will be analysed: enterprise control over the labour process; market structure and the composition of demand; the relation of manufacturing enterprise to financial institutions; and finally, the relation of manufacturing enterprise to government.

However, before we can re-pose and attack the question, it is necessary to begin at the beginning and justify the question. First, we have to justify the choice of poor manufacturing performance as an explicandum. Here it will be argued that our explicandum is preferable to the other objects of investigation in the field of applied economics (poor overall economic performance, de-industrialisation, etc.). Second, we have to justify the presumption that the British are bad at manufacturing. This will be done by reviewing the evidence and the first section of this essay turns to this task of justification by defining the nature, extent and consequences of poor performance in British manufacturing.

1   The nature and consequences of British manufacturing's relative failure

It is only since the late 1970s that applied economics has become preoccupied with the specific issues of British manufacturing performance. The earlier and more general object of investigation was poor overall economic performance. This explicandum materialised in the textbooks in the form of those national league tables which rank Britain *vis-à-vis* her national competitors since 1945 in terms of growth of national income and manufacturing output, share of world trade, growth in labour productivity, rate of investment, and so forth.

This presentation of the problem may be time-honoured, but it is not very helpful. To begin with, it usually encourages discussion of the causes of economic growth. This is a profitless issue because economic growth, in neo-classical terms, has theoretically under-specified factorial concomitants rather than identifiable causes. More seriously, the problematisation of overall performance denies the curate's egg quality of national economic performance. It is presupposed that there is something unitary called 'economic performance' and the various economic indicators are simply so many signs of one fundamental state of the economy. If this essentialist fallacy is rejected, then overall economic performance is a diffuse explicandum which defies economical explanation.

It is therefore immediately encouraging that the specific problems of British manufacturing have been recently problematised as part of a syndrome of 'de-industrialisation'. Competing definitions of the de-industrialisation syndrome are offered by the two Oxford economists Bacon and Eltis (1978) and the Cambridge economist Singh (1977). De-industrialisation may represent a progressive problem shift in applied economics, but both the competing definitions of de-industrialisation mis-specify the problem and thus the ensuing discussion has been disappointingly inconclusive.

For Bacon and Eltis, de-industrialisation is about the malign expansion of the government sector as government spending pulls resources, like labour and investment funds, away from manufacturing industry. Bacon and Eltis did draw attention to the loss of employment from the manufacturing sector. But the weakness of their definition was that it foreclosed the question of the causes of this employment loss by introducing a causal mechanism (crowding out by government) which is in the end implausible. It ignores the basic point that, from the later 1960s, the government sector was bidding for female labour in an increasingly slack labour market where male manufacturing employment was declining autonomously. Bacon and Eltis deny this autonomous decline: but it is precisely this decline which has to be explained.

For Singh, de-industrialisation is about a relative inefficiency whereby a nation's manufacturing sector is unable to sell enough of its products abroad to pay for the nation's import requirements at socially acceptable levels of output, employment and exchange rate. Singh did draw attention to the foreign trade constraint established by an inefficient manufacturing sector. But the weakness of his definition was that it located manufacturing efficiency in an idealised textbook world where the reasonably efficient should always be able to attain trade equilibrium through the export of manufactures. It ignores the basic point that, since the oil crisis pushed up import bills, the advanced industrial economies have generally been unable to pay for full employment imports. If they are all de-industrialising, then the Singh definition is simply not restrictive enough.

If we criticise the definitions of de-industrialisation as premature and unsatisfactory, we are left with the more modest problem of poor manufacturing performance in Britain. Before we go on to examine the nature and extent of this relative failure, we must establish the preliminary point that poor manufacturing performance does matter. It does so for at least two reasons. First, the evidence shows that the British economy has an important manufacturing sector whose fortunes depend on maintaining international competitiveness. Second, reflection shows that poor performance by this manufacturing sector will have important adverse effects.

Britain has a mature industrial economy with a large manufacturing sector which accounts for a significant proportion of total employment and output. From the early 1950s onwards, manufacturing has accounted for around one-third of employment and output, although the proportion of employment in manufacturing industry has latterly declined towards one-quarter. By any standard, the British economy is very open. The British manufacturing sector is increasingly heavily committed to export business which accounted for 20 per cent of UK manufacturing sales in the mid-1950s and over 30 per cent by 1980 (appendix A, table 4, col.vi).

Over the same period, foreign manufacturers dramatically increased their share of the British home market from under 10 per cent to around 30 per cent.

The present pattern of exchange is that Britain relies on receipts from exported manufactures which cover the bill for imported manufactures and leave a small surplus for finance of some imported foodstuffs and raw materials. Manufactures continue to dominate our commodity exports as they have always done. In the 1950s, manufactures accounted for four-fifths of our exports. In 1980, even with North Sea oil, manufactures still accounted for three-quarters of our exports (appendix A, table 2, col.xi). On the import side, the main change since the early 1950s has been a dramatic rise in the relative importance of manufactured imports as a proportion of our total imports. In the early 1950s, manufactures accounted for 20 per cent of our total imports, by 1970 they accounted for 50 per cent and by 1980 for almost 65 per cent (appendix A, table 1, col.x).

Changes in the pattern of exchange have been associated with geographic shifts in the relative importance of different trading partners. With the rise of manufactured imports, traditional Commonwealth trading partners have become very much less important as import suppliers; in 1951, 22 per cent of our imports came from the Overseas Sterling Area, which by 1980 supplied only 10 per cent of our imports (appendix A, table 1, col.ix). This decline was more or less exactly matched by the rise in importance of industrial countries as import suppliers; the Common Market and Japan accounted for 36 per cent of our imports in 1951 and 52 per cent in 1980 (appendix A, table 1, cols ii and v). Rather less predictably, there has been a parallel geographic shift on the export side with advanced industrial countries becoming very much more important as customers for British exports. The Overseas Sterling Area took 52 per cent of our manufactured exports in 1951 and only 24 per cent in 1980 (appendix A, table 2, col.ix). The Common Market which took 15 per cent of our exports in 1951 was taking 37 per cent by 1980.

British entry into the Common Market in 1973 formally recognised and practically reinforced changes in trading patterns which were already taking place. The Common Market's importance as an export customer had already increased dramatically before we joined; between 1951 and 1970 the Common Market's share of our manufactured exports practically doubled to 28 per cent (appendix

A, table 2, col.ii). Membership of the Common Market locked us into a free trade area where we competed with similar sized economies, principally France and West Germany, which by the 1970s had trading patterns something like that of Britain. The French and West German economies were open, like the British economy, with exports accounting for 20 to 30 per cent of gross domestic product. Furthermore, the French and West German pattern of commodity trade was very similar to the British pattern, with manufactures accounting for three-quarters of exports and more than half of imports (appendix A, tables 1 and 2).

Until we withdraw from the Common Market, and/or unilaterally set up import controls, we are locked into competition with our West European neighbours. And we must now pose the question, why does it matter if we do badly in this contest? By way of answer, we will argue that an uncompetitive British manufacturing sector, which is relatively unsuccessful, handicaps us in two ways: first, relative unsuccess has a secular long-run impact on the total volume of resources available for social and private consumption and investment; second, relative unsuccess has a short-term impact on the possibility of using the given resources available at any one moment of time.

If we consider the long-run impact of manufacturing uncompetitiveness on the quantum of available resources, our starting point is that an uncompetitive manufacturing sector will be or become relatively small and perhaps will also be achieving modest levels and rates of increase in productivity. This has repercussions because the manufacturing sector is the privileged locus of productivity improvements; in agriculture and service activities, it is inherently much more difficult to make continuous efficiency gains by increasing the capital intensity of production. If the manufacturing sector is small and inefficient, then, in the long run, the resources available for private and social purposes will as a result be more limited. The consequences are particularly serious in a mature and long industrialised economy like Britain, where peasant agriculture and craft manufacturing sectors are very small. Here efficiency gains cannot be made by redeploying labour from the 'pre-industrial' sectors into machine manufacturing (Denison, 1968). Such a mature economy could only hope that exportable natural resources (such as coal or oil) would provide the purchasing power to buy in efficiently produced manufactures from overseas.

More immediately, relative unsuccess in manufacturing has a short-term depressive and constraining effect on the use of available national resources. The basic point here is that relative unsuccess will usually manifest itself in the form of manufactured imports which are not compensated for by increased manufactured exports. At the simplest, this will induce a relative or absolute contraction of the domestic manufacturing sector which will, in orthodox Keynesian terms, have multiplied effects on the level of domestic activity. This is particularly serious because, if the level of domestic activity is flagging for this reason, it will be difficult or impossible to apply demand management policies of the sort popular in 1950s and 1960s Britain. If the national manufacturing sector is weak, the economy may have to be constrained below full employment since attempts to stimulate domestic activity will draw in manufactured imports and cause a balance-of-payments crisis. Continuous depreciation of the currency might in the short run stabilise the payments situation, but only at the expense of unacceptable consequences for domestic inflation as imports become continuously more expensive. No orthodox policy instrument will shift the external constraints which are likely to be established by a relatively unsuccessful manufacturing sector. And, outside Cambridge, there is no academic consensus that import controls will work.

If abstract reflection suggests that a relatively unsuccessful manufacturing sector has a depressive and constraining effect on the economy, the evidence suggests that Britain was already suffering these effects in the early 1980s. A relative decline in the importance of manufacturing employment appears to be normal in the mature industrial economies. But there has been a large absolute decline in manufacturing employment in Britain since the mid-1960s. With the workforce then and now numbering just over 25 million persons, manufacturing employment has declined by some 3 million (Thirlwall, 1982). Perhaps a significant proportion of this loss could be attributed to the world recession of the 1970s rather than to secular national decline in manufacturing. But why should the British manufacturing sector be so vulnerable, if it is not uncompetitive? And, if world recession is an active force, the deteriorating balance of trade in manufactures is all the more worrying because world recession and depressed levels of domestic activity should have slowed import growth.

The British balance of trade in manufactures has deteriorated very rapidly. Back in the mid-1950s, the value of manufactured exports was more than 2½ times as large as the value of manufactured imports (appendix A, tables 1 and 2), but by 1980, manufactured exports only just covered the bill for manufactured imports (appendix A, tables 1 and 2) leaving only a small surplus on manufacture trade. Payments crises of the sort that dominated the 1950s and the 1960s have now receded. But, if the world recession were to lift and if the British economy were to recover from its present depressed level of activity, the windfall gain of North Sea oil could not compensate for the relative unsuccess of British manufacturing (Thirlwall, 1978). At full employment, there would be a massive deficit on current account and we would face a terminal payments crisis. In this sense, the British economy is still fundamentally balance-of-payments constrained.

It is in the context of these arguments that we can decide how to measure the performance of British manufacturing industry relative to its competitors. This performance could be measured in many different ways – profitability, growth of output, productivity and patterns of specialisation and structural change, could all be considered. But, given the practical constraints on the British economy which we have already analysed, measures of our relative success against the rest of the world in the international trade in manufactures must be privileged as the most sensitive and relevant indicators of the performance of British manufacturing industry. As for interpretation of results, all the various economic indicators of performance do not show a failure relative to our international competitors at all times since the Second World War. The record on growth of industrial production is dismal, with British industrial production growing at half the rate of French and West German industrial production which both trebled in size over the twenty-five years 1955 to 1980. On the other hand, as we shall argue later, from the end of the 1950s, the British rate of labour productivity growth was steadily rising towards the European norm of 4 per cent per annum. But, if we consider the privileged indicators of trade performance, the record is one of relative failure. The remainder of this section will attempt to establish this point.

Graph 1 summarises the evidence on import penetration of the British market for manufactures. It shows that, in the 1950s, British manufacturers completely dominated their home market and imports were negligible; the import penetration ratio was low and did not increase from its level of 6 or 7 per cent until the early 1960s (appendix A, table 4, col.v). From then onwards, however, import penetration increased rapidly, albeit unsteadily: there were clear upward steps in 1962–4 and 1967–8 which raised the import ratio towards 15 per cent; and in ten of the eleven years after 1970 import penetration increased. By the beginning of the 1980s, import penetration had thus reached 25 per cent. British manufacturers were therefore increasingly unsuccessful at resisting imports on their home market. There has been a dramatic increase in import penetration, which is obvious to all British consumers in the High Street electrical shop or the local car park.

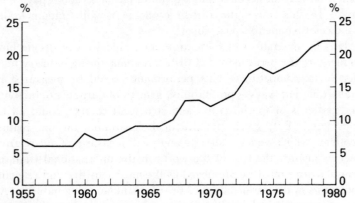

GRAPH 1   Import penetration ratio* for products of manufacturing industry in the UK

Source: Appendix A, table 4, col.v.
*Imports are here calculated as a percentage of home demand and exports. The ratio therefore registers UK manufacturers' commitment to exports and rising exports-to-sales ratios which partially offset increasing import penetration.

These national changes have been so dramatic that it is important to get them into a clear international perspective. From the early 1950s to the early 1970s, there was a long boom in international trade; over these twenty years, the volume of developed-country exports grew at a phenomenal 8 per cent per annum (Maddison, 1977). During this period there was a massive increase in the exchange of manufactures between the developed countries and import penetration was rising rapidly in all of them except Japan. Up to the early 1970s, in relative international terms, import penetration levels in Britain were not unreasonably high. If APM is the ratio of imported manufactures to gross domestic product, in 1972 the British APM was 13·3 per cent; in West Germany and France, the two countries most comparable to Britain in terms of size and trade specialisation, the APMs were 11·0 and 9·5 per cent respectively (Panić, 1975). If the strong German national manufacturing sector was unable to stem import penetration of its home market, the conclusion must be that rising import penetration in the developed countries after the early 1950s must be explained by demand characteristics rather than by the weakness of the indigenous suppliers. Consumers were sensitive to the minor packaging details which differentiated otherwise identical durables (like cars and washing machines) while firms increasingly bought producer goods on non-chauvinist price and performance criteria.

If increased import penetration was not a direct index of a weak British national manufacturing sector, nevertheless, there was always underlying weakness in the British position. By the early 1970s, the dynamic prospects were unfavourable because the UK had a relatively high income elasticity of demand for manufactured goods. For every 1 per cent increase in national income, imports of manufactures increased by 3·09 per cent in Britain as against 2·14 per cent in West Germany and 2·19 per cent in France (Panić, 1975). And by the middle or late 1970s, after we had joined the Common Market and set up a free trade area with our immediate competitors, the worst did seem to be happening; from 1970 to 1978, there was a 40 per cent increase in the volume of finished manufactured imports and only a 10 per cent increase in our manufactured exports (Dornbusch and Fischer, 1980). The contrast between export and import volume growth establishes the crucial point; given her unsuccess as an exporter of manufactures, Britain cannot afford an average propensity to import and a high income elasticity of demand for imports.

Graph 2 summarises the evidence on Britain's share of world trade in manufactures. It shows that during the long boom of the 1950s and 1960s, Britain's share of world exports of manufactures declined precipitously; our share slumped from 19·8 to 10·8 per cent in the fifteen years after 1955 (appendix A, table 3, col.ii). This is the key indicator which shows the relative weakness of British manufacturing in the 1950s and 1960s when all the comparably sized industrial economies (like France, West Germany, Japan and

Italy) maintained or gained trade share (appendix A, table 3, cols iii–vi). It is gratifying to find that this slide was halted in the 1970s; after 1973, our share of world trade in manufactures seems to have stabilised at around 9 per cent (appendix A, table 3, col.ii). Nevertheless, too much should not be made of that 'improvement'. In the 1950s and 1960s, when world trade was expanding rapidly, British exporters were losing relative share, but did achieve substantial absolute increases in volume; by 1960 the volume of British exports was 2½ times the 1938 level. In the rolling recession of the 1970s, with a depression in world trade, maintenance of trade share did not translate into substantial increases in volume; as already noted, the volume of British manufactured exports increased by only 10 per cent up to 1978.

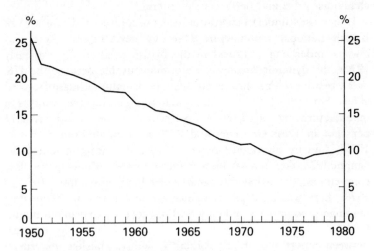

GRAPH 2   Britain's share of world export trade in manufactures

Source: Appendix A, table 3, col.ii.

To be fair to British manufacturers, as we have emphasised increased import penetration, it should also be noted that exports accounted for an increased percentage of British manufacturers' sales over our period. Through the first half of the 1960s, exports accounted for 17–18 per cent of UK manufacturers' sales, while by the end of the 1970s they accounted for around 30 per cent (appendix A, table 4, col.vi). The essential point remains however, that, even if British manufacturers exported a larger proportion of their output in the late 1970s, they did not export enough to recover any of the world trade share they had lost in the previous two decades.

It should also be remembered that British manufacturing is unusually heavily involved in overseas manufacture as well as direct export from its home base.

TABLE 1 *Overseas production as percentage of exports in 1971*

USA	393
UK	215
France	94
West Germany	37
Japan	37

Source: United Nations (1978).

In the 1960s, British firms manufactured abroad twice as much as they exported from Britain. But the fragmentary evidence does not show that foreign manufacturing was being purposively substituted for direct exports in the period of rapidly declining trade share. Britain was not investing more in particular foreign markets where our exports were rapidly losing share (*National Institute Economic Review*, 1961). More generally, as Channon (1973) suggests, there was little foreign green-field site development of the sort that would be required if overseas factories were being built up at the expense of the British base. And, in any case, if foreign manufacturing were being substituted, that would not be an acceptable solution from the national and social point of view. To pay for our imports we need the large receipts from direct export of manufactures where the value is added in Britain; the remittable profits from overseas manufacture will be much smaller.

To sum up, the evidence of export failure is thoroughly dispiriting even if it does not show a continuous decline in the British share of world trade in manufactures over the past thirty years. It is all the more depressing because, as we will now argue, there are no extenuating circumstances which can be invoked to explain or excuse decline. To be more specific, neither specialisation in the wrong product lines nor uncompetitive costs and prices excuse the export failure.

If British manufacturers were specialised in industrial lines where world demand was slow growing, that might excuse poor export performance and incidentally help explain increased import penetration. Panić and Rajan (1971) grouped manufactures into five categories from category 1 'very fast growing' to category V 'very slow growing'.

TABLE 2   *Percentage share of faster-growing manufactured exports (categories I – III) in total national exports*

	1960	1968
USA	60·3	73·9
West Germany	55·0	63·8
UK	53·0	59·4
France	45·3	55·7
Japan	31·4	47·5
Belgium	21·6	36·1

Source: Panić and Rajan (1971).

By this measure of industrial specialisation, the UK occupies an intermediate position and it is impossible to argue that Britain was seriously handicapped in these terms *vis-à-vis* her European competitors, France and Germany. In any case, even if Britain was handicapped, that is not an adequate excuse for poor export performance because unfavourable product specialisation in a national manufacturing sector is not a given but a variable which can be changed, as the Japanese showed in the 1960s.

If British manufacturers were being priced out of markets because their costs were increasing faster than those of their competitors, that again might excuse poor export performance and also excuse increasing import penetration. The question of wage costs is crucial here because this is where international differences in rates of cost increase are most likely to arise. For more than twenty years, the going rate of wage inflation in terms of the domestic currency has been higher in Britain than among our competitors; from 1963–80, domestic wage costs roughly doubled in the USA, Canada, West Germany and Japan, while they virtually quintupled in the UK (*Economic Progress Report*, June 1982). But, as graph 3 shows, according to the standard IMF measure, British unit labour costs in terms of a common currency do not increase faster; indeed, the graph shows an erratic improvement in our competitiveness over the whole period 1960 to 1976. Above-average domestic wage inflation has not damaged our international cost competitiveness because, as graph 4 shows, sterling was devalued in 1967 and then depreciated more or less continuously from 1971 to late 1976.

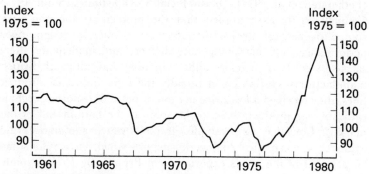

GRAPH 3 Unit labour cost competitiveness

Source: *Economic Progress Report*, no. 146, June 1982, p.7.

It may be unsatisfactory to rely on a depreciating currency to maintain cost competitiveness and this point may be proved by our experience when sterling appreciated moderately from 1979 to 1981 and unit labour costs rocketed upwards. Nevertheless, out-of-control labour costs cannot be used as an excuse for our poor export performance before the end of the 1970s.

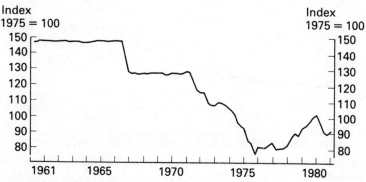

GRAPH 4 Sterling's effective exchange rate

Source: *Economic Progress Report*. no. 146, June 1982, p.7.

Far from excusing our export performance, if the evidence on cost competitiveness and product specialisation is examined in more detail, it focuses and reinforces our concern about export failure. If costs were not out of control, the price of British manufactured exports was right but still foreigners preferred not to buy them (Fetherston, et al. 1977). Quasi-official NEDO studies (Stout, 1977; Connell, 1979) have argued that the problem is the non-price competitiveness of British manufactures – inferior design, poor performance, bad marketing, late delivery and inadequate after-sales service. It is therefore understandable that, although British manufacturers specialised in broadly the right industrial product lines, they received a low price per ton or per unit exported; technically inferior products have to be sold 'at the bottom end of the market'. Consider, for example, graph 5 which summarises the evidence on mechanical engineering exports which account for some 20 per cent of the goods exported from Britain. By 1975, 1 tonne of German mechanical engineering exports was worth 60 per cent more than a representative tonne of British mechanical engineering exports and, as graph 5 shows, this differential has increased dramatically over the past twenty years.

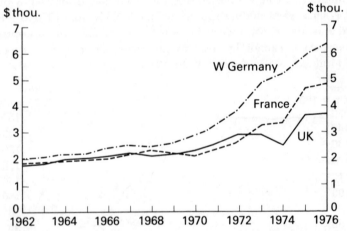

GRAPH 5　Average value per tonne of exports of mechanical engineering products

Source: Connell (1979), p.19.

All this is worrying because a deficiency in quality is an intractable micro problem which is not easily amenable to central policy regulation. This also incidentally establishes the irrelevance of Thatcherite economics: disciplining the working class through mass unemployment will not solve a problem of non-price competitiveness even if it does make British manufactures more price and cost competitive.

If the problems of the past thirty years are so fundamental, we must now consider whether and how they form part of a secular trend. Our share of world trade has been falling since the early 1870s, and some would argue that this fall was inevitable because British exporters were defending an historic position of relative importance which was bound to be eroded by the development of other major industrial nations. On this issue, it is necessary to insist on the basic methodological point that, if the British trade share goes down in two successive periods, we should not presume that *one* secular set of conditions is responsible. This point is of some practical importance. For example, the British economy was over-committed to export staples like cotton and shipbuilding in the 1920s and 1930s but, as we have already argued, the pattern of industrial specialisation was favourable in the 1950s and 1960s. If the historical inevitability argument has to be scrutinised period by period, it can be refuted in the post-1950 period by examining the evidence at a disaggregated level and looking at the success and failure of exports on a market-by-market basis.

The disaggregated evidence shows that losses in some markets were inevitable but that an overall loss of trade share was not inevitable. In the early 1950s, Britain accounted for up to three-quarters of the manufactures imported by Commonwealth countries like Australia and New Zealand or Nigeria and Ghana (*National Institute Economic Review*, 1961). We could not expect to maintain this position of dominance; here we were bound to lose. But we also exported manufactures to developed countries like France, Germany and the USA, where, in the early 1950s, we seldom accounted for more than 15 per cent of the manufactures imported into these countries (*National Institute Economic Review*, 1961). We lost overall share because we were unable to build from a position of relative weakness in the advanced industrial markets. Indeed, the evidence shows that we lost share in the advanced markets, albeit at a slower rate than in traditional markets.

The British loss of share in European and more generally, in industrial markets, was not inevitable. Successful direct exporters, like the Germans or Japanese, increased their share of world trade exactly because they did build from a position of weakness in tough markets.

TABLE 3   *UK percentage share of industrial countries' exports to different trading blocs*

	1962	1976
To world	12·7	7·6
To industrial countries	9·2	6·7
To other European countries	21·4	14·4
To Australia, New Zealand and South Africa	42·6	18·5

Source: Connell (1979).

To sum up on trade performance, there is evidence of failure for which there are very few excuses. The argument that there really is nothing to be explained cannot be accepted. The British *are* relatively bad at manufacturing and this failure needs to be explained. In this case, we are going to have to decide on an explanatory framework inside which we can pose and answer the question about failure. This framework is outlined in the next section.

2   Explanatory frameworks

This section begins by analysing the orthodox frameworks in which the question of poor manufacturing performance has been and could be posed and answered. Through such criticism we will finally establish the basis for an alternative framework of our own. We will begin by considering orthodox economics where, because of the rift between micro and macro theory, two kinds of explanation are possible: the causes of poor manufacturing performance are usually discussed in an ethereal abstracted way on a disembodied macro plane; alternatively at another level, the theory of the firm could be invoked in explanation. Both these explanations will now be considered and criticised.

If we begin on the macro plane, our starting point must be that the academic analysts of de-industrialisation have been conspicuously unsuccessful at explaining the process. Consider, for example, the contributions to Blackaby's (1979) symposium on de-industrialisation. In these essays we can observe the three kinds of inadequate quasi-explanation which are commonly offered in applied economics.

(i) *The national character explanation.* Here, long-standing and pervasive national attitudes and institutions are identified as the cause of a 'British disease'. For example, Balogh and Thatcher blame Britain's class-bound institutions and especially the educational system. These social attitudes and institutions may be important, but we doubt whether they should be invoked in this way to explain industrial decline. Such explanations make an unjustifiable leap to an underlying social cause. They are unsatisfactory because they offer a speculative identification of a quasi-idealist sort.

(ii) *The circular explanation.* There is general enthusiasm for a vicious circle of decline. The editor (Blackaby) endorses Singh's emphasis that cumulative and circular causality leaves Britain even further behind. Stout's essay advances a more technical variant on this explanation; successful and fast-growing countries obtain dynamic economies of scale which make further innovation easier. These explanations are not very useful. When there is a confusion about cause and effect, it is simply compounded by general assertions that everything goes round and round. Technical arguments about economies of scale (or learning by doing) are more interesting. But, if these mechanisms were decisive, then late-comers and slow-starters would stand no chance at all.

(iii) *The factorial explanation.* As exemplars of this approach, we may consider Brown and Sherriff who list immobility of labour, poor industrial relations, lack of innovation, non-responsiveness to demand and lack of appropriate skills. They then end by noting that underpaid management may be responsible. The problem is that this is a factorial list of symptoms not an explanation. There is no concept of how some factors might fit together to form specific obstacles at particular points in the operation of the manufacturing sector.

Subsequent work on de-industrialisation has not brought us any closer to a credible macro explanation. Thirlwall (1982), for example, emphasises that the cause is our unsuccess as an exporter. But that does not explain poor manufacturing performance, it only specifies the immediate mechanism underlying job loss. This only highlights the deficiencies of all the orthodox macro explanations. Applied economics is preoccupied with the symptomatalogy of poor manufacturing performance; it endlessly analyses the symptoms of the disease. Applied economics does not provide an aetiology; this branch of economic discourse seems unable to define the preconditions and origins of poor manufacturing performance.

On a different micro economic level, the theory of the firm could perhaps be used to provide an explanation. This immediately raises the question about which theory of the firm. Orthodox neo-classical theory of the profit-maximising firm survives in the textbooks. But it is generally agreed that such theory is irrelevant to contemporary advanced capitalist economies like Britain where one hundred giant firms account for nearly one-half of manufacturing output. In Britain, as elsewhere, there has been a massive abridgment of the market with the rise of such giant firms which internally co-ordinate production and distribution by bureaucratic means. Partly in response to this perceived irrelevance, in the past twenty years there has been a confusing proliferation of new theories of the firm or managerial capitalism. We do not have the space to review the various theories of Baumol, Cyert and March, Galbraith, Marris, Williamson and others. We shall, however, make some general points which are applicable to most of them and which will establish the inadequacies of such theories for approaching the particular questions which concern us. This should not, of course, be construed as a general judgment on such approaches for other purposes.

To begin with, the new theories do not make a radical break with the framework of classical theory. The new theories situate the firm on the same terrain as the old theory because they assume that the firm operates in a theoretical environment which might be called the capitalist economy in general since it abstracts from the specific institutional features of particular capitalist national economies. Furthermore, the new theories, like the old, are teleological in that they assume the firm is goal-directed. Classically, the new theories simply replace profit maximisation with a different goal – growth or sales revenue or managerial utility. And in the new theories, these goals are enforced externally or exist internally for reasons which are at least reconcilable with orthodox theory. Some of the new theories suppose that goals are enforced externally by the processes of the product or capital markets; for example, take-over can eliminate the slow grower just as surely as price competition eliminates the unprofitable in the old theory. Other new theories of the firm reject an environmental explanation of firm goals and, instead, root the motivation of the firm in the existence of particular personalities (managers, shareholders and workers) who make calculations of their interest. These differentiated personalities are, however, only sub-species of economic man whose rational calculus underpinned the whole structure of the old theory.

In sum, the new theories of the firm are basically variants on the old rationalist teleology. The differences about objectives, motivations and enforcement mechanisms do not add up to a fundamental break, because the new theories conserve the old object of investigation (the firm in the capitalist economy in general) and the old teleological style of explanation. With this point made, we can now argue that, largely because of their conservatism the new theories are, for our purposes, no more successful than the old. It is important to emphasise there that the new theories will not be criticised as untested or untestable. For example, no attempt will be made to consider whether the evidence shows firms are sales-rather than profit-maximising, nor to consider whether sales-maximising behaviour can be distinguished from profit-maximising behaviour. We would argue that the capacity of the old or new theories to rationalise the 'empirical evidence' is a side issue because the central problems concern the nature and scope of the theoretical abstractions in old and new theories of the firm. This exemplifies the more general methodological point that, in all the more important theoretical choices, it does not matter whether theories account for more observations (Williams, 1975). Criticism of theory must always ultimately take the form of argument about how phenomena are and should be constructed, interpreted and explained.

We may therefore begin by asking whether we need an explanation of enterprise behaviour in teleological form. Even if we do not pursue that question, there is the immediate internal problem that it is difficult to establish the existence of a teleological goal. In the new theories, personalities and their interests as managers or shareholders are supposed to exist within, or in relation to, organisational structures. But individuals are not supports (or Träger as Marx would have said) of places in an organisational form. There is always scope for variable perception, construction and identification of personal and organisational goals. If we admit these possibilities, the teleological goal can only be saved by introducing a mechanism of external environmental enforcement which renders the motivations and calculations of personalities ultimately irrelevant. But the existing critique of neo-classical theory shows that fierce conditions must be met before the product and capital markets will enforce goals like profit-maximisation. Winter's (1964) classic article showed that profit-maximisation requires not only perfect competition but also constant returns to scale, a series of states to test firm behaviour, equal financial strength and a specified cut-off point beyond which firms are not allowed to incur information costs. It should also be noted that the process of eliminating unfit firms will be very much more complex if the firm is identified as an embodied organisation with particular functions, rather than as the disembodied production function of traditional theory. In this case, it is presumably necessary that enterprise organisation as well as behaviour must both vary systematically and be subject to environmental selection.

The criticisms so far made are not trivial but perhaps some of them could be resolved by theoretical specification. As Cutler et al. (1978, vol.2) have recently argued, a much more fundamental series of problems arises because the firm with its goals of profit or growth is situated on the terrain of the capitalist economy in general when the theory abstracts from the specifically national institutional conditions. The problems that arise here are inherent in the object of investigation defined by orthodox economies. In principle, it may be laudable, or at least harmless, for economists to improve the refinement of their abstractions about the behaviour of firms in the capitalist economy in general. In practice, the resulting universal abstractions necessarily do not have much power to explain the behaviour of firms in specific capitalist national economies.

To begin with, if we pose the issue of the giant firm in the capitalist economy in general, it is difficult to avoid getting caught up in a profitless argument about the relative efficiency of co-ordination by market or by bureaucratic organisation. Orthodox neo-classical theory incorporates a strong presumption in favour of the market. Some recent theorists of the firm have simply inverted this logic; for Williamson (1981), the rise of the giant firm over the past 150 years establishes the general presumption that the administrative co-ordination of production and distribution is more efficient than the market system which he claims it has superseded. Against all this, it must be insisted that, unless fierce preconditions are met, it is unlikely that one form of productive co-ordination (market or administrative) has an invariable result in terms of efficiency. Furthermore, the problem which has to be resolved in applied economics is the national variability in results in different advanced capitalist economies where giant firms are equally important.

More crucially, if we situate goals like profit or growth on the terrain of the capitalist economy in general, they are defined as universal operational goals. But, as Cutler et al. (1978) have argued, profit and growth are not universals because these aims and the means to their achievement are differently defined in specific national economies and, in practice, the variability is such that generalised injunctions or motivations to pursue profit or growth are meaningless. This point can be developed by briefly examining the issues of profit and growth which are both pertinent to our question and problem-situation.

In the capitalist economy in general, profit can be either in traditional terms the difference between marginal cost and marginal revenue or, more neutrally, the difference between earnings and expenditure (including provision for repairs and renewals). But in specific national economies, profit is something disclosed in company accounts and variably defined by national conventions and accounting practices which determine how earnings and expenses must be entered before a profit figure is struck. A firm's profitability can be very different if, for example, its depreciation provision is calculated under historic or current cost conventions. Under historic cost rules, depreciation is related to the original purchase price of the capital equipment, while under current cost rules depreciation is related to the current cost of replacing those assets. In an age of 10 per cent inflation, for example, depreciation allowances will be very much higher under current cost rules, and profitability will therefore be correspondingly lower. This point is of great practical importance when different conventions about depreciation and stock valuation are enforced in different national economies. On depreciation, for example, Britain at present maintains modified historic cost accounting with current cost results given in an appendix to the main company report. Countries like the Netherlands have adopted current cost rules. The national differences are, in fact, still greater than the preceding discussion implies since neither the historic nor current cost approaches can be identified with a single set of rules. Furthermore, at least one advanced capitalist national economy, Italy, does not have a national set of rules which is enforced by a system of external audit for company accounts (*Financial Times*, 4 December 1981).

As for the means to ends like profit or growth, these means also vary on a national basis. For example, an objective like growth can be pursued by merger if, and only if, the national rules of the game allow merger. It all depends on specific institutional and legal preconditions which vary on a national basis. Merger is permitted and encouraged where large manufacturing companies are normally publicly quoted companies with a wide dispersion of share ownership achieved through a stock exchange which has an active secondary market in issued shares. These institutional conditions are most clearly met in Britain and the United States where the stock market is a much more important institution than in many other advanced capitalist countries. On the other hand, government rules on merger have historically been very different in Britain and America. In Britain in the 1960s, mergers between companies in related manufacturing activities were directly allowed and even promoted by government which indirectly also encouraged merger by penalising practices which restricted competition between independent companies. In America, anti-trust laws have long discouraged all forms of collusion and merger between firms in related activities. This policy undoubtedly limited the extent of mergers and shaped the form of those mergers which did take place by encouraging conglomerate merger between firms in un-related activities; by the 1970s, pure conglomerate mergers accounted for half the assets acquired by merger in the USA (Williamson, 1981).

Our conclusion must be that neither the old nor the new theories of the firm can help us answer questions about the poor performance of British manufacturing because these theories credit all firms with overly general objectives in an under-specified environment, the capitalist economy in general. The universality of such theories ensures that they cannot explain the particularity of national experience. More positively, when we have identified the deficiencies of the theory of the firm, we can see more clearly what kind of alternative framework we are looking for: our alternative framework should be able to conceptualise the firm's discretionary calculations made under the specifically national rules of the game. For this purpose we could try some ready-made concepts. Specifically, we could adopt the concepts of enterprise structure and strategy which have been developed by American historians and management theorists.

The classic concepts of structure and strategy were formulated by Chandler (1962, 1977) in his two major historical studies of the development of the modern American corporation. Strategy here is 'the determination of the basic long-term goals and objectives of an enterprise' (1962). This concept is a kind of military metaphor whose virtue is that it allows choice – the firm can choose its long-term objectives. Business strategy is counterposed to enterprise structure, which is equated with formal organisation because every organisation can be epitomised by the chart which shows the hierarchical and vertical chain of command. It is also argued that strategy and structure are systematically related because 'structure follows strategy' (1962). Certain kinds of business structure allow effective strategies; for example, multi-divisional organisation allows a giant firm to run a diversified business.

Chandler develops these concepts and arguments in the course of an historical analysis of the development of nineteenth- and twentieth-century American business enterprise whose strategies and structures have (with a lag) migrated to other national economies. Multi-unit business enterprise developed in America after the 1840s; in Singer or Armour a hierarchy of managers in a network of offices co-ordinated production and distribution for a mass market. The task of co-ordination was complicated by vertical integration and diversification; from the 1920s onwards an increasing number of giant firms were operating in many product markets. Growing problems of co-ordination were resolved by the introduction of multi-divisional organisation in firms like General Motors or Jersey Standard; here a general office concentrated on strategic decision-making while product (or geographic) divisions handled routine operating decisions.

For our purposes, there is more substance and relevance in Chandler than in economists' theories of the firm. Nevertheless, if we separately consider his concepts of strategy and structure, they have serious limitations. In describing enterprise calculation, Chandler (1962) concentrates on strategic decisions about the firm's organisation and product lines. By implication, it is these boardroom decisions which matter. He ignores business tactics; for example, in his account of the 1920s, he ignores Taylorism and scientific management which manipulated the labour process at plant level in order to cut costs. The problem with Chandler's concept of structure is that it takes the organisation chart at face value and uncritically assumes that authority and initiative come from above. We know that in Japanese corporations, under the *ringi* system, junior managers have the power of initiative and their proposals move upwards, with superiors adding their seal of approval. Is the Western firm so very different?

The most fundamental problems, however, concern the way in which Chandler (1977) couples the concepts of strategy and structure together in a mechanical schema of challenge and response. For Chandler conceives the business corporation as Toynbee conceives civilisation; it develops in response to challenges imposed by the environment and its subsequent growth depends on the creative efforts of an elite. In nineteenth-century America, the external challenge was first technological innovation (railways, telephone, machine manufacture, etc.) and second, growth of a mass market (Chandler, 1977). The institutional response was multi-unit business whose strategy was to exploit and extend the mass market through low-cost production and distribution. This schema of challenge and response depends on defective and unexamined presuppositions about the relation between formal organisation, strategic calculation and innovation.

On organisation, Chandler's conventional concept of the firm as a unitary sphere of bureaucratic co-ordination is far from convincing. Against this view it can be argued that the large firm is usually a quarrelsome thing – with conflicts between divisions and functional departments and a great divide between senior and middle management. In such cases, the individual firm does not necessarily have any coherent locus of decision-making; strategy and tactics on production and sales, for example, are not necessarily organised into an overall design. It is difficult to accept Chandler's presupposition that this kind of disorder can be controlled by the choice of an appropriate formal organisation. Efficiency in the long run depends on innovation in production and marketing and, as Kanter's (1982) recent work shows, innovation by middle managers depends on politically improvised informal structures. The formal hierarchial organisation authorises and provides the resources for routine action. The innovative break with routine is disruptive and requires the mobilisation of a coalition of organisational backers who will provide information, resources and authority. It is not surprising therefore that Kanter concludes, from her study of five corporations, that innovation is helped by the absence of a well-defined, formal hierarchical organisation; middle managers innovate most easily in an unstructured environment where information moves freely, responsibilities are loosely defined and there are many centres of power.

On strategy, Chandler, like most other theorists of the firm, assumes that strategic response to the environment is systematic but does not explain how and why this is so. If there is to be a systematic response by manufacturing firms in a national economy, the necessary precondition would seem to be the existence of general forms of enterprise calculation which guide strategic decision-making in the different firms. It will now be argued that this precondition is implausible or hard to satisfy. We can do this by examining the effects of the return on investment (ROI) techniques which are now almost universally used by large American corporations in appraising investment projects. Without going into technicalities about discounting calculations, companies using ROI techniques will only adopt an investment project if it shows a rate of return greater than a 'hurdle rate' which is often 25 per cent or more; the same criteria can be expressed in a different way where firms insist that investment projects must pay back in a specified time period like 3 to 5 years. In two recent articles, Hayes (Hayes and Abernathy, 1980; Hayes and Garvin, 1982) has argued that ROI techniques are a defective and unreliable guide to strategic decision-making.

At the level of the individual firm, ROI techniques are biased against large-scale strategic investment. All ROI techniques estimate future returns which will be uncertain, especially where the company is investing in radically new products or processes that open new markets or re-structure old ones. Where a firm is concerned to obtain short-run predictable returns, such strategic innovation will often be unattractive. The rate of return calculation may support re-packaging an existing product and lowering production costs rather than developing a new product, while patching and replication of existing production facilities will usually be more attractive than green-field site development. More important, at the level of the industry, there cannot be a systematic response because a company applying ROI techniques to reject a project may be strategically outmanoeuvred by a competitor who goes ahead after applying a lower 'hurdle rate' or after ignoring ROI criteria. If the competitor, through investment, established a technically superior lower-cost product, then the firm which initially rejected the investment project may find it difficult to make up the leeway because profitability is depressed. The implication of this is that, if strategic decisions cannot be easily reversed, the lagging firm may be caught in a disinvestment spiral. Furthermore, it may be difficult to justify breaking out of this spiral in ROI terms; when firms are moving into a position of technological backwardness, simultaneous investment in several different projects is often necessary to achieve an acceptable return.

In conclusion, these arguments suggest that there are unlikely to be similar strategic responses to a given technological or market opportunity. Indeed, we can develop our argument further by inverting the assumption of systematic and mechanically predictable response; what we have to explain is exactly differences of strategic response to a given situation. Consider, for example, the current strategic issues in the photographic market; here the question is whether and how to introduce electro-magnetic image recording as a complement to, and substitute for, the traditional chemical emulsion processes of image recording (*Financial Times*, 5 February 1982, 8 April 1982).

The American Eastman Kodak company dominates the world market in conventional photographic film and paper; Kodak has over 60 per cent of the free world market for conventional amateur film and 40 per cent of the colour paper business. Kodak has considered electro-magnetic systems but rejected them as unmarketable because the electronic camera is complex and expensive and the end result is a television picture with poor image quality and no print-out copies. Kodak has therefore decided to respond by re-packaging the chemical process for the 1980s in the new 'disc' camera and film system which provides sharper idiot-proof pictures than the previous 110 cartridge system. Mass sale of the heavily promoted disc camera should lock consumers into chemical photography and Kodak materials.

After making a similar analysis of the problems of electro-magnetic photography, Sony Corporation of Japan has nevertheless decided to launch the electro-magnetic 'mavica' camera and film system in 1983 and to develop the mavica over the next ten years. Initially, the mavica will be sold in small quantities at a high price for specialist 'industrial' uses such as press photography where poor image definition is not a problem and the possibility of transmitting pictures by telephone line is a major advantage: meanwhile, development teams will work on improving the product; Sony has already announced the 'mavigraph' printer which turns the electronic image into a conventional print photograph (*Financial Times*, 26 March 1982). According to Sony's chairman, Akio Morita, the company strategy is to improve the process and the product while lowering its price to widen demand until Sony Corporation can start mass production for the consumer market.

A difference of time horizon clearly explains the different strategic responses of the two companies. According to its chairman, Sony was looking for a new major product line because its last major product innovation (the video recorder) was approaching market saturation. In this situation Sony was prepared to allow ten years for a development project to become a commercial business and then to wait another ten years to recover its investment. The interesting question is why should there be this difference of time horizon? Partly, no doubt, it is simply a matter of variable calculation; Kodak applies American style ROI techniques and concludes that the immediate returns from electro-magnetic image recordings are too small. This consideration can be important. As Hayes argues, and as our essay on GEC will show, the pursuit of short-term financial results can inhibit innovation. Nevertheless, this is not a complete explanation because we must recognise that many Western firms are not free to choose long-run objectives. This point is very nicely brought out by the case of the collapse of the British motor-cycle industry in the face of Japanese competition.

The Boston Group (1975) report on the British motor-cycle industry placed much emphasis on the difference between British and Japanese 'market philosophies'. The Japanese pursued long-run market share and sales volume while the British were concerned with short-term model by model profitability. These differences in market objective produced different enterprise strategies. The Japanese firms developed ranges of bikes with a model in every displacement class, while the British firms all withdrew small displacement bikes in the face of Japanese competition and ended up producing only 'super bikes' of over 700 cc. On Boston's account, the British firms chose the wrong time scale and the wrong market objectives. On our interpretation, Boston's account is unacceptable because the British never had a choice: material conditions enforced short-run objectives in the British industry and dictated a strategy of segment retreat on to super bikes.

The position of the British industry was defined by a massive relative inferiority in scale and efficiency. All the British firms had traditionally made small numbers of bikes by craft methods. By the mid-1970s, the maximum annual output of the British industry as a whole was around 50,000 bikes with productivity of approximately 15 bikes per man year. The big three Japanese firms moved sideways into the full-size bike business from their base in mass production of small commuter bikes by capital intensive methods. By 1974 Honda, Yamaha and Suzuki each made 1 to 2 million bikes with productivity of 100 to 200 bikes per man year. It is equally clear that the British firms did not have the managerial resources to take on the Japanese mass producers. The existing British managements had run small firms; the total British bike *industry's* workforce was around 3,000. Furthermore, management controls had been primitive or non-existent in the British firms; bikes were not cost-engineered at the design stage, while under-production and 'sell-out' policies had been used to control inventories.

In principle, new management and capital equipment could have been bought in to stage an offensive against the Japanese. But, in practice, at least until the NVT merger, the independent British firms did not have the financial resources even to defend themselves by maintaining a full range of bikes. Under the British financial rules of the game, sustained losses over several twelve-month accounting periods would have put a firm like BSA into the hands of the receiver. As the low-cost Japanese mass producers were price leaders all round the world, British craft firms got slim margins on every bike they sold. Unprofitable models could not therefore be cross-subsidised without prejudicing the future of the firm. The British firms had to withdraw their smaller models as and when Japanese competition made them unprofitable.

The example of motor-bikes demonstrates the importance of two sets of conditions. The existence of managerial and financial constraints in motor-bikes raises the broader issue of the national conditions of enterprise calculation. The relative inferiority in terms of scale in motor-bike production raises the broader issue of the position of the enterprise in the national industry and the position of that industry in international terms. In the rest of this essay, and in the case studies which follow, our analysis will be organised around these broad issues which can provide us with an alternative framework. As a preliminary, the rest of this section outlines in skeletal form our schema of the conditions of enterprise calculation operating upon differentiated segments of national manufacturing capital.

If we consider the conditions of enterprise calculation, our primary object must be the conditions of execution rather than conceptualisation. In any firm, 'having ideas' is easy, but securing their development, adoption and execution is difficult. Fundamentally this is so because execution of a business strategy depends on specific material preconditions. For an individual firm these might include, for example, access to outside finance or a suitable distribution network. We would emphasise the degree to which each national environment provides to some extent a different set of institutional conditions; for example, the supply of outside finance is very differently organised in the various advanced capitalist national economies. We have already argued that no general theory of the firm can explain why the British are bad at manufacturing. Instead of this, we will offer a specific description of the national conditions of enterprise calculation. In the British case four relevant conditions will be emphasised.

(1) *Management control over the labour process.*
All manufacturing firms must accept or try to modify the control of the workforce over the labour process. Larger British manufacturing firms normally have to deal with an organised unionised workforce. If this is often the case abroad, union prerogatives do vary significantly between countries. For example, British unions conventionally claim the right to negotiate manning levels when new machinery is introduced; their German or Swedish counterparts do not.

(2) *Market structure and the composition of demand.*
Manufacturing firms must serve a characteristic market structure and a specific composition of demand in their home market. In Britain over the past thirty years, two-thirds or more of manufacturing output has been sold on the home market. As we shall see, the characteristics of the home market conditioned and constrained enterprise calculation in British industries as diverse as cars and shipbuilding. It is also important to remember that if companies export, they must enter foreign markets (usually one

at a time) and adjust to the rather different requirements of those countries.

(3)   *Relation of the enterprise to financial institutions like the banks and the stock exchange.*

Enterprise calculation is conditioned by the quantity of funds supplied by financial institutions and, more importantly, the terms on which such funds are supplied. Many commentators on British banking have observed that banks in Japan and Germany have a different relation to manufacturing industry. Less well examined, but equally important, is the question of the stock exchange and the development of secondary markets in issued shares. An unusually developed secondary market in issued shares in Britain permitted the merger boom of the 1960s.

(4)   *Relation of the enterprise to the state whose economic policies impinge at many points.*

Britain is now a part of the Common Market but that supranational organisation is mainly a free trade area and farmers' benefit club. Most relevant economic policy matters are still settled on a national basis. Conditions such as the level and composition of demand are influenced by government policy. More than this, the government has economic policies (in the plural) on such matters as competition and industrial structure.

The emphasis on the national conditions of enterprise calculation may seem provocative and needs some justification when there is such a vast recent literature on the multi-national company. However, the existence of the MNC is not such a problem for our analysis as at first appears. The most that could be argued is that, if multi-nationals all make the same strategic calculations, they standardise the response to variable national conditions of calculation and these national conditions remain a legitimate object for investigation. Furthermore, we would argue that the existence of MNCs does not standardise the strategic response.

We would reject the radical's stereotype of the MNC as representative of a homeless supra-national capital which alights where it pleases according to some simple one-dimensional calculation of interest. For example, the evidence does not support the thesis that, because all other major costs of production are similar in a variety of locations, MNCs simply migrate to wherever labour costs are low. Arguably, the need to be near large high-income markets is a more powerful motivation. Thus, to a significant degree, direct investment is a two-way interchange between the developed countries just like the export trade in manufactures; in 1975, 41 per cent of the total stock of investment from developed countries was invested in only four developed countries (USA, Canada, UK and West Germany) (Hood and Young, 1979). Furthermore, how a MNC serves, or exploits, foreign markets is powerfully conditioned by the home base of the parent in a specific national economy. In this respect, Swedish Volvo is not like British Dunlop or American Ford. As Pratten (1976a) shows, with a small home market, Swedish multi-nationals must concentrate production in their home base to obtain the economies of scale and they therefore tend to use their foreign subsidiaries for distribution rather than production. Again, the particular nationality of the parent must complicate the operation of mechanisms like transfer pricing where they are used to repatriate profit to the parent company. Thus, when both parents are struggling and in some financial difficulty, American Ford has a motivation to repatriate profits from the UK while British Dunlop has a motivation to repatriate profits to the UK.

Multi-nationals must have a place in our analysis, but they must be differentiated according to parent company and then situated as one segment among several different segments which make up the British manufacturing sector. To raise the analysis of the firm's variable position to a sufficient level of generality, we will consider the whole issue of the variable position of the firm in terms of the firm's affiliation to one of a series of segments of national capital. We would emphasise that the different segments of the national manufacturing capital are differently affected by the primary force of the national conditions of enterprise calculation; for example, a large publicly quoted company and a small individually owned manufacturing firm will have different sources of outside finance. And these segments are themselves important in a secondary way because they have different capabilities and they can and do make different calculations of their interest; an American MNC operating on a world-wide basis and a British firm with no overseas manufacturing capacity have different short-run options.

If we are analysing segments of manufacturing capital in Britain, the primary distinction in the private sector is between big business and small business segments. The share of a small number of giant firms in British manufacturing output increased rapidly over the

1950s and 1960s. According to Prais (1976), the 100 largest manufacturing enterprises accounted for 22 per cent of UK net manufacturing output in 1949 and 41 per cent in 1970. Subsequently, the
share of the giant firms has not increased, but it remains true that
100 giant firms account for the better part of half UK manufacturing
output and employment. By this measure, British manufacturing is
unusually concentrated and big business is more dominant than in
other capitalist national economies.

The big business segment is itself differentiated into sub-sections.
Most big manufacturing firms are diversified and operate across
several related or even unrelated product markets; on Channon's
(1973) calculations, 60 of the top 100 UK firms were diversified in
this sense and only 6 of the top 100 could be classified as single-
product firms. The diversified giant firms are often market leaders
and have a strong position in the product markets where they
compete; in 12 of the 17 (SIC) manufacturing industrial orders, the
share of the 100 largest firms is over 30 per cent (Johnson, 1980).

By 1970, a clear majority of the top one hundred firms were also
multi-national in that they were parents or subsidiaries in enterprises which manufactured inside and outside Britain. The subsidiaries of American multi-nationals are important; by 1970, 300 large
US multi-nationals accounted for just over 15 per cent of UK
manufacturing output (Hood and Young, 1979). And these
American subsidiaries were more important in Britain than elsewhere in Europe; in Germany and France they accounted for only
8–10 per cent of output in 1970 (Hood and Young, 1979). But,
quite contrary to popular stereotype, British-owned multi-nationals
are actually numerically more important in the top 100. Channon
(1973) defines a multi-national as a company which has more than
six overseas manufacturing subsidiaries, and on this criterion, by
1970, 58 of our top 100 companies were British-owned multi-
nationals. The British big business segment is unusually committed
to multi-national operations. British big business owns twice as
many giant multi-nationals as either French or German big business; 49 of the world's 260 largest MNC's are British-owned while
only 21 are West German and 19 are French-owned (Hood and
Young, 1979).

The dominance of the big business segment in British manufacturing is such that the trade performance of British manufacturing
is largely the result of the business strategy and the market place

success or failure of 100 or 200 giant firms. If we consider exports, for example, in 1977, three-quarters of UK exports were accounted for by just 189 enterprises (Prest and Coppock, 1980). Foreign-owned UK firms, principally the British subsidiaries of American MNCs, had an important position in this export business; foreign-owned UK firms accounted for 30 per cent of our exports in 1977 (Prest and Coppock, 1980). These foreign-owned companies and the giant British multi-nationals make many of their sales to foreign affiliates and, thus, a significant proportion of our foreign trade now takes place on an intra-firm basis; in 1973 30 per cent of UK exports were intra-firm transactions (Hood and Young, 1979). If there are, therefore, strong positive links between big business conduct and poor British trade performance, we should also remember that, negatively, the relative under-development of the small business segment in Britain may be an important part of an overall explanation of poor trade performance.

This relative under-development must be put into perspective. The dominance of big business in Britain is qualified by the existence of a substantial small business segment; in mid-1976, manufacturing firms employing 200 or fewer employees accounted for 22 per cent of manufacturing employment in the UK (Bannock, 1981). Big business may dominate most product markets, but there is a large tail of small firms in many manufacturing industries. It is difficult to say much more about the small business segment because most of the available national and international evidence concerns small plants or establishments rather than firms, and the relation between the number of small firms and small establishments is complicated when many larger firms own some small plants. Nevertheless, the evidence does suggest two important conclusions. First, the relative importance of the small manufacturing segment has declined dramatically in Britain since the Second World War. If, for example, one considers the workshop end of manufacturing and small plants employing fewer than 10 persons, there were 93,000 establishments of this size in Britain in 1930 and only 35,000 such establishments in 1960 (Prais, 1976). Second, the small-business segment is smaller in Britain than in any other advanced country. In the 1970s, 29 per cent of UK manufacturing employment was in small establishments and only in West Germany was the percentage anywhere near as low as this; all the other advanced industrial countries had 40 to 65 per cent of employment in establishments with fewer than 200 workers (Bannock, 1981).

3   Enterprise control over the labour process

Every pub and club in Britain contains at least one drinker who will tell you that 'it's the bloody-minded workers and their unions who have ruined British industry'. If this argument is to be considered seriously, we must define the nature of the labour problem and its conditioning effects on manufacturing capital. We can begin by challenging the popular non-academic definition of the problem which focuses on strikes and lost working days; on this view the problem is that the British worker will not work and downs tools for trivial reasons. This view may be confirmed by the media presentation of news, but it is decisively contradicted by statistical evidence on strikes and industrial disputes.

The available statistical evidence does not show that Britain has had an unusually severe strike problem, and this conclusion stands even if we include the industrially troubled years of the early 1970s which culminated politically in the coal miners' strike of 1974. Relatively, even in the period 1967–76, Britain came somewhere near the middle of the developed countries' strike league table in terms of days lost per 1,000 workers (Smith, 1980). Absolutely, most manufacturing plants have not lost a large number of working days through stoppages; the Department of Employment calculated that, in the years 1971–5, 98 per cent of manufacturing establishments employing about 80 per cent of manufacturing employees experienced no work stoppages in an average year (Department of Employment, 1978). The official statistics understate the extent of the strike problem because they do not record the small unofficial stoppages which are particularly prevalent in Britain. It must also be admitted that there are general problems where plant-size is large; as Prais (1981) has shown, in Britain strike frequency is almost directly proportional to size of plant. Nevertheless, when all these qualifications have been noted, it would be hard to argue that lost working days are a major condition of poor manufacturing performance.

If there is a labour problem in Britain, it arises from what British workers do when they *are* working. The descriptive literature on

British manufacturing since 1945 has clearly documented a variety of bad work practices. Across a broad range of British industries, machines, installations and assembly lines have been affected by several factors:

(1) They are *overmanned* by the standards achieved in manning comparable equipment in other countries. Unnecessary semi-skilled operatives are retained or demarcation rules about 'who does what' artificially maintain jobs for craftsmen and their mates.

(2) They are *run slowly* so that the equipment habitually works at speeds below those which it is technically capable of and does sustain in other countries.

(3) They are *poorly used* in other ways so that process throughput suffers. For example, the absence of effective preventive maintenance can lead to frequent breakdowns and excessive downtime, or machines may regularly turn out defective products which require expensive rectification further down the line.

At any moment of time, the existence of such work practices reflects past union success in defending custom and practice when new technology is introduced.

If we put these observations about work practices into a more formal framework, it could be argued that in British manufacturing over the past thirty years there has been a general failure of management control over the labour process. This failure could be a significant constraint on enterprise calculation. We can begin to examine whether this is so by considering Kilpatrick and Lawson's (1980) argument that poor control of the labour process is a major factor in our 'industrial decline' since the late nineteenth century.

Kilpatrick and Lawson's article must be welcomed as a progressive problem shift in applied economics. They problematise the important question of the struggle between management and labour over the organisation (and re-organisation) of the labour process within which labour power is expended. This is a necessary corrective to the orthodox neo-classical concept of production as a process combining factors in variable proportions rather like the ingredients in a cake mix. Neo-classical analysis ignores the central point that the efficacy of labour power is variably determined by micro-institutional conditions in the labour process. If they are right to re-conceptualise production in this way, Kilpatrick and Lawson are wrong in trying so single-mindedly to relate our industrial decline to the labour process; they end up providing one more single-factor explanation of Britain's poor manufacturing performance. This line of argument is not only methodologically dubious, it also cannot be brought to a decisive conclusion. Kilpatrick and Lawson positively demonstrate that British employers have long accepted union prerogatives and they cite mainly nineteenth-century instances where the introduction of new technology was delayed and obstructed by organised groups of workers. But they never systematically confront the issue of the extent to which resistance to new technology and the resulting bad work practices imposed significant penalties in terms of cost, output or quality.

From our point of view, this neglect of effects is a crucial weakness. If we are interested in the question of how the observed failure to control the labour process conditions enterprise calculation, it is not enough to show that bad work practices exist. It is necessary to show that bad work practices had damaging consequences which manufacturing firms had to suffer as constraints on their operations. Before we can examine this crucial issue, it is necessary to specify what these consequences might be. We will suppose that the direct adverse effects of bad work practices would be low physical output and/or high costs. The indirect effects could include low product quality and other non-price deficiencies because, for example, poor assembly and quality control compromises reliability. We will not ignore these indirect effects, but to begin with we will concentrate on the direct effects of bad work practices on output and costs. There are two reasons for starting here. First, orthodox economic theory incorporates strong presuppositions that price and cost disadvantages can decisively handicap a national manufacturing sector. Second, Thatcherism politically privileges industrial problems of low output and high costs; the government gives priority to reducing inflation and holding down wage rises because it presupposes that we must become more competitive in cost terms. Against all this it will be argued that there is little evidence that we have been seriously handicapped by low output and high costs and there is little reason to suppose that, in so far as British manufacturing has such a problem, it is either caused by bad work practices or could be resolved by their abolition. Low output and high costs may be important for particular enterprises and segments of capital, but it is not the crucial constraint on manufacturing as a whole.

If we are concerned with low output and its relation to work practices, the evidence on labour productivity is immediately relevant. The available measures here relate a physical quantum of manufacturing output expressed in value terms as value-added to the quantity of labour input expressed in person years. As a point of reference, we can consider the productivity achievements of France and Germany. The measures show that, when post-war reconstruction was largely completed in the mid-1950s, labour productivity in Britain was higher than in France or Germany. But, for the past twenty years there has been a productivity gap with Britain lagging behind France and Germany; as the table below shows, by 1970, output per employee in manufacturing was over 50 per cent higher in France and Germany. 50 per cent seems to be a large gap, so it is worth remembering that, in dynamic terms, the gap is not all that large. By 1973, Britain had attained the levels of value-added per man hour which France and Germany had attained in 1965–6 (Jones, 1976). So Britain was behind by less than a decade.

TABLE 4 *Gross value added per person employed in year 1970 (on puchasing power parity basis)*

Belgium	155
France	164
Germany	155
Italy	105
Netherlands	183
EEC	147
Britain	100

Source: Jones (1976).

Furthermore, if absolute levels of output per man were lower in British manufacturing, the gap was not increasing dramatically by the later 1960s because the British rate of growth of labour productivity had accelerated towards the European norm. Back in the 1950s, the British trend rate of labour productivity growth was well below that achieved by our European competitors. But, as Jones (1976) shows, labour productivity in the UK grew faster in each sub-period from 1955–60 to 1963–73 and by the early 1970s, the

British rate of productivity growth had more or less doubled and reached the 4 per cent per annum level which France and West Germany had maintained since the early 1950s.

TABLE 5   *Per cent per annum increase in output per person employed in manufacturing*

	1955–60	*1969–73*
France	4·40	4·58
Germany	4·92	4·37
UK	2·1	4·46

Source: Jones (1976).

Other studies (Wragg and Robertson, 1978; Wenban-Smith, 1981), give slightly different results but confirm the overall picture of rising British rates of productivity increase which reached 3–4 per cent levels in the 1960s. Wragg and Robertson (1978) bring out the point that the rising rate of productivity increase was particularly commendable because it was an intra-industry achievement. Very little of the British productivity increase was obtained the easy way by redeployment of labour from low to high productivity industries; from 1954 to 1973, 90 per cent of the productivity growth was achieved within industries.

Longstanding international differences in physical output levels must also be set in the context of substantial international differences in labour cost levels. If we look at prevailing national levels of labour costs, by the 1970s, the UK had become a low-wage economy.

TABLE 6   *International comparison of labour costs**

Germany	231
USA	194
France	138
Italy	138
Japan	125
Britain	100

Source: Blackaby, ed. (1979).
*Total cost of labour involved in manufacturing production at current exhange rates.

If physical output levels were lower in Britain, suitably modest wage levels provided enterprises with some compensation. And, as we have already argued in our discussion of trade performance, there was never a secular problem about the rate of increase of labour costs in Britain. By the early 1970s, Britain had settled down into a kind of equilibrium as a low-wage, low-productivity-level economy.

In so far as Britain is a low-wage economy, perhaps labour's low physical output is a characteristic rather than a fault. In orthodox theory, there is no reason why all national manufacturing sectors should converge on one productivity level if the size of national market and the relative cost of labour and capital varies. Firms are supposed to adjust their production techniques according to differences in the relative prices of inputs, and, if labour is relatively cheaper, then larger quantities of labour should be used to produce a given quantum of labour. The relative cheapness of labour in Britain does make labour-saving investment very much less attractive. Pratten (1976b) shows that in 1972, given a payback period of three years, expenditure of about £12,000 could be justified if it saved one employee in the USA; in the UK the equivalent figure was £5,000. It would be wrong to put too much emphasis on this neo-classical line of reasoning; the debate on Habakkuk's thesis about British and American technology in the nineteenth century shows that you cannot read choice of technology off a difference in wage level. Nevertheless, it is important to recognise that orthodox theory does not support the conclusion that a high level of labour productivity is invariably good and that a low level is invariably bad.

So far we have concentrated on the labour productivity record up to 1973, and it must be admitted that the record afterwards is somewhat confusing. After 1973, there was a slow-down in the British rate of growth of labour productivity. But, with the oil crisis and the subsequent rolling recession, this trend was to some extent apparent in all the industrial countries. Almost all British industries experienced declining rates of productivity growth and this suggests an underlying conjunctural problem of demand deficiency (Wenban-Smith, 1981); cyclical downsavings in post-war Britain have classically depressed output growth which in turn feeds through to reduce growth of output per person. Paradoxically, however, when demand fell away precipitously in the major downturn after mid-1979, productivity growth rates improved; by the end of 1981, output per person in manufacturing had increased by 3 per cent while manufacturing output had declined by 15 per cent (*Economic Progress Report*, January 1982). It may be that rates of labour productivity increase are returning to the relatively high levels of the 1960s. But the significance of 3 per cent per annum growth of labour productivity is now entirely different. In the 1960s, faster productivity growth was part of a virtuous cycle of expansion in the economy. In the early 1980s, with no signs of genuine recovery in manufacturing output, faster growth seems to be an effect of a permanent contraction in our manufacturing base. If that appears melodramatic, we should remember that major British industries like steel-making are clearly in a vicious circle of decline with ever lower levels of output associated with ever more remarkable improvements in labour productivity.

If we exclude this kind of 'achievement', the slow-down in productivity growth after 1973 must mainly serve to focus our attention more generally on the connection between the rate of output growth and the rate of productivity growth. Verdoorn's law postulates, and studies of the British economy (Wragg and Robertson, 1978; Wenban-Smith, 1981) confirm, that there is a strong positive relation between rate of growth of output and rate of growth of labour productivity. We know that, through the long boom of the 1950s and 1960s, output in British manufacturing grew relatively slowly. According to Jones (1976), British manufacturing output grew at about 3 per cent per annum, while in five other EEC countries it increased at about 6·5 per cent. If manufacturing output growth was independently constrained in the British economy, then this would excuse low rates of productivity increase and make the 1960s achievement all the more commendable. The problem, of course, is to know whether low output growth was an independent constraint or a symptom and result of low productivity growth. On this point, the argument in the later sections of this essay is relevant; we will argue that British manufacturing faced demand problems about market limitations which were not surmounted because financial institutions and government were unhelpful. The implication of our argument is that output growth was independently constrained.

At this stage in our discussion of productivity, we can establish the basic contrast between British manufacturing's marketplace performance and its workplace performance. Our international marketplace performance is very bad; the evidence on trade share and import penetration is depressing and it is very difficult to find extenuating circumstances. But, after our review of the evidence and arguments about labour productivity and costs, we could conclude that British industry's workplace performance is quite reasonable. The evidence shows that labour productivity performance is respectable in relative international terms. Furthermore, our argument suggests that there are extenuating circumstances (such as wage levels and slow output growth) which could explain the observed deficit in labour's output. Even if this interpretation and argument about 'low' productivity were to be completely rejected, one thing is certain: there is no way in which existing labour productivity measures can be used to justify the inference that bad work practices are the cause of low labour productivity. This crucial point will now be established.

Ultimately, the problem with all measures of labour productivity is one of attribution. Labour productivity measures relate a quantity of output to a quantity of labour input. Any deficiency in output could be attributed either to poor-quality labour inputs or to deficiencies in the quantity and quality of other inputs, especially capital. But, given the heterogeneity of capital goods, it is very difficult to measure the input of capital into the production process. We have some crude indications about the quantity and quality of capital in British manufacturing. For example, the proportion of manufacturing output which is re-invested is not much lower in Britain than in Germany or the USA. And if there is a capital equipment problem it is not simply a matter of vintage; in the key area of machine tools, British capital equipment is not older than that in use elsewhere. But we do not have any aggregate measure of productivity which reliably discloses whether a difference in the quantity and quality of capital equipment explains part or all of the observed deficit in national output. If we were able to resolve these problems and show that British capital equipment was not inferior, that might suggest the problem was poor-quality labour input. But, in this case, available measures of labour productivity would still not allow us to determine whether the poor quality of labour input was primarily caused by bad work practices. There may be other significant causes of national differences in the quality of labour input. We know, for example, that technical and vocational education is very variably developed in different advanced capitalist countries. In Germany, vocational training is legally obligatory for all 15–18-year-olds not otherwise in full-time education; whereas in 1973 in Britain, 60 per cent of those aged 16 to 19 were undergoing no form of further education whatsoever (Prais, 1981). We simply cannot assess the impact of this kind of difference on quality of labour input; attempts such as those of Denison to weight labour input by years of education and age/sex characteristics remain controversial and unconvincing.

The uncertainties about attribution are so great that we must finally conclude that the privileged status of the labour problem in British manufacturing may simply reflect a measurement illusion. Economic discourse may privilege the labour problem because the quantum of labour input is all that can be measured easily and related to the quantum of output. Here, as elsewhere, economic science may be diversionary as well as dismal. No doubt, an uneasy awareness of this point explains the recent interest in process comparisons rather than orthodox productivity measures. From an empiricist point of view, the central problem with orthodox productivity measures is that they do not hold other factors constant so that we can isolate the variation in output attributable to different quantity and quality of labour input. But this *ceteris paribus* condition is approximately satisfied if analysis focuses on one manufacturing process which is undertaken using similar or identical capital equipment in different countries in two plants which are perhaps managed by one multi-national company. This does not completely solve the problem because differences of plant layout may complicate matters where production processes are continuous and interlinked. And the quasi-solution is obtained, as always in this kind of control-the-variables empiricism, by narrowing down the frame of reference so that it is difficult to ascend to generalisation. Nevertheless, the precision of attribution is such that it is worth taking process comparisons seriously.

By way of illustration, we can consider the widely cited process comparisons given in the 1975 Central Policy Review Staff Report on the British car industry which examined the whole process of final assembly and some specific operations such as body framing and door production. On final assembly the CPRS (1975) concluded that 'even with the same capital equipment, plant lay-out and working procedures, it takes almost twice as many labour hours to assemble a car in the UK as it does to assemble the same or a very similar car on the continent.' In single-process comparisons it was again a case of divide by two to find the output of the British worker; in door production using identical machines British output of doors per shift was approximately half continental output. A follow-up investigation by the *Sunday Times* into Ford's British and European operations showed clearly that bad work practices explained larger labour input and/or smaller process output. In Britain, output was lower because lines and machines stopped more often; the main assembly line routinely stopped when shifts changed over and press machines and welding gear broke down more often because of poor preventive maintenance.

Here, at last, we have a definite link between bad work practices and lower output in one of Britain's problem industries. But, when we consider the repercussions for costs and the feed-through from labour cost penalties the picture is complex, and the evidence from process comparisons does not support popular economic prejudices about the damaging consequences of bad work practices. Alarm about these consequences rests on a failure to interpret the evidence of process comparisons and specifically on a failure to discriminate the very variable repercussions of bad work practices for manufacturing capital at different levels. First, it is important to register a systematic discrepancy between (a) the major importance of cost control problems in the labour process to the individual enterprise, and (b) the often minor importance of such problems to the industry. Second, it is important to register another systematic discrepancy between (a) the motivating force of national labour cost variations for some segments of manufacturing capital such as American-owned multi-national companies, and (b) the minor importance of labour cost (or total cost) variation for national manufacturing capital as a whole.

We can first consider the enterprise/industry opposition by examining the case of motor cars. From the enterprise point of view, control of bad work practices could reduce labour costs and dramatically increase profits for Ford or control losses by changing the break-even point for British Leyland. In 1975, when a family car cost £1500, the total net cost penalty from using British labour was £25. This was a glittering prize in a low-margin volume-sale operation and it was the only no-investment change which could transform enterprise profitability. On the other hand, control of bad work practices is not necessarily crucial to the industry, because industries where bad work practices impose cost penalties often have larger cost handicaps arising from other causes. This was true of cars because in 1975 average sales per British model were just over half of continental levels, so the high fixed costs of new model development had to be spread over a small volume of output. In 1975, the cost penalty arising from low-volume production was estimated at £90 per car, or nearly four times as large as the £25 penalty arising from bad work practices. At the industry level, control of bad work practices was an irrelevance because their abolition would not have turned the industry into a low-cost producer. The British industry's major problem was not work practices but the fragmented structure of the industry and its failure to win volume in export markets.

The argument so far already suggests that control of costs through the elimination of bad work practices may not be very important for national manufacturing capital as a whole. This interim conclusion is qualified and reinforced when we analyse the opposition between the segment of capital and national manufacturing capital as a whole. Relatively high labour costs arising from bad work practices may be important in the calculations of some segments of capital. Even if, as we have already argued, multi-nationals are not generally retreating to low-wage developing countries, it may still be the case that labour cost considerations influence American multi-national decisions as to where they site the subsidiaries which will supply the EEC countries. There is anecdotal evidence that American multi-nationals have switched some kinds of consumer good production to mainland Europe because they can source more profitably from non-British factories with superior work practices. This no doubt explains why Ford is not only market leader in the British car market, but also Britain's leading car importer. More subtly, in other cases, British plants have been increasingly used to assemble for the British domestic market rather than to manufacture for British and overseas markets; this is the history of General Motors' British subsidiary (Vauxhall Cars) over the past ten years.

The aggregate impact of such production-switching changes on export performance and import penetration is obscure. If we consider exports, American multi-national subsidiaries are often used as export platforms from which several markets are served. It is not surprising therefore that Dunning finds that the subsidiaries of American multi-nationals in Britain generally have a higher propensity to export than British companies. However, this is not altogether reassuring because the subsidiaries of American multi-nationals are heavily concentrated in some sectors of British industry; in 1970-1, American-owned multi-nationals made 60 per cent of their sales in seven industrial sectors (food, tobacco, minerals, oil-refining, instrument engineering, other electronic apparatus and motor vehicle manufacture) which accounted for only 38 per cent of the sales of all UK companies (Dunning, 1973). This industrial distribution may explain the apparently high propensity to export in British subsidiaries of American multi-nationals. Solomon and Ingham (1977) have shown that *within* the mechanical engineering sector, British subsidiaries of American multi-nationals have a significantly lower propensity to export than indigenous companies. At the end of this argument we can only conclude that significant production switching *may* have taken place. However, it is certain that this effect cannot be the central or single cause of poor British trade performance because the American-owned MNC segment simply is not large enough. Even if it does account for a larger proportion of exports, a segment which since the early 1950s accounts for 10-15 per cent of output can only act as one depressive influence on trade performance. Production switching can only be part of our overall explanation and more empirical work would have to be done before we could determine its exact importance.

Furthermore, we must emphasise that relatively high labour costs (arising from bad work practices or any other cause) do not have great significance for national manufacturing capital. The predictions of classical theory in this matter are decisively contradicted by the empirical evidence which shows that over the past thirty years, changes in relative cost competitiveness do not explain national success and failure in the international trade in manufactures. The Fetherston et al. (1977) analysis of the 1960 to 1976 period shows that a 40 per cent rise in relative unit labour costs did not prevent West Germany's share of world trade in manufactures increasing. By way of contrast, the USA lost share dramatically despite an almost 50 per cent reduction in relative costs, and Britain again lost share dramatically despite fairly stable relative unit labour costs. The implication is that non-price factors are crucial to success in the international trade in manufactures. And the knock-on effects of bad work practices for labour costs cannot be crucial for national manufacturing capital as a whole.

If this conclusion is accepted, there is only one way in which bad work practices could be important for national manufacturing capital as a whole; it would have to be demonstrated that the non-price considerations which account for our poor export performance were primarily caused by bad work practices. Such work practices can only directly explain a small proportion of the quality deficiencies of British manufactures. Strikes can cause late delivery and frequent plant breakdowns can lower assembly standards and thus cause reliability problems. But management is responsible for poor design or weak marketing and it is necessary therefore to specify a mechanism whereby management's poor performance in these areas is indirectly determined by bad work practices. We know that junior and middle management in British problem industries often spends a disproportionate amount of time sorting out labour problems; plant managers in the British car industry claim to spend almost half their time dealing with labour disputes while their counterparts in Belgium and Germany spend 10–15 per cent of their time on such problems (CPRS, 1975). Do bad work practices and labour disputes distract British managers with damaging consequences for non-price competitiveness?

Our arguments in the later sections of this essay suggest that this distraction effect is less important than is commonly supposed. Ineffectual management is immediately responsible for the non-price deficiencies of British manufactures. But in the 1960s the effectiveness of management was being undermined by a variety of developments. As we will argue later, the relation to financial institutions conditioned a merger boom in big business which created large and unwieldy organisations with long spans of control. If such developments made the task of management objectively more difficult, is it necessary to invoke a subjective distraction effect as a major cause of ineffective management? In any case, the work-practice distraction effect must be limited since it primarily affects junior and middle-line management which is responsible for production at the factory. But the non-price deficiencies of British manufactures are not simply a matter of the quality of the product which leaves the factory gate; the deficiencies are at least as much a matter of marketing. If marketing failure stems from management ineffectiveness, the culprits are senior managers with their development and marketing staffs who are all well away from the factory floor. Furthermore, in marketing, from the 1950s onwards, the problems facing management had nothing to do with the British worker because there were difficulties about market limitations which will be analysed in the next section.

4   Market structure and the composition of demand

The marketing function in a broad sense includes a wide range of activities. It begins with the definition of customer requirements and the development of products to meet those requirements. It then goes on to include pricing policy, sales promotion techniques, setting up appropriate distribution channels and providing technical back-up and after-sales service. In recent years, some economists have belatedly recognised that inefficient marketing may be more of a handicap than inefficient production in British industry. Connell (1979), for example, has argued that British industry's sales revenue and profits could perhaps be most effectively increased by better marketing and a more general effort to improve the non-price deficiencies of British manufactures. Nevertheless, Connell continues to define the market problem in orthodox supply side terms as a matter of the response of British enterprise to a given environment; in his analysis, the problem is that British enterprises typically devote too few resources to marketing and diffuse their efforts too widely across a range of different geographic markets. This analysis is undoubtedly correct as far as it goes. Case studies (British Overseas Trade Board, 1977) show that concentration of effort is the key to export success; in fields as diverse as cutlery and metal masts, successful exporters identify the particular foreign markets which offer the best growth potential and then adjust their product and develop the distribution channels to serve those markets. But these observations avoid the crucial question as to why is the concentration of effort necessary? Our answer would emphasise underlying problems about the nationally variable composition and character of demand which have been ignored in current economic discussion.

Economic discussion ignores such problems because it operates in a problematic of Keynesianism where the key consideration is the volume of demand on the national and international market. Thus, demand problems on the British national market of the 1950s and 1960s have been largely discussed in terms of stop/go and fluctuations in the aggregate level of demand. As for the international market, this is usually assumed not to be a problem because the extent of the market for any product is ultimately set by the world's large and growing current needs for a particular product. On this Smithian assumption, international demand cannot have been a problem for twenty years after the mid-1950s during a long boom when trade flows were increasingly liberalised. These presuppositions are dubious. Demand problems on the home market will be discussed in our section on government. In this section, therefore, we will concentrate on the international market and the assumption that the extent of the market is ultimately limited by the world's needs. On this point, the Marxist debate about the principle of economic determinism provides us with an analogy. When Engels, as an old man, was trying to clarify and define the principle, he hit upon the formula that the economic was determinant in the last instance. As Althusser observed in the 1960s, that formula is perfectly acceptable, provided it is recognised that the last instance never comes. The ultimate extent of the world's needs is as irrelevant in many product markets as the role of the economic in the last instance in the Marxist social totality. In practice, the extent of world needs is irrelevant because national markets for many products are neither undifferentiated nor costlessly open.

More specifically, it will now be argued that the variable composition and character of national demands from the mid-1950s onwards often conditioned British enterprise calculation and could render irrelevant favourable trends in the aggregate volume of world demand. On our analysis, two distinct kinds of market problems confronted British firms and their foreign competitors – problems of differentiated national demand and problems of international distribution. We will examine the failure of British enterprises to surmount these problems by considering the cases of shipbuilding and cars where classic demand difficulties presented themselves. It may not be very satisfactory to discuss cases, but it is hard to see how else particular problems about the character of demand can be analysed. Furthermore, we would argue that such difficulties are commonplace in the British problem industries. The immediate reason for decline in the problem industries is not that world demand is declining, but that the British manufacturers in those industries are unable to adjust to the composition of demand. For example, the British bike industry was overwhelmed in its major export market (the USA) because British firms failed to adjust to the requirements of the booming secondary use market where motor bikes were being bought for leisure use rather than for low-cost basic transport. British bikes suited the traditional owner-mechanic who was concerned with rebuildability. But British bikes lacked the styling, features and fuss-free reliability which the Steve McQueen look-alikes in the American secondary-use market demanded.

We can begin by considering differentiated national demand. In many product lines, customers in different national markets and trading blocs demanded goods with specific qualities and characteristics which were not demanded in other markets. We should remember that, for example, in consumer products many American multi-nationals originally set up subsidiaries in Britain or mainland Europe to meet the demand for the distinctly European type of car, white goods or biscuit by manufacturing on the spot. There may have been convergence in some product lines such as motor cars where American manufacturers are increasingly developing world cars. But differences in the character of demand still persist; the small European front-loading automatic washing machine is a very different product from the large American top-loader which is only saleable in Europe in heavy-duty form for commercial launderette use. Furthermore, market demands can be even more particular and specifically national in character. Here, in some cases, such as shipbuilding, British manufacturers could adopt product and production facilities to meet the demands of the home market and end up with a product which was not attractive to foreign buyers.

For much of the 1950s and 1960s, the annual output of the British shipbuilding industry was static at 1·0 to 1·25 million tons. In the same period, world shipbuilding demand and capacity was growing rapidly at a rate of 10 per cent per annum. But that was in practice irrelevant because, although British shipbuilders did make some export sales to foreign shipowners, they concentrated on supplying British shipowners. Between 1945 and the early 1970s, more than 70 per cent of the tonnage built in British yards was built for British owners. And the adaptations to British demand were exactly what disqualified British shipbuilders from competing effectively for foreign orders. To establish this point, we must now demonstrate how the demand linkage to British shipowners conditioned the structure and stategy of the British shipbuilding industry. In the interests of simple exposition, we will ignore the complication of British government orders for warships; such orders did not really help the industry because government did not concentrate orders on specialist yards and the British navy often specified warships which were relatively unsaleable abroad.

British shipowners' demand for merchant ships was fragmented and dispersed largely because there were many British shipowners with relatively small fleets. In 1976, no fewer than 23 owners had fleets whose total tonnage fell between 100,000 and 500,000 tons. In the same year, one-fifth of the total British fleet was still under family ownership. British owners were slow to move into the operation of the newer type of vessels such as large tankers and bulk carriers; in 1963, the average British-owned tanker built in UK yards was still only 13,000 tons. A variety of vessel types was required – tramp freighters, cargo liners, refrigerated vessels, ferries, passenger liners, etc. These were always ordered on a one-off or small series basis with vessels made to measure for particular owners; in a freighter, for example, the owner would expect to specify not only tonnage and performance but also the arrangements of decking, hatches and cargo handling gear which were preferred for a particular trade. Much of the demand was replacement demand because British shipowners were not dramatically increasing the size of their fleets before the late 1960s. But the flow of replacement orders from British shipowners was erratic and unpredictable because many of the smaller owners over-reacted to variations in freight rates and placed speculative contracts with British yards when freight rates were rising.

This pattern of demand fundamentally conditioned British shipbuilding. If we begin by examining the structure of the industry, fragmented demand was met by a supplying industry which was also highly fragmented. In 1965, there were 27 shipyards in the UK which regularly built vessels of more than 5,000 gross tons or equivalent naval vessels. Many of these yards were small independent firms which survived until government-sponsored reorganisation had created regional groupings by the early 1970s. Demand patterns also conditioned enterprise strategy. Most of the yards were 'jobbing shipbuilders' who deliberately maintained their ability to make a variety of types of merchant ships; this was simply the best insurance in a risky business where the specialised yard might not obtain orders. The strategy of non-specialisation in turn conditioned investment decisions. The jobbing shipbuilder wanted the flexibility of a traditional shipbuilding yard dominated by open berths where craftsmen built whatever vessels were on order. When the shipbuilding industry already possessed such facilities it did not need to invest heavily and, in any case, the costs of new investment could be burdensome if orders became hard to find. Hence the industry's investment peaked at £20 million per year in the late 1950s and subsequently declined as British shipbuilding yards generally moved into a position of relative technological backwardness.

The importance of this demand linkage is confirmed by the experience of the one British firm which avoided this fate and by the experience of continental yards which adapted to the new demands. Prior to nationalisation of shipbuilding, the Sunderland firm of Austin and Pickersgill had found a specialised niche in the factory-style series production of the SD14 utility freighter. But Austin and Pickersgill were not building for typical British owners; the outline specification of the SD14 was determined, and early production vessels were bought, by the Greek Mavroleon family who ran London and Overseas Freighters and saw the potential international market for series production of a Liberty freighter replacement. Elsewhere in Europe, national merchant fleets were usually much smaller than the British fleet and other national fleets probably did not make such reactionary demands on their home builders. There were therefore cases where European yards successfully adapted to changing international demands; Kockums of Sweden had some success with Japanese-style computer-controlled plate fabrication for big tankers and bulk carriers.

The demand-induced problems of British shipbuilding may have no direct parallel elsewhere in the shipping world. But a detailed examination of the recent history of other advanced capitalist countries would doubtless disclose other instances where the character of national demand induced retardation in a supplying industry. Such considerations may, for example, be important in the collapse of the traditional French textile industries in the 1970s. The potential for demand-induced retardation is present in all the advanced capitalist countries because the home market is predominant in France or West Germany just as it is in Britain where, before 1970, four-fifths of manufactures were sold on the domestic market. What is perhaps really distinctive is the British response to demand difficulties; in Britain the problems are not resolved, or even identified, and the outcome is disastrous. This was certainly so in the case of shipbuilding because in the 1970s British shipowners took their orders elsewhere, leaving British shipbuilders with few customers for merchant vessels; between 1974 and 1976 less than one-third of the tonnage registered by British owners was British-built and, at present, no other major shipbuilding nation supplies a smaller proportion of the requirements of its national merchant fleet. This disastrous outcome was clearly conditioned by certain national peculiarities. In British shipbuilding there was no linkage (other than custom) between the supplying industry and its home customers, while neither financial institutions nor governments were prepared to enforce the conventional relation and maintain national demand at the same time as the supplying industry was forcibly reorganised.

The tragedy of British shipbuilding is that the commitment to British shipowners was practically irreversible for the yards although this relation could be easily and costlessly dissolved from the owners' point of view. By the 1960s, British shipbuilders were increasingly locked into supplying British shipowners. The builders could not find other customers who would make the same demands and their production facilities prevented them moving effectively into more capital-intensive product lines. In particular, to build supertankers in the 1960s, British shipbuilders would have had to make a quantum jump into large-scale factory production on green-field sites. The scale of the change required is indicated by one statistic; in 1965 one Japanese yard at Nagasaki produced a tonnage which was equivalent to three-fifths of the output of the entire British industry. Of course, such Japanese yards were discomfited when world demand for supertankers collapsed after 1974. But that rebounded to the disadvantage of the British because the Japanese responded by modifying their technology to compete more directly in the production of high-value-per-ton vessels which required complex hull structures and more outfitting.

British shipowners were not locked into British shipbuilders by any kind of financial linkage. Owners and builders were not subsidiaries of one parent corporation as they might be in Japan, nor did British shipowners usually own shipbuilding yards. Significantly, the one successful British shipbuilding company was an exception to this rule; Austin and Pickersgill was an associate of London and Overseas Freighters which therefore had a direct financial interest in the success of the Sunderland yard. Generally, however, although many British shipowners conventionally placed orders with one or a few yards, British shipowners were free to sign contracts with non-British yards. This was what British owners did when they finally moved into big tankers and bulk carriers at the end of the 1960s. By the mid-1970s, Britain had the world's third-largest tanker fleet and there were several British owners who separately operated more than 1 million tons of tankers and bulk carriers. These vessels were generally bought in from foreign yards which had specialised in these product lines and could therefore offer better prices and delivery dates. At this point, the relation to government becomes important. The British government reacted to shipbuilding's difficulties by aiding ailing yards which had no customers and finally by nationalising the whole industry. Although it intervened over particular orders for ships and did offer British shipowners some financial inducements to build in Britain, the figures show quite conclusively that the British government failed to ensure that our shipowners bought British while the British shipbuilding industry was reorganised to meet new patterns of demand.

So far we have discussed differentiated demand, and we can now turn to the distinct problem of distribution. Many consumer and producer goods can only be sold in a national market, if the manufacturer has a supporting network of distributors and dealers to hold stock, promote the product, make the sale and provide the customer with after-sales service and technical back-up. This is not so much of a problem with heavy producer goods where the supplier sells a sophisticated and expensive machine or indeed a whole factory or power-station on a turn key basis with installation, running in and subsequent back-up supervised by the supplier's own staff. But, wherever products are mechanically or electrically complex and the manufacturer gets turnover by selling many relatively low value units, distribution is a problem. Although international trade was increasingly liberalised in the 1950s and 1960s, foreign markets were not costlessly open even when tariffs and quotas had been removed. If British manufacturers wanted to enter new national markets abroad, they had to incur heavy 'front end' expenses. For example, they had to set up distribution and service networks which would initially handle small volumes. And, if foreign customers required new or modified products, both production and marketing had to be got together in one act. Foreign markets were, and are, open to British manufacturers only if they identify and solve the relevant distribution problems in particular product markets. The difficulties of achieving this were often considerable. By way of example, we can consider the distribution problems of the British car industry or, more specifically, the problems of BMC/BLMC, the major independent British car firm between 1952 and 1975.

Between 1952 and 1965, BMC deliberately expanded production from approximately 300,000 vehicles per annum to 1 million vehicles per annum. The company's strategy of expansion created demand problems; where were 1 million vehicles to be sold every year? In the 1950s and 1960s, the company's increased output was sold at home. Home vehicle sales increased much more rapidly than export sales; from 1951–2 to the record year of 1964–5, home sales increased more than five times (+ 577%) while export sales did not double (+ 131%). This was the line of least resistance when car use and ownership was rapidly increasing on the British home market where the company had a large dealer network. When BMC was formed in 1951, 138,000 new cars were registered; just over ten years later, in 1964, 1,216,000 new cars were registered. The company's problem was that growth in new car registrations slowed down subsequently as the British car market matured. By the 1970s, replacement demand was dominant in a market which was approaching saturation at the European level of one car for every three to four persons. Even in the best years of the 1970s (1973 and 1979), just under 1,750,000 new cars were registered in the UK and the new car market was usually substantially smaller than this.

Quite apart from its limited overall size, the composition and character of demand on the home market created increasingly severe problems for BMC which was the market leader with nearly 40 per cent of British new car registrations. At home, BMC's fundamental problem was the British private car buyers' taste for diversity which was nurtured in the 1950s by a fragmented British supplying industry where five major manufacturers each offered a range of models. In Germany, Volkswagen could persuade one-third or more of new car buyers to buy just one model, the Beetle. But a British bestseller seldom claimed more than 10–12 per cent of the market. Thus, after 1959, BMC had to produce two bestselling small cars (the mini and the 1100) which in their heyday together took some 25 per cent of the car market. To defend its normal market share of nearly 40 per cent, BMC had to develop and keep in production a variety of other models. What BMC needed was a bestselling larger (1500–1600 cc) car, but this was impossible because of the limited British demand for larger cars. With one-third of sales in the 1100–1300cc displacement class, the British market was large enough to sustain several bestsellers in this class; the BMC 1100/1300, the Ford Escort and the Vauxhall Viva all sold well from the late 1960s onwards. But showroom 1500 and 1600cc cars consistently accounted for under one-fifth of new car sales; in this displacement class there was only room for one bestseller and ever since it was moved upmarket (in the late 1960s), the bestselling 1600 has always been the Ford Cortina. Ford's position in this market sector was virtually unassailable because Ford usually had a good product and always had the distribution network to make fleet sales of a new car which had to be sold to business users since it was too large and thirsty for the private unsubsidised buyer.

More generally, the growing importance of the company car sector from the mid-1960s was a factor which worked against BMC. In most European countries, business users buy their own cars and claim a mileage allowance for company use. In Britain, as a way of avoiding income tax and pay policy restrictions, business employees have increasingly been provided with a company car as a perk, even if they do not use a car on company business. In 1965, only 37 per cent of all UK executives received a company car; currently, according to Inbucon consultants, 85 per cent of company executives earning over £10,000 a year now have a company car. The private unsubsidised car buyer who traditionally bought BMC was of declining importance and by the early 1970s only accounted for some 60 per cent of purchases in the new car market. At this point, the British private buyer's taste for diversity dramatically aggravated BMC/BLMC's problems. This taste for diversity was now served by car importers who provided a wide choice of small cars distinguished by marginal packaging differences (VW Polo and Golf, Renault 5, Fiat 127, Datsun Cherry, etc.). By 1975, 45 per cent of private buyers bought a foreign car.

After the Leyland takeover of BMC at the end of the 1960s, the company's home market problems were becoming acute: with the rise of the company car and the growth of imports, the share of the home market available to BLMC was shrinking rapidly. When the British car market turned down after 1973, the inevitable result was an absolute loss of production and sales. Austin-Morris sold nearly 700,000 cars at home and abroad in 1972 and 1973; by 1975 sales were down to 450,000 and they never recovered. Home market problems led to a dramatic loss of sales because of the long-standing failure to develop export markets. Here the story up to the late 1960s is of BMC's opportunistic switches from one export market to another. This postponed disaster, but did not find adequate outlets for the increasing number of cars coming off the lines at BMC's British factories. A disaggregated market-by-market analysis highlights the problems. BMC, and its successor BLMC, lacked the distribution and the products to achieve volume in its two major export markets – Europe and North America.

In the early 1950s, BMC made most of its export sales in the Commonwealth; but export markets like Australia were spoilt by regulations insisting on manufacture with substantial local content. The BMC's next gambit was to develop the North American market which had traditionally taken sports cars in small volume. As late as 1954–5, the USA and Canada together took only 19,000 cars or just 12 per cent of BMC's total vehicle exports. By 1959–60, the North American market took 110,000 cars or 39 per cent of total vehicle exports. But its product lines were such that BMC could not find a stable place in the American market. Like all the other European importers except Volkswagen, BMC was overwhelmed in 1960 when the American manufacturers introduced their 'compacts'. In 1960–1, the North American market took only 41,000 vehicles. Subsequently the company staged a partial recovery, although it was in something of a dilemma about product lines. The small front-wheel drive cars which had been developed for British tastes and conditions were not very saleable in America.

But with its new product lines, the BMC was able to switch markets again and to take sales in Europe. From a small base, production for Europe built up so that European markets by 1964 took 130,000 units or 40·6 per cent of BMC's world exports. To get round tariff barriers, the company developed European assembly of British 'knocked-down' kits in Italy, Belgium and Spain. The weakness of this strategy was that the company had sub-contracted these assembly operations; BMC did not own or control the activities of the two major assembly operations in Italy and Spain. Furthermore, BMC and its successor BLMC were not well placed to make volume European sales because it had a non-existent or patchy distribution network in many European markets. The company was strongly represented in some small peripheral markets like Eire and Denmark, and it had volume sales in Belgium and

Italy where cars were assembled locally. But, unbelievably, BMC and BLMC never had a dealer network in France and Germany, two of the big three national markets. Consequently, in 1975, when 3,500,000 new cars were sold in France and Germany, BLMC managed to sell just 7,204 cars in those countries. It was this failure to solve distribution problems and the resulting low volume sales in near West European markets which distinguished BMC/BLMC from the other major European national producers (Fiat, Renault and VW) and which ultimately determined BLMC's failure.

Clearly, the enterprise itself must take prime responsibility for failing to solve distribution problems. Successive management teams at BMC and BLMC failed to maintain and build the European dealer networks which were essential for volume sales. This failure relates also to poor product planning. The company never developed a range of cars which was highly saleable in Europe; through the 1960s and into the 1970s, one model (the mini) consistently accounted for two-thirds or more of BMC/BLMC's European sales. But the relation to government does become important with the company's failure and effective nationalisation in 1975. The Ryder report was the crucial official document which outlined the future strategy of the newly nationalised company. Ryder completely ignored the market limitations which had frustrated the company for nearly twenty years and based a strategy of expanded car output on the assumption that increased output could be easily sold at home and abroad. The subsequent history of the company has shown the falsity of this assumption; in 1981, BL sold 80,000 cars in Europe when Ryder had projected it would sell more than 300,000.

In conclusion, therefore, many British enterprises in the difficult industries faced problems about market structure and the composition of demand. It would be hard to argue that these problems were unlike or worse than those facing enterprises in other capitalist nationalised economies. In cars, shipbuilding and motor-bikes, producers in other European national economies faced similar problems but managed to resolve, or come to terms with them more successfully. British enterprises were hindered from doing this by governments which did not take market problems seriously. And, in some cases such as shipbuilding, there was the further problem of an absence of financial linkages between the supplying industry and other segments of capital; such linkages could have played a crucial role in controlling traumatic dislocation and promoting adjustment to new patterns of demand. However, it would be wrong to appraise financial institutions and government simply in terms of their negative impact on problem industries with market difficulties. In the next two sections of this essay, we will consider how British enterprise calculation was much more generally conditioned by relations to financial institutions and government. We will argue that these relations operated to constrain enterprises and segments of capital even where there were no industrial problems about the composition and character of demand.

5   Relation to financial institutions (a) external finance from banks and stock exchange

The relation of manufacturing to financial institutions is important in all the advanced capitalist countries. This is because the financial system generally provides investment funds for manufacturing or, more precisely, performs certain channelling and transformation functions in the supply of funds for manufacturing. Financial institutions collect savings from the mass of small savers and then make them available to manufacturers in large blocs. As intermediaries, financial institutions also classically fulfil a transformation function because in many cases the form and duration in which savers prefer to hold their savings will differ from the needs of manufacturing. The question to be answered in this section is: how does the performance of these channelling and transformation functions by British financial institutions condition the calculations of British manufacturing? We must begin by noting that this question can only be answered by piecing together the available evidence on finance which, unfortunately for our purposes, often covers the corporate sector as a whole and includes distribution as well as manufacturing. More seriously, there is a problem of interpretation; much of the evidence is undisputed but difficult to interpret. We will try to resolve this problem by constructing an argument from the evidence.

The British pattern of flows of funds between the personal and business sector has been unlike the pattern which prevails in other advanced capitalist countries. As Hu (1975) has demonstrated, the national income accounts of other advanced countries from the early 1950s onwards show the corporate sector is running a financial deficit which is covered by a massive channelling of resources into the corporate sector from the personal sector and sometimes from government. But until the mid-1960s, in the UK, the corporate sector had a financial surplus in most years; that is to say, the corporate sector did not usually receive resources from other sectors but was in a position to invest in them. It is true that since about 1964 the corporate sector has been in deficit, but, until the mid-1970s, this deficit was relatively small in relation to gross fixed investment and investment in stocks. The British deficit did cover fixed investment, but more than 80 per cent of investment in stock was internally financed until the inflation-induced stock appreciation crisis in 1974. Yao Su Hu shows that in other advanced capitalist countries the deficit covered a larger proportion of investment in fixed equipment plus stocks.

If the pattern of flows of funds into the corporate sector was different in Britain, it follows logically that the sources of funds available to manufacturing and other companies were also different. To a remarkable degree, British companies have financed investment out of internally generated funds, that is, depreciation provision plus retained profits. If one considers the apparent situation, under the prevailing historic cost-accounting rules which have always defined profit in Britain, internal funds have been clearly the dominant component of the total funds available to industrial and commercial companies; the Wilson Committee's evidence (vol.2, 1977) showed that from 1964 to 1975 retained earnings averaged 70 per cent of total funds available and in no year accounted for less than 59 per cent.

The two major sources of external funds were bank lending and new issues on the stock market. It is difficult to generalise about the relative importance of these two external sources since the volume of new issues was very variable. But most studies suggest that in secular terms up to the mid-1970s, the banks and the stock exchange supplied roughly equal proportions of the 25 per cent of available funds which were externally provided.

This rough parity is unusual because in other advanced capitalist countries the banks have been relatively more important than the stock exchange as suppliers of long-term loans to manufacturing. This point emerges clearly from any comparison of the ratio of bank debt to stock exchange equity in different advanced capitalist countries.

TABLE 7   *Bank debt as percentage of stock exchange equity for industrial and commercial companies in 1970*

Japan	85
West Germany	57
France	39
USA	31
UK	22

Source: Carrington and Edwards (1979).

This peculiar situation did not arise because British companies were unusually well supplied with new equity by the stock exchange; over the period 1969–73, the stock market supplied less new equity finance in relation to GNP in the UK than it did in France, Germany, Japan or the USA.

TABLE 8   *New equity finance as percentage of gross national product, 1969–73*

France	0·87
West Germany	0·52
Japan	1·50
USA	0·65
UK	0·49

Source: Hu (1975).

It is necessary to be cautious about interpreting these figures because they cover equity issues of ordinary shares when fixed interest securities (debentures) were favoured by British companies; in their heyday in the later 1960s, debentures accounted for well over half of all British commercial and industrial issues (Thomas, 1978). But that does not really change the picture since the conventional figures on equity issue grossly overstate the amount of cash which British manufacturing realised from this source. Meeks and Whittington (1976) have shown that from 1964 to 1971 only one-third of the total value of new equity issues by UK quoted companies were issues for cash; in a period of merger boom the rest were equity issues made in exchange for the shares of other companies which were being taken over.

If the relative importance of the banks and the stock exchange has been different in Britain, the more important point is that the banks and stock exchange in Britain *together* do not offer access to sizeable medium and long-term external finance as West German and United States institutions do. If one considers all medium- and long-term capital funds provided to corporate enterprise, in percentage of gross domestic product terms, at the end of the long twenty-year boom British provision was less than half as generous as in West Germany or Japan.

TABLE 9 *Medium- and long-term capital funds, externally provided to non-financial corporate and quasi-corporate enterprises (% GDP)*

	France	Japan	W. Germany	UK	USA
1970	4·51	7·99	7·60	3·09	3·98
1971	4·79	9·65	9·04	4·35	4·99
1972	4·92	8·33	9·64	2·75	4·86
1973	5·00	8·46	8·67	1·77	4·01
1974		3·87	6·06	2·67	3·65

Source: Carrington and Edwards (1979).

We are of course concerned with how this national peculiarity conditions and affects manufacturing enterprise. From this point of view, the significance of a deficiency in external resources depends on the adequacy of industry's internal resources. If industry's own resources are substantial, an inadequate external supply of funds will not constrain the rate of expansion of the manufacturing sector. The rate of expansion that can be sustained from the corporate sector's own resources depends on two considerations, liquidity and profits. If industry has a stock of liquid assets, this can be run down to finance expansion. But in the British case we would argue that the crucial consideration was profitability. British companies did emerge from the Second World War flush with liquid assets, and reserves were considerable through the 1950s; in the mid-decade cyclical peak year of 1954 marketable securities, tax reserve certificates and net bank balances amounted to 14·1 per cent of net assets of all quoted companies in manufacturing and distribution (Meeks, 1981). But, by the mid-1960s, this liquidity reserve was exhausted; in the mid-decade cyclical peak year of 1964, liquid reserves had fallen to just 1 per cent of quoted company net assets (Meeks, 1981). From the early 1960s onwards therefore, the sustainable rate of expansion in the corporate sector depended on profit, or the surplus earned on existing assets.

The question of profit is complex because the size of this surplus depends on how it is measured and, as we have already argued, in any specific national economy the size of the declared corporate surplus depends on the prevailing accounting conventions. If there is no one correct way of measuring the accounting rate of return, nevertheless one conventional definition is most suitable for our purposes. In an inflationary age, this relevant rate is the current or replacement cost rate of profit. Such a rate makes allowance for the need to replace fixed capital equipment and working capital stock at current replacement prices, which as a result of inflation will be higher than those prevailing when capital equipment was originally purchased and stock was previously bought in. Such replacement cost allowances must be made if we are to make realistic provision for maintaining the value of existing fixed and working capital assets in the corporate sector. The residual post-deduction figure gives us a measure of the accounting profit or surplus on existing assets and, from our point of view, this provides us with the best available measure of industry's real capacity to expand from internal resources in an inflationary age. Such a current cost measure is not, of course, the declared accounting rate of return disclosed in British company reports of the 1950s or the 1970s. This declared rate of return was, and is, measured under historic cost conventions which increasingly, as inflation accelerated, tended to overstate profit and thus give a false impression of the sustainable rate of industrial expansion. This point can be simply demonstrated by considering the hypothetical case of an individual manufacturing company which applied all its declared historic cost profit to financing expansion in the form of a new branch factory. In an inflationary period this company would then be unable to maintain stock levels or replace its existing machinery in the old factory.

The available data on current cost profit give a pre-tax rate of return since 1960 for private manufacturing companies as well as for industrial and commercial companies (Martin and O'Connor, 1981).

As graph 6 shows, a downward trend in manufacturing profit begins in 1960 just when company liquid reserves were running out; from nearly 13 per cent at the beginning of the decade, the rate sagged through the 1960s so that by the early 1970s it was under 8 per cent. There was then a further sharp drop in 1974 towards the 3 per cent rate of profit recorded in the years 1974 to 1976 inclusive. A weak recovery towards 5 per cent profit in 1978 was followed by a drop back to under 3 per cent as the present recession set in.

GRAPH 6   Rate of return* in British manufacturing

Source: Martin and O'Connor (1981), table B2, p.23.
*Current cost rate of profit = gross trading profit less stock appreciation less capital consumption at replacement cost, as percentage of net capital stock (fixed assets other than land) at replacement cost plus book value of stock.

These low and declining profit rates are not necessarily a symptom of terminal illness; as current experience shows, the manufacturing sector can survive low or zero profit for quite long periods of time provided enterprises carefully monitor cash flow. From our point of view, the relevant point is that low and declining profit means that the short-run rate of expansion which British manufacturing could sustain from internal resources was always modest and becoming increasingly negligible. Very low positive rates of return are only significant if they are sustained in the long run; thanks to the magic of compound interest, a steady 3 per cent per annum growth translates into a doubling of size every twenty-five years. This is small consolation when rates of return and thus short-run expansion possibilities are substantially greater in all the other advanced capitalist countries. Hill's (1979) work for the OECD shows that there is a general secular trend towards declining rates of return in all these countries. But the effects of relative decline have been much more severe in Britain since British rates of return have long been substantially lower than those elsewhere. At the upper end of the range of variations in corporate profit rates, the United States and West Germany had rates of return of around 20 per cent in the twenty-year boom from the mid-1950s to the mid-1970s; these rates were nearly twice as high as those which were being sustained in the British economy at the same time (Martin and O'Connor, 1981).

International differences in the rate of return do not therefore compensate for differences in the provision of funds from external sources. On the contrary, in the British case, low British rates of return reinforce the deficiency in external resources. In this, as in other matters, the comparison with our closest competitors, France and West Germany, is really striking. In our view, this deficit of internal plus external finance in Britain is something which has to be explained, although it is not easy to construct an interpretation of how it arises and how it conditions enterprise calculation.

TABLE 10   *Total medium- and long-term finance (internal plus external funds) available to non-financial corporate and quasi-corporate enterprises as percentage of gross domestic product*

	France	West Germany	UK
1970	17·7	22·39	9·9
1971	17·24	22·34	11·8

Source: Carrington and Edwards (1979).

For the apologetic marginalist or the apocalyptic Marxist, there is, of course, no interpretative problem here because the significance of a low and declining rate of profit is clear: for the marginalist it forecloses all further discussion because a low rate of return is a sufficient reason for low investment; while, for the Marxist, it is an assurance that the terminal crisis of capitalism is just around the corner. Both these interpretations must be rejected since they rest on gross intellectual confusion as to exactly what rate of profit is (or can be) observed to be declining. For the marginalist, profit is the difference between marginal cost and marginal revenue or the price that has to be paid to obtain capital; for the Marxist, it is the ratio of surplus value to constant plus variable capital. Both these opposed concepts of profit are ultimately metaphysical in that their function is to vindicate the possibility of allocative efficiency in the one case and the necessity for exploitation in the other. More immediately relevant is the point that both Marxist and marginalist concepts exist in the theory of the capitalist economy in general and have no operational counterparts in specific capitalist national economies. Even if Marxist or marginalist operational categories and measures were to be developed, there is no reason to suppose that they would show a profit level or trend which coincided with the declared (or any other) accounting rate of return in a specific national economy.

If the marginalist interpretation rests on confusions about the category of profit, it is important to emphasise at this point that the interpretation cannot be sustained, as some suppose, by invoking the low capital/output ratio in the British economy as an alternative problem-free measure of inefficiency which shows that investment in Britain is just not worthwhile. In the case of capital/output ratios, we encounter again, in particular form, problems about the measurement of capital input which we have already noted in our discussion of labour productivity. It is clearly necessary to calculate an incremental capital/output ratio which relates an input of extra capital equipment to a net increase of output. The overall capital/output ratio is a meaningless measure because its value directly depends on variability in the ratio of replacement investment to total investment; where most investment is replacement investment, the overall/capital ratio will necessarily be low. This point is highly pertinent in the British case because the low current cost rate of return which we have analysed implies that in Britain an unusually large proportion of our corporate investment has been replacement investment. Unless one is satisfied that this complication has been properly and accurately allowed for, our poor relative international performance in capital/output terms may be a matter of mis-specification and arithmetical logic rather than inefficiency. Furthermore, it must be admitted that it is extremely difficult to separate replacement investment when much of it takes the form of investment in new and technically superior equipment.

It might be possible to salvage the orthodox economic interpretation of low profits by shifting the argument about the inhibiting effect of low profit on to the terrain of econometrics where opportunist operationalisation rules. This is the gambit which the Treasury tried, in its 1977 evidence to the Wilson Committee. For the Treasury, the key to investment is the expectation of (accounting) profit, the basic assumption being that businessmen will invest when it is profitable to do so. Econometric studies show that investment changes relate positively to recent changes in capacity utilisation and expectations of short-run growth in the volume of sales; the Treasury believes these variables are significant because they determine the short-run expectation of profit. We would argue that this may be true but it is not very informative. At an observational level, low investment and low borrowing are associated with low profit in British manufacturing. This does not, however, say anything about the rationality of other modes of calculation; it simply rationalises what British manufacturers actually did as the only possible course of action. Furthermore, it abstracts from the supply side and the whole question of the terms on which funds are made available. In its evidence to Wilson, the Treasury constructed the supply side in terms of the one operational issue of variations in the rate of interest which were devalued, because econometric studies do not show the cost of funds to be a significant determinant of investment. This simply does not tell us very much about the terms on which finance is supplied to industry; the term for which loans are granted or the criteria which are applied in appraising borrowers may well be more important than the rate of interest.

If we discount existing economic interpretations, we must nevertheless confront the question of whether a low and declining constraint rate of profit is a sufficient reason for low investment. We can begin to answer this question by making a general point about the incentive to invest where accounting profit is low. In the theory of the capitalist economy in general, low profit only removes the incentive to invest on certain very restrictive assumptions and classically on the assumption that profit is determined by the *given* technical and cost considerations which determine the relation between marginal cost and marginal revenue. There seems to be no good theoretical reason to suppose that this givenness is a problem in the long run; by strategic investment, a large manufacturing enterprise will shift the moveable technical and cost constraints and adjust to the immoveable ones. Thus, recent theorists of the capitalist economy in general such as Wood (1975) have argued that profit is generally a dependent variable because firms can choose a higher rate of return to finance growth strategies. If we turn to the situation in particular national economies, we cannot however take such a generalised and sanguine view of firms' ability to choose a higher accounting rate of return. The crucial point here is that an individual firm's return on a strategic investment programme is likely to depend on a variety of specific considerations such as market share or the burden of new product introductions. We will consider Gale's (1980) evidence and arguments on these points in our final section on government and manufacturing: there we will argue that the enterprises and industries which government nationalised in the 1970s shared characteristics which made it unlikely that large-scale strategic investment would produce a decent rate of return. At the same time we would argue strongly that the futility of strategic investment in sectors of manufacturing cannot legitimately be deduced from a low average rate of return in manufacturing as a whole.

In this context it is also important to emphasise the particular point that low and declining profitability did not immediately compromise the manufacturing sector's ability to finance investment by borrowing from the banks or other financial institutions. Flemming et al. (1976) have produced a composite measure of the cost of capital which is directly comparable with the measures of current cost rate of return which we have already discussed. The Flemming series shows that real interest rates were low and falling; the post-tax real cost of capital declined from nearly 9 per cent in 1960 to around 4 per cent in the 1970s. Therefore declining cost of capital paralleled a declining rate of manufacturing profit until the mid-1970s. In each of the fifteen years between 1960 and 1974, the (post-tax) cost of capital was always below the manufacturing sector's (pre-tax) current cost rate of return and the average difference was a fairly substantial 3·8 per cent. It was the *post-tax* rate of return, of course, which was more relevant to enterprise calculation. But company taxation probably did little more than reduce the gap which we have noted because (as we will argue in our section on government) the burden of company taxation was never heavy and the system was almost certainly increasingly generous to companies. In any case, in the short run, it did not matter if the post-tax current cost rate of return was at, or marginally below, the cost of capital, because the perceived rate of profit was a historic cost rate which led both borrowers and lenders to an optimistic view of corporate profitability. British industry's declared profits were measured on a historic cost basis which increasingly made industrial profitability look better than it was; for all industrial and commercial companies, the pre-tax historic cost rate of return held up at around 15 per cent until the mid-1970s (Clark and Williams, 1978).

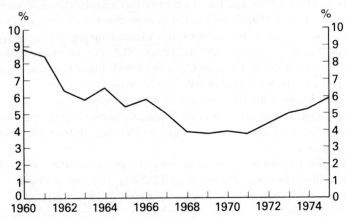

GRAPH 7   cost of capital in Britain

Source: Flemming (1976), table C, p.197.

We have now argued that low accounting profit in British industry up to the mid-1970s was not generally a sufficient reason for low investment, and our next question must be: why was the observed level of external finance so low and how did the available supply condition enterprise calculation? We can begin to answer these questions by considering supply side conditions and lending practices. First, there are the national institutional conditions which determine the overall volume of long- and short-term funds available. Second, there are the criteria according to which money was made available to borrowers; these criteria are not determined by the volume and term of funds available since they reflect the exercise of discretion by lending institutions working within a specifically national legal and accounting framework. We will consider in turn the volume of funds supplied and the loan criteria applied by the High Street banks and the stock exchange new-issue market – the two institutions which we have already identified as the major suppliers of external finance for British industry.

To begin with the banks, the immediate problem here was not that the volume of advances was restricted because the banks did not have access to substantial deposits; at worst there were credit squeezes in the stop phases of economic policy in the 1950s and 1960s. The more serious problem was that the banks took the view that it was imprudent to lend long to firms when they borrowed short from private customers. This line of reasoning was always rather dubious when the building societies, which financed house purchase in Britain, lent long and borrowed short very successfully by varying the rate of interest to attract deposits. Nevertheless, before 1971, whatever the High Street banks would lend was lent short-term; overdrafts might sometimes be allowed to roll over but the bank could legally enforce repayment. Notionally at least such short-term loans could only be used to finance the enterprise's demand for working capital. Unlike the banks in all the other advanced capitalist countries, through the long boom of the 1950s and 1960s, British banks did not lend money over periods longer than two years for the purchase of capital equipment like machine tools. It is important, therefore, that in 1971 under the Tory government's new policies for the banking system, a variety of restrictions were lifted and the High Street banks obtained access to medium-term deposits from the wholesale money market which they were prepared to lend to manufacturing for terms of six or more years. There was then a remarkable change of practice so that by 1976 medium-term loans accounted for 40 per cent of total lending to industry (Wilson evidence, vol.2, 1977).

In any case the banks never changed the conservative and formalistic criteria which were used in the determination of how much could be advanced and on what conditions to particular clients. The American Banks Association of London in its submission to the Wilson Committee (evidence, vol.2, 1977) usefully discriminated two alternative sets of criteria which might be applied to lending.

(i) *The going-concern approach* is concerned with the future viability of the borrowing firm and the lender asks: 'will the business generate a sufficient flow of funds to make repayment?' The key action is surveillance of a series of liquidity and gearing ratios which are set at specific levels after a detailed examination of the client's business.

(ii) *The liquidation approach* is concerned with the fixed assets which the borrowing firm can offer as security and the lender asks: 'does the firm have assets which could be sold off to repay the loan after liquidation?' The key action is the taking of security in the form of, say, the deeds to freehold factory property.

From Hu's (1975) description of differences in bank lending practices, it is clear that German, French and American banks adopt a going-concern approach, while only British banks adopt a liquidation approach. Our High Street banks may no longer apply mechanical rules about not lending more than one-third of asset value as they did in the 1950s and 1960s, but they must continue to operate a liquidation approach geared to security on fixed assets because this approach is enforced by British accounting conventions on disclosure and by the national legal system. Requirements and conventions about the disclosure of information by companies are very much less rigorous in Britain than in America or Japan; it is symptomatic of this difference that the Japanese banks in London told Wilson that their lending to British companies was limited by the reluctance of such companies to disclose information to their bankers. More fundamentally, the English legal system privileges the creditor who takes security on fixed assets. Under English law, it is easy to take security on fixed assets but difficult to take security on moving goods; by way of contrast in America, for example, inventory liens can be readily obtained. Furthermore, English law privileges the secured creditor as against the unsecured creditor; most importantly here, only a secured creditor can petition to have a company put into receivership.

The conservative lending practices of the banks made the lending practices of the new issue market all the more important. In principle, this market was an alternative source of finance for quoted companies in the big business segment. In practice, the volume of funds available from the new issue market was restricted because of the peculiar way in which savings have been channelled by the British financial system. Contractual savings have been more important in Britain than in other advanced capitalist countries. In the mid-1970s, life assurance and pension funds accounted for 35–40 per cent of household gross financial savings in the UK as against 11–16 per cent in West Germany and 3–4 per cent in France (Hu, 1975). The importance of contractual saving in Britain is underpinned by the peculiarity of a national taxation system which makes it attractive to save through institutional intermediaries. Regular premiums or contributions are allowable against income tax and the ultimate benefits are normally free of the capital gains tax which a private investor in shares often has to pay.

Contractual savings could have been an engine for growth if they had been channelled into manufacturing industry. But the life assurance companies and pension funds did not sustain a massive new issues market for two reasons. First, institutional funds on the stock exchange have been largely diverted into buying existing issued shares from the personal sector rather than new issues from the company sector. The personal sector has been a persistent net seller of shares; in the mid-1950s, private investors owned around two-thirds of ordinary shares in quoted companies but, by the mid-1970s, private investors only owned one-third of these shares. Meanwhile the proportion of securities owned by savings institutions (insurance companies, pension funds, investment and unit trusts) rose from under one-quarter to just over one-half (Wilson, evidence, vol.3, 1978). The second major consideration is that institional funds are spread across a wide range of investments including property and government securities. As one-third or less of institutional funds may go into company shares, the proportion which finds its way into new issues of company shares is very small indeed. In the three years from 1971–3, new issues of shares and loan capital (net of redemptions) by UK industrial companies amounted to just 14 per cent of the net increase of funds of the life assurance companies and pension funds.

If the volume of funds available to companies on the new issue market was restricted for these reasons, the lending practices of the new issue market were crucial. It is notable therefore that the new issue market did not provide a regular, stable source of funds for industry, nor did the market concentrate the available supply on profitable firms. Through the 1960s and 1970s, there were erratic fluctuations in the availability of new issues depending on the state of the market. New issues are most easily floated in a brisk market when share prices are high and rising; they can miscarry in a nervous market and cannot be made at all during a stock market slump. Thus in the depressed market of 1974, less than £200 million of shares were issued, but in 1975, as the market recovered, more than £1500 million were issued (Wilson, evidence, vol.3, 1978). Furthermore, the new issue finance which was erratically available was not channelled to companies with unusually good profit records. Meeks and Whittington (1976) have shown that companies with high rates of growth by equity issue were not unusually profitable.

There can be no doubt that the lending practices of the banks and the new issue market powerfully conditioned the calculations of manufacturing enterprise. In developing our argument on this point, we will immediately concentrate on the lending practices of the High Street banks. When every manufacturing enterprise had a bank account, these lending practices were relevant to the whole of British industry.

To begin with, short-term loans made borrowing extraordinarily unattractive. Economists have traditionally been preoccupied with the issue of variations in the rate of interest, but variability in the term of the loan will usually be more important for borrowing enterprises where profitability is low and cash flow has to be watched. The term of the loan is crucial since the attractiveness of borrowing always depends in practice on the size of the regular repayments (of principal plus interest). As all hire purchase and finance companies know, the borrower will happily pay a high rate of interest if the individual instalments are low because the term is long; the annual repayments on a six-year loan at 16 per cent are less than the repayments on a three-year loan at 2 per cent. The shift to medium-term loans after 1971 is therefore a significant change; from the point of view of manufacturing, however, the High Street banks almost certainly offered too little and too late. A substantial proportion of the new term loans was immediately diverted into the finance of property speculation; the rather unsatisfactory series on the proportion of bank loans going into manufacturing shows this falling away from its normal level of 40 per cent after 1971. After the property bubble burst, an increasing proportion of what manufacturing took up was distress borrowing in increasingly hard times.

Meanwhile, the damaging consequences of the liquidation approach persisted. A going-concern approach enforces certain kinds of calculation by borrowing firms whose managements must calculate in specific goal-oriented terms about the future if they are to conform to a particular set of ratios. On the other hand, a liquidation approach is much more permissive. This is 'rubber stamp' lending subject to the constraints of prudence and any company with good assets should be able to borrow. From the liquidation standpoint, giant firms with no goals and many assets are acceptable borrowers, while small and rapidly growing enterprises are more doubtful propositions. If Soichiro Honda had turned up with his accounts at a Barclays branch in West Bromwich in the 1950s, the manager would have interpreted the progress of Honda Motor Company as a cautionary tale of over-trading and would have suggested, not a bank loan, but the appointment of a receiver. Furthermore, there is a strong suspicion that the liquidation approach has encouraged British banks to support fixed-asset trading rather than manufacturing. The final result of the British bankers' mindless obsession with security was the British property boom of 1972–3; clearing banks such as National Westminster (as well as the 'secondary banks') lent heavily to property speculators who had 'first-class security' in the form of office blocks.

The constraints established by the banks pressed most heavily on small business. Big business could perhaps tap the new-issue market but, in practice, the High Street bank was the one and only source of external finance for the vast majority of small businesses. There are other suppliers such as the Industrial and Commercial Finance Corporation, but these other sources are of marginal importance. A survey undertaken for the Bolton Committee at the beginning of the 1970s showed that 92 per cent of respondent small firms had not made any attempt to obtain outside finance from any financial institution other than their High Street bank. Furthermore, the banks insisted on stricter conditions for loans to small business which were regarded as more risky than loans to large business. The conditions about security in the form of assets or personal guarantees were more onerous; classically, the banks would want the small businessman's private house pledged as security. Rules about the permissible ratio of advances were also stricter for small business according to the Association of Independent Businesses; in the 1970s in Britain, a small businessman wanting to start or expand a business would normally be expected to finance at least half of the assets from his own resources, whereas in Europe the comparable percentage would be 20 or 30 per cent (Wilson, evidence, vol.2, 1977). The conclusion must be that in Britain small business has been meanly treated by the banks. This is confirmed by the Bolton Committee's striking finding that smaller firms in manufacturing were actually net *lenders* of funds to the banking system in the 1960s; as Table 11 below shows, cash in hand and at bank in smaller manufacturing firms (employing less than 100 persons) was actually greater than bank borrowing, although this was not true of larger manufacturing firms.

TABLE 11   *Cash as percentage of bank credit received in manufacturing firms*

	1964	1968
1–24 employees	217	108
25–99 employees	166	124
100–199 employees	66	42
all small firms	141	92
all quoted firms	74	58

Source: Bolton Committee (1971).

We have already argued that Britain has a relatively under-developed small business segment. There has been a historic decline in the relative importance of this segment in all advanced capitalist countries. But in Britain this trend has gone further so that in share of employment and output terms, the British small business segment is smaller than in any other advanced capitalist country. The mechanics of this decline are under-researched. We do know that in all advanced capitalist countries there is a high turnover with many births and deaths in the small business segment. Although British small business appears to have a relatively low death rate, the small business segment has declined because the birth rate has not risen to match or exceed the death rate. Consider, for example, the Bolton Report's evidence on a period (1958–63) when the decline of the small firm was not proceeding unusually rapidly. In the six years from 1958, the population of small manufacturing firms was declining by about 1,000 firms a year; four firms per working day failed and were not replaced by new firms. In this situation, there can be little doubt that the conservative lending practices of the High Street banks have been the immediate external condition of the low birth rate in the small business segment.

The final question that we must ask in this section is: how did manufacturing firms respond to the conditions set by the financial institutions which supplied external finance? This is really a question about how frustrated demand manifested itself. There are two possibilities: first, there could be overt frustration with the banks actively refusing loan propositions put up by manufacturing enterprise; second, there could be repressed demand which would manifest itself in forms such as public protests about the terms on which loans are available.

The question of frustrated demand has been examined in two recent major official inquiries – the Bolton Committee on small firms which reported in 1971 and the Wilson Committee on the City which reported in 1978. Bolton commissioned a special survey which tried and failed to find small firms which needed and deserved finance but had been turned down after making serious efforts to raise it. Bolton's Report (1971) therefore concluded that 'in spite of considerable efforts, we have identified no body of legitimate unsatisfied demand significant enough to require radical changes in the market'. In a larger context, the Wilson Report came to similar conclusions at a more recent date and added the point that there was actually evidence of excess supply of funds; in 1975 and 1977, only about one half the loan facilities notionally available to industry was actually taken up. We do not find the official evidence and conclusions as reassuring as the authors of these reports intended them to be. Both Bolton and Wilson Committees were apologists for our existing financial institutions; the Wilson Committee in particular seems to have interpreted its brief as to find out what the City was doing and tell them to carry on with it. Neither report seriously considered the possibility that manufacturing enterprises are unlikely to waste effort in putting up loan proposals which are 'no-hope' under the existing British rules of the game as defined by our financial institutions.

If we are looking for frustrated demand, it is altogether more instructive to read the evidence submitted to Bolton and Wilson where representatives of manufacturing had the opportunity to protest against the conditions set by external financial institutions. Interestingly enough, some representatives of manufacturing did protest while others did not, as the evidence to Wilson shows very clearly. The Association of Independent Businesses representing small business criticised British bank loan practices fairly comprehensively: the banks had 'an obsession with security' in the form of assets of personal guarantees; they were over-cautious about how much they would lend in relation to asset value and they still made too many short-term loans. Given what we know of British banking practices, this criticism is not surprising. Altogether more remarkable is the written evidence which the Confederation of

British Industry representing big business submitted to Wilson; this contained no significant criticism of the banking and financial system. To support its position, the CBI presented the results of a survey of 181 member firms of varying sizes. This showed conclusively that 'industry generally is not merely satisfied with but often complimentary about its relation with those who supply it with funds' (Wilson, evidence, vol.2, 1977). 89 per cent of respondents had not 'in recent years' been prevented from carrying out a potentially profitable investment project by problems about external finance. 78 per cent of respondents rated the services of the clearing banks as good rather than bad or indifferent. These results cannot be dismissed as aberrant when other surveys, for example by the Engineering Employers' Federation, confirm the overall picture.

Our conclusion must be that, as the AIB evidence shows, there is evidence of repressed demand. But there is not as much public protest as one might expect and, in particular, big business seems to have learnt to love its financial chains. However, this does not absolve financial institutions from all blame. If we take the argument one stage further, we must ask: why did big business acquiesce in financial constraints imposed by limited external finance? The answer must be two-fold: first, British big business acquiesced in financial constraint because it was increasingly fazed by organisational problems about scale; second, these scale problems were largely the result of a merger boom which was conditioned by the stock exchange's hyperactive market in issued securities. The apparently anomalous evidence about acquiescence in financial constraint does not therefore threaten our position because this evidence simply indicates the effects of another adverse conditioning influence established by financial institutions. This influence will be examined in the next section.

6   Relation to financial institutions (b) the merger boom and the stock exchange market in issued securities

Before we can develop our own explanation of the merger boom and its conditioning effect on the big business segment, we must begin by considering the orthodox explanations of mergers between manufacturing firms. Orthodox economic theory of the capitalist economy in general takes a mainly productionist view of the manufacturing enterprise. Most textbooks suppose that enterprises pursue trading profit (or perhaps sales volume) through the production of goods for sale. But this position is unsustainable when, in the capitalist economy in general, assets double as production and financial assets. Enterprises may therefore pursue trading profit or growth through the purchase of assets as well as, or instead of, using those assets to produce final products. When enterprises legally own specific blocs of assets, the possibility of merger activity where enterprises buy other enterprises is inscribed in the capitalist economy in general. Since the phenomenon of merger is widespread in advanced capitalist national economies, this theoretical possibility can hardly be denied. Orthodox economic theory therefore accommodates mergers by subsuming them under its general teleological explanations of firms' production behaviour: mergers, like everything else, reflect the purpose which they are designed to fulfil. Thus the classic view is that mergers are undertaken for profit which can be achieved through the realisation of scale economies or the exploitation of increased monopoly and market power. On the radical or Marxisant variants of this view, mergers represent a necessary move towards the control of competition under capitalism.

It is hard to see how mergers in specific capitalist economies can be explained in this way as a result of the general logic of the capitalist system. To begin with, mergers always take place in a particular national economy where the extent and nature of any existing merger activity will depend on national policy and institutions or, more specifically, on government policy with regard to mergers and the financial institutions which define the terms on which enterprises can be bought and sold. These specific national conditions vary widely through time and between different countries. As we have already argued, the US government has long been hostile to mergers between companies manufacturing similar products, while the British government freely allowed and even encouraged such mergers in the 1960s. It might be argued that these national considerations only modify and qualify the operations of the basic motivation. The considerations that we have mentioned, however, suggest an alternative explanatory strategy; we could try to explain mergers in terms of the national logic of the situation rather than in terms of the teleological purpose which they were designed to fulfil.

The proposed change in problem situation can be explained by looking at the analogous but separate phenomenon of the rise in home ownership in Britain since the Second World War. This phenomenon can be explained in terms of the logic of the situation. Tax subsidy ensured that those who took out a mortgage paid a relatively low rate of interest on the sum which they borrowed. In an inflationary period, the burden of their debt diminished in real terms, while the value of the house/asset bought increased. It is unnecessary to credit British house-buyers with universal objectives. Their behaviour is explained when one has analysed how ownership was made available to the middle-class public who could buy appreciating assets with depreciating money on the easiest of terms. Given the national conditions on which home ownership was made possible, it would be surprising if there was not a boom in house purchase. Exactly the same point could be made about company purchase in the British merger boom after the late 1950s. In the case of British mergers we would explain the underlying situational logic in terms of two minor permissive conditions and one major active condition. The minor conditions were government acquiescence in company mergers and a wide dispersion of share ownership in major companies. The major condition, as in the case of home ownership, was the purchase consideration or the terms on which public joint stock companies could be bought. We will analyse these conditions separately and in turn.

Some economists, such as Aaronovich and Sawyer (1975), have argued that the British government actively encouraged mergers. Certainly, in the late 1960s, the Labour government's Industrial Reorganisation Corporation directly promoted some large mergers such as GEC and BLMC. More generally, government may have indirectly encouraged merger by allowing takeover while it outlawed most forms of collusion between independent firms; after 1956, so called 'restrictive practices' which maintained prices or shared markets were prohibited unless they had been officially approved. In practice, this effect does not seem to have been very important; Elliott and Gribbin (1977) showed that concentration did not increase unduly rapidly where restrictive practices had been outlawed. Government, therefore, seems mainly to have figured in a permissive way by acquiescing in mergers which were conditioned by other considerations. At the peak of the merger boom around 1967 and 1968, twenty public company mergers a month or one per working day were being announced. But from the beginning of the merger boom in the late 1950s, only two to five mergers a year were referred to the Monopolies Commission and only half of these were found to be against the public interest.

Joint stock organisation along with dispersion of share ownership was a second permissive condition of merger. When large companies were threatened with takeover, there was often no large bloc of shareholders which wished to preserve the identity of a particular firm. Directors were seldom in a position to block takeover; in half of the hundred largest companies of 1976 the board of directors held no more than 0·5 per cent of the ordinary voting capital (Prais, 1976). Furthermore, over the period of the merger boom, shares in the largest companies were increasingly owned by financial institutions such as pension funds, insurance companies and unit trusts. As we have already noted, the proportion of ordinary shares owned by financial institutions was approaching one-half by the mid-1970s. British financial institutions are not sentimental and they generally take the view that they invest in securities rather than companies. This point is proved by the recent popularity of 'dawn raids'; provided they are offered a premium over the current market price, reputable financial institutions will sell blocs of shares on a 'no-questions-asked' basis to a broker who is acting on behalf of a takeover raider.

Neither of the permissive conditions which we have analysed explains why companies should have wished to buy other companies. We would argue that this is explained by the purchase considerations, or the terms on which companies could be bought. These terms were effectively defined by the stock market which allowed takeover raiders to pay with their own company paper when buying other companies. Kuehn (1975) has analysed the methods of payment used in the takeover of publicly quoted companies between 1957 and 1969. During the British merger boom, acquiring companies did not have to pay cash. In Kuehn's comprehensive survey of 1,557 takeovers, the percentage of take-overs financed by cash was under 40 per cent over the whole period and fell to under 30 per cent at the height of the boom in 1966, 1968 and 1969. By implication, therefore, in more than 60 per cent of takeovers from 1957 to 1969, payment was made partly or entirely in company paper. The basic currency for company purchase was the ordinary share; share exchange (with or without a cash sweet-ener) was the method of payment in 46 per cent of takeovers and ordinary shares alone were offered in rather more than half these cases. Some acquiring companies also issued debentures or convertible unsecured loan stock. In the aggregate, over the period 1957 to 1969, debentures were used as a means of payment in only 12 per cent of takeovers. But this kind of paper was becoming very much more popular through the 1960s and by 1968–9, loan stock was being issued in 30 per cent of takeovers.

If companies could through takeovers buy good assets with a kind of paper money which they printed themselves, this was very attractive when mediocre profitability ensured most British manufacturing companies were not generating large cash reserves. If the takeover raider's company paper was acceptable, it was possible to acquire other companies without damaging the takeover raider's liquidity. Furthermore, the two kinds of paper which were issued during the merger boom cost the takeover raider very little since they did not mortgage future earnings. Where ordinary shares were exhanged or issued, the acquiring company did not enter into any fixed commitment to pay interest or to repay the principal; ordinary shares are serviced out of future profits if and when they are earned. From this point of view, it may seem paradoxical that, as the merger boom gathered pace in the 1960s, acquiring companies increasingly preferred to issue debentures, a kind of loan stock which committed them to paying a fixed interest charge for a period of years. Why should any company willingly raise its gearing ratio, or the proportion of its capital financed by long-term debt, rather than by share capital? The answer is that this long-term debt cost the acquiring company almost nothing. There were important tax advantages because debenture interest was calculated as a charge before profits and thus was not subject to profit or corporation tax. More important, real rates of interest were low through the 1960s; companies could sell debentures offering around 7 per cent when inflation was running around 4 or 5 per cent.

In so far as ordinary shares were the currency of the merger boom, there was considerable scope for striking tactically advantageous deals. The terms of any kind of share exchange or conversion can only be defined by the prevailing prices of the ordinary shares of the acquiring and the acquired companies. If the ordinary shares of company A have a high price/earnings ratio and the ordinary shares of company B have a low price/earnings ratio, then company A can take advantage of this difference in market valuation to buy the assets of company B relatively cheaply. Acquisition was thus particularly attractive for companies with highly valued paper. As Jim Slater said when asked to explain Slater Walker's acquisitions, 'it was a pity not to use the shares.' Nevertheless, studies by Kuehn (1975) and Meeks (1977) show that merger did not generally involve firms with high stock-market valuations taking over firms with low stock-market valuations. This was doubtless because many firms with mediocre earnings and nondescript share prices put in defensive bids of one sort or another during a period of intense merger activity. This is consonant with Kuehn's findings that attack was the best form of defence if management wished to ensure the continued existence of a company; from 1957 to 1969, quoted companies which made at least two takeovers more than halved the risk of being taken over. The important point therefore is that *all* publicly quoted companies, with or without exceptional market valuations, could pay painlessly with company paper.

The stock market not only made it easy for acquiring companies to buy other firms, it also undermined the possibility of resistance by firms which were threatened by takeover bids. As long as takeover raiders could pay with cheap company paper, they could afford to buy companies at relatively high prices without agonising about how much the acquired business was worth. Takeover raiders were thus able to make an attractive offer which the threatened company would ultimately find hard to refuse, although its board might well play 'hard to get' in the hope of securing an improved offer. Takeover battles were few in number and normally occurred only where there were rival bidders, as when both Plessey and GEC bid for English Electric. The number of contested bids was small and the number of successful defences was tiny; at the height of the boom, from January 1966 to December 1969, the financial press records 637 successful takeovers and only 44 failed takeovers.

If the stock market conditioned publicly quoted companies into buying other companies, the result was a massive merger boom which started in the late 1950s and peaked at the end of the 1960s before petering out in the early 1970s. It is unfortunate that the available evidence on mergers does not distinguish the sub-group of manufacturing companies from the larger group of all publicly quoted companies. However, general trends in the sub-group were undoubtedly similar to those in the larger group. If we consider the question of disappearance through merger, takeover accounted for the disappearance of the better part of half of all the publicly quoted companies in Britain. In Kuehn's (1975) survey of 3,500 quoted companies which existed for all or part of the period 1957–69, 43 per cent of the sample were taken over and ceased to exist. If we consider expenditure on acquisition, mergers were a major object of expenditure from the late 1950s. In Meeks's (1977) sample of 893 companies which continued in existence through the 1950s and 1960s, expenditure on acquiring other companies outstripped new investment (whether measured gross or net) at the height of the boom in the late 1960s. It is not surprising therefore that Meeks finds that the typical continuing company, in the 1964–71 period, grew more through external means (acquisition) than through internal means (investment).

TABLE 12   *Expenditure on new subsidiaries as percentage of investment expenditure*

	As per cent of gross new investment	As per cent of net new investment
1949–55	9	17
1956–62	30	63
1963–69	46	118

Source: Meeks (1977).

Having established the dimensions of the merger boom, we must now observe that there was a dramatic increase in the relative importance of the big business segment in British manufacturing over the same time period from the late 1950s to the early 1970s. The Prais (1976) series on CR 100, or the share of the 100 largest manufacturing enterprises in UK net manufacturing output, gives a straightforward measure of the rise of the giant firm in British manufacturing.

This rise in CR 100 from 27 to 41 between 1953 and 1968 shows that the relative importance of the big business segment was increasing dramatically. It should also be noted that this measure does not indicate the extent of the broader structural changes in British manufacturing which were incidental to the rise of the big business segment. As the CR 100 rose, many smaller firms which were outliers from the top 100 were absorbed by the giant firms in

TABLE 13 *Percentage share of the 100 largest firms (CR 100) in UK net manufacturing output*

Year	CR 100
1909	16
1924	22
1935	24
1949	22
1953	27
1958	32
1963	37
1968	41
1970	41

Source: Prais (1976).

the top 100. By 1970, 100 firms were responsible for the better part of half of manufacturing output; just twelve years earlier, in 1958, 420 independent firms had produced half of manufacturing output (Prais, 1976).

The end result was that, by the early 1970s, Britain had a big business segment which was unusually large by the standards of other advanced capitalist countries. In the United States, for example, the share of the 100 largest companies in the 1960s was stable at somewhere above 30 per cent, while the British share was rising to over 40 per cent and rising. This national peculiarity is of vital importance to us when trying to answer the question why the British are bad at manufacturing. A relatively small number of giant firms in the big business segment must bear a large and increasing share of the responsibility for poor manufacturing performance. We will argue that the poor performance of the big business segment was conditioned by the merger boom. But first we must establish the preliminary point that the growing importance of the big business segment was a direct result of the merger boom.

Economic discussion has raised the issue of whether, and to what extent, the growing predominance of large firms is a spontaneous drift effect produced by random variation in firm growth rates. Gibrat long ago demonstrated that changes in the distribution of firm sizes can be caused by a dispersion in the growth rates within a population of firms. This point has since been much elaborated in an increasingly scholastic discussion of abstract possibilities. If we focus on the British national economy, it is easy to show that spontaneous drift is not the immediate cause of the observed increase in CR 100: in Britain in the 1960s, as in earlier periods, merger largely or entirely explains the observed increase in concentration. This point emerges very clearly from Hannah and Kay's (1977) investigation of three sub-periods using large samples of publicly quoted companies.

TABLE 14   *Merger's role in the rise of CR 100*

	Overall rise or fall in CR 100	Change in CR 100 due to merger
1919–30	+21	+16·1
1930–48	− 8·8	+ 1·9
1957–69	+14·8	+15·2

Source: Hannah and Kay (1977).

On Hannah and Kay's calculations, the CR 100 would actually have fallen slightly between 1957 and 1969 without mergers. Another study by Aaronovich and Sawyer (1975) took a different sample and sub-period and did not confirm the conclusion that mergers were the sole cause of increasing concentration; nevertheless, Aaronovich and Sawyer did conclude that more than half the increase in CR 100 concentration between 1958 and 1967 was due to merger.

It is sometimes argued that these results are not conclusive since they depend on an implied counter-factual about what would have happened in the absence of mergers; both Hannah and Aaronovich assume that without merger, the concentration increases which did result from merger would not have occurred. This assumption is not defensible in the theory of the capitalist economy in general where enterprises can freely switch between the internal investment opportunities represented by new projects and the external investment opportunities represented by acquisition and merger. But we would vigorously defend the validity of the Hannah and Aaronovich results in the British national economy of the 1950s and 1960s. Given the under-developed new issue market and the conservative banking system, large British manufacturing firms had to finance internal growth from their own modest resources, while the hyperactive market in issued shares allowed British firms to use the stock exchange to finance acquisition on the easiest of terms.

Here, national financial institutions made external growth an easy option and internal growth a difficult option. It is pointless to speculate about what might have happened if national institutional conditions had been different; what did happen was the predictable result of prevailing national conditions.

If the stock market via merger determined the increasing predominance of big business, our next question must be: what impact did this have on the performance of the big business segment? We must begin here by criticising the stereotyped economic way of problematising the repercussions of increased concentration for enterprise performance: is increased concentration a good thing because a general social advantage results from gains in efficiency made by larger firms which can exploit economies of scale; or is increased concentration a bad thing because only sectional private advantage results from the exploitation of monopoly by large firms which have greater market power? These twinned questions are naive since they are unanswerable even on the terrain of the theory of the capitalist economy in general. The nature and extent of any 'economies of scale' must be uncertain as long as economics cannot decide exactly what these economies are and how they arise. Are the economies of scale primarily technical or organisational, and are they accessible to all enterprises of a particular size, or do they depend on a rate of growth, or a dynamic process of learning by doing? The extent of monopoly is equally uncertain; in most industries, if the product market is defined broadly to include substitutes and if the supplying industry is defined geographically to include foreign producers, substantial industrial concentration does not necessarily indicate market power. Furthermore, even if monopoly could be operationally defined, the consequences of increased monopoly would still be unclear; welfare economics will only support the agnostic conclusion that, if there is monopoly anywhere else in the economy, an increase in monopoly may increase rather than decrease welfare (Hannah, 1979).

Instead of pursuing these issues, it is more profitable to begin by examining what happened in the British big business segment after mergers had taken place. Our argument so far is that increasing concentration was primarily and initially a matter of financial logic, not production logic. Nevertheless, company paper bought production assets and manufacturing facilities; all takeover raiders had to do something with the assets once they were bought. Acquiring companies had two alternative courses of action. First, a 'financial' profit could be taken in the short run by treating the acquired firm as a collection of financial assets which should be sold off as and when a financial gain could be realised. Second, a 'productive' profit could be earned in the medium and long run by treating the acquired firm as a collection of productive assets which could earn trading profit for the takeover raider. At the end of the takeover boom, asset strippers like Slater attracted considerable adverse publicity. More generally, however, the facilities of the taken-over firm were retained, albeit in rationalised form, and the takeover raider tried to earn profit through manufacturing. This choice was reasonable since the mergers which produced giant British companies were not entirely lacking in industrial logic. Conglomerates, such as ITT whose subsidiaries are active in unrelated production and financial activities, may be important in America, but conglomerates were virtually unknown in Britain until the late 1960s. Most British takeover raiders bought firms whose activities complemented or parallelled their own. On Kuehn's (1975) classification, 74 per cent of mergers between publicly quoted companies from 1957 to 1969 were horizontal within the same stage of one industry.

Horizontal mergers between manufacturing firms obviously left scope for realising profit from rationalisation of competing product ranges, duplicate production facilities and overlapping distribution systems. It is therefore reasonable to ask what success takeover raiders had in racking greater accounting profit out of merged businesses. The accounting rate of return is of course a conventional measure, but it is significant in this context because accounting profit is the measure which has always been considered inside and outside the firm when mergers between manufacturing firms are justified. The case of GEC shows this very clearly; a merger which justifies itself in terms of profit is universally applauded and perceived as a success. Meeks (1977) has produced the definitive study of profit before and after takeover during the British merger boom, and we can now review his conclusions.

Before we examine post-merger profit performance, we can consider the pre-merger performance of acquiring and acquired firms. The basic point here is that merger was not a method whereby highly profitable firms took over unprofitable firms. Meeks (1977) shows that the typical acquired firm had an average profitability record by industry standards while the typical acquirer had a profitability record which was one-quarter higher than average for the industry. This is not a result which is produced by a freakish distribution; Meeks subsequently shows that companies with high acquisition records were fairly evenly distributed as between high, middle and low profitability groups. In general, therefore, we can only conclude that British takeover raiders had learned how to grow rapidly without earning the high profits which, under British rules, would otherwise be necessary to finance growth. In Meeks's 1000 firm sample, over twenty years, the top 100 public companies in the ranking by acquisition growth achieved an average overall growth rate some 10 per cent higher than the top 100 in the ranking by investment and some six times higher than the scarcely less profitable zero acquisition group. From 1948–64, the average member of the top 100 companies in the ranking by acquisition was practically doubling in size every two years.

Given that takeover raiders had not obtained high profits from their own firms' assets prior to merger, it is perhaps not surprising that profits after merger were usually very disappointing. With his sample of approximately 1000 firms, Meeks begins by calculating the pre-tax accounting rate of return for pairs of companies in the three years prior to merger. He is then able to show that profitability typically improves slightly for the amalgamated firms in the year of the merger. Nevertheless, even with the benefit· of adjusted accounting periods which often allowed one of the partners to enter 15 or 18 months' profits in the 'first year's' results, more than 40 per cent of the sample reported a drop in profitability in the year of merger. More strikingly, in a majority of cases, the amalgamated company's profitability in the next seven years is typically below the level attained by the separate companies in the three years before takeover. On average, the drop in profitability is maintained even if we allow for the accounting bias introduced by the way in which, during the merger boom, takeover raiders were increasingly willing to buy the assets of other companies above book value. Aaronovich and Sawyer (1975) show that for all quoted companies the ratio of takeover purchase price to book value was 1·08 in 1957–9 and 1·61 in 1966–8. This depresses profit rates in consolidated post-merger accounts since it raises the value of the assets which are used as denominator in calculating the profit ratio. Meeks shows that adjusting for purchase of assets above book value reduces the size of the fall in profitability but does not reverse the trend.

Our final question must be why merger and enterprise buying was so unsuccessful by the profitability yardstick. Some theorists such as Penrose see merger as a fairly costless way of raising the firm's maximum rate of expansion because it reduces the managerial co-ordination required to sustain a given expansion of productive capacity. In a specific national economy this may be so in the particular case of expansion by replication, as when a brewer or brick manufacturer contemplates expanding the geographic area which his enterprise serves; here it is in many ways more attractive to buy in an existing enterprise rather than build a branch factory. More generally, however, merger raises the requirement for management co-ordination; if the merged companies are to be operated as one productive unit, management's tasks become more difficult because the company is larger in size and its operations more complex. In this way the merger boom in the big business segment of British manufacturing seems to have created intractable problems which defeated management's best efforts.

After the merger boom, many British companies were absolutely very large by international standards. Table 15 indicates the contrast with France and Germany which had comparably sized economies. If merger in British big business increased the span over which management control and co-ordination was exercised, it also increased the complexity of company operations because post-merger companies were increasingly diversified and multi-national. We have already argued that the British merger was typically a horizontal affair between firms in related activities. Nevertheless, merger normally increased diversification since many large British companies were already active in several different product markets before they merged; on Channon's (1973) classification nearly 45 per cent of the top 100 British companies were diversified by 1960 before the merger boom really got under way. The rise to 60 per cent diversified by 1970 must largely reflect the amalgamation of firms whose activities only partially overlapped. There was also the complication that many large British companies brought foreign manufacturing operations into their mergers. Channon (1973) classified a company as multi-national if it had six or more overseas subsidiaries. Primarily as a result of merger, an increasing number of the top 100 companies qualified as multi-nationals; there were

30 domestically owned multi-nationals in the top 100 of 1960 but the number had increased to 50 by 1970.

TABLE 15   *Number of companies in 1970 with more than 40,000 employees*

89 American	6 Italian
30 British	5 Benelux
12 German	3 Swiss
12 French	3 Swedish

Source: Hannah and Kay (1977).

Management theorists would argue that the problems caused by longer spans of control and more complex operational decisions could be dealt with by choosing an appropriate organisational form and re-organising the management hierarchy. This argument assumes that firms are (or should be) spheres of rational bureaucratic co-ordination and, as we have already argued, this assumption is controversial. Nevertheless, given the facts of increasing size and complexity, it is significant that large British companies did change structural form in the 1950s and 1960s. Initially, at least, British big business seems to have dodged the problem of integrating the productive operations of companies which merged; before the mid-1960s, many big British companies (like AEI) were loose federations of quasi-independent production organisations which remitted profits to head office. By 1960, the holding company had replaced the functional organisation as the predominant organisational form in the top 100 companies; the formation of 19 new holding companies in the 1950s brought the total number of companies of this type to 40 by 1960 (Channon, 1973). But, in the 1960s, the financial federation represented by the holding company was supplanted by productive co-ordination represented by the multi-divisional organisation. During this decade, m-form organisation rose to predominance so that, by 1970, Channon could classify nearly three-quarters of the top 100 companies as multi-divisional in form. This reorganisation can be seen as a rearguard attempt to control the problems of increasingly large and unwieldy productive enterprises by introducing the universal panaceas recommended by American management theory. In this connection, it is significant that most of these ideologically motivated reorganisations of the 1960s were externally sponsored by management consultants; the one firm of McKinsey was used by nearly one-quarter of the top 100 British companies between 1950 and 1970.

We have now identified structural reorganisation as an attempt to control the increasingly uncontrollable and we earlier identified diversification as a contingent result rather than a purposive strategy. This allows us to explain what is for management theory the paradoxical recent history of British manufacturing; in Britain by the early 1970s modernity of enterprise strategy and structure co-existed with poor performance in product markets. As Channon (1973) showed, by 1970, British big business was dominated by large, diversified multi-divisional firms, just like American big business, which was then supposed to be the very model of efficiency; 60 of our top 100 companies of 1970 were diversified and 72 had adopted multi-divisional organisation. Paradoxically, however, by almost every standard, large British manufacturing firms performed worse than American firms in Britain and worse than European firms on the continent which were often more traditional in strategy and structure. This shows only that, contrary to the suppositions of analysts like Chandler, there is no universal and necessary link between performance and, for example, the adoption of particular organisational structures. In the British case, poor performance is readily explicable because, as we have seen, modernity of enterprise strategy and structure was largely a meretricious appearance produced by the merger boom in the 1950s and 1960s.

If reorganisation of the management hierarchy was an inadequate response to the problems created by merger in the big business segment, perhaps a brutal rationalisation of production facilities in the merged companies could have solved the problems. However, the case of GEC under Weinstock suggests that while this kind of rationalisation could transform profitability, it did not necessarily establish the conditions for success in product markets which would sustain a long-run growth of employment. As we will argue in our essay on GEC, rationalisation was a negative response which set up a double bind; the financial controls which guided rationalisation almost certainly inhibited the company's response to market opportunities. In any case, GEC was an exception since most large British companies did not undertake major rationalisation after merger. This is strongly suggested by Newbould's (1970) survey of 38 firms which had merged; 21 of these firms did not shut down any plant and 30 shut down less than 5 per cent of their plant of any particular type.

More general indirect confirmation of this point is provided by census of production data on plant size which shows that the British big business segment did not concentrate production in a small number of giant plants. There has been no rise of the giant plant parallel with the rise of the giant firm. From 1930–68, the share of the 100 largest plants in manufacturing net output was constant at around 10–11 per cent while, over the same period, the share of the 100 largest firms increased from 23 to 41 per cent (Prais, 1976). Furthermore, in the 1960s, the typical giant firm was burdened with an increasing number of small plants. In 1958, the 100 largest firms owned an average of 28 plants each employing 750 men; by 1972, the 100 largest firms owned an average of 72 plants which typically employed only 430 persons (Prais, 1976). Prais (1981) has recently argued that construction of large plants and, therefore, concentration of production was inhibited by labour control problems and fears that large plants were unmanageable. This argument, however, does not fit the historical evidence. In heavy industry, there are long-standing international differences in size of plant; in steel or cars, the largest plants in Britain before the Second World War were unusually small largely because of fragmented patterns of ownership. Furthermore, the persistence of small plants in the big business segment of the 1950s and 1960s was overdetermined by the merger boom; one or both partners brought a tail of small factories into the combined operation and these small plants were not immediately closed so that production could be rationalised.

Our conclusion must be that the stock exchange conditioned poor manufacturing performance in the big business segment where merger created unmanageable production organisations. By making takeover easy, the financial sector conditioned big business into the pursuit of short-run financial advantage. The medium-term consequences in big business were problems of control which nullified any financial or production benefits. At the same time the small business segment was constrained when, for much of the period, it was difficult to borrow long-term for production purposes from the High Street banks. In Britain, neither small nor big business has been intelligently supplied with generous amounts of long-term finance by the banks and the stock exchange.

7   Government economic policies

This section examines whether and how government economic policies conditioned enterprise in different segments of British manufacturing. Before we analyse the conditioning effects of different policies, however, we must in a preliminary way establish some concept
of government economic policies and where they come from. On
these issues, our position can be summarised in two theses which
are in part defined by our rejection of the views of economic policy
which are current in applied economics of the orthodox or radical
type. Each of these current approaches has its own synoptic view
of government economic policy. For orthodox applied economics,
the choice between policy objectives establishes and unifies the
field of economic policy. In the radical alternative, the existence of
economic interests establishes a principle of identity and unity in
the policy field. In either case, the policy activities of governments
in the advanced capitalist countries may be diverse but they are
also coherent. Our theses challenge this assumption of coherence.

*Thesis 1   National governments have a plurality of economic policies and
these policies are not necessarily mutually consistent and compatible*

Orthodox economic discussion commonly presupposes that
governments have, or at least should have, a coherent and unitary
economic policy. Within such a policy, the ends and objectives are
supposed to be neatly arranged in a hierarchical order which then
determines the appropriate use of policy instruments. The main
objectives are usually supposed to be more or less common to
all the advanced capitalist countries whose governments generally
accept the desirability of policy objectives such as low unemployment, control of inflation, external payments equilibrium and a
reasonable rate of economic growth. On this view, economic policy
is defined by, and co-extensive with, the possibility of making
informed choices between objectives; in the textbook cliché, policy
is about the 'trade-offs' between different objectives.

Even if we bracket the question of why policy has to be
approached in terms of objectives, there are several fundamental
objections to this approach. It is intellectually suspect because it
treats the cultural and variable objectives of government policy as

natural universals; it is worth reminding ourselves here that the concept and problem of unemployment has been with us for less than a hundred years, while the objective of 'full employment' is less than fifty years old. Furthermore, and more crucially, choice-based coherence in the policy field is, in practice, impossible or, at least, unlikely. Modern national governments have at their disposal a large variety of technical policy instruments – orthodox fiscal and monetary measures, direct intervention and moral suasion. These tools can be used for a variety of different ends and, in practice, are likely to have many unanticipated consequences. The adjustment of means to ends is therefore a complex, contradictory process with an unpredictable outcome. Matters are further complicated by contradictions between objectives which are likely to arise because there is not a single locus of control in a modern national government's economic policy. Different parts of the government apparatus will normally use different technical instruments to pursue different ends.

These practical obstacles to coherence have been of some import-ance in Britain over the past thirty years. The point about conflicts between different loci of control was most obviously illustrated under the 1964 Labour government. In the experimental phase of 'planning by enlightenment', the Department of Economic Affairs was set up to promote growth *via* the National Plan. However, the Treasury still retained full responsibility for internal demand management and the external exchange rate. The Treasury's defla-tionary policies directly frustrated the DEA's promotion of growth. Clashes of this sort are not, however, the main difficulty. Because they are dramatic and visible, they can (at least, in principle) be removed or at least resolved in a *de facto* way by the exercise of political power. In the case quoted, the conflict was resolved by allowing both the DEA and the National Plan to atrophy. A variety of other subtler conflicts and contradictions is more immediately relevant to our purposes in this section because they were less easily resolved. The overall management policies of the Treasury which aimed to maintain employment co-existed uneasily with the indus-trial policies pursued by the Board of Trade or the Department of Trade and Industry; while, within the field of the trade department, location and anti-monopoly policies could often conflict with attempts to promote rationalisation. Weinstock's GEC provides a classic instance of conflicts and contradictions in the policy field after 1968. The cabinet suspended long-standing anti-monopoly policies to permit the creation of one giant firm which would pursue efficiency; GEC immediately did so through a programme of rationalisation which involved plant closures and wholesale redundancy. The implication must be that the British government is bound to have economic policies in the plural and the government has to suffer the contradictions between different policies.

Thesis 2   National economic policies are practices which have specific preconditions in the material and institutional conditions of government calculations

Many radicals and Marxists would argue that the plurality of government policies has an underlying principle of unity; that it is the interests of capital in general, or of specific segments of capital, which determine the nature of government economic policies. Some Marxists would argue, at a high level of generality, that government economic policies can be referred to general stages in capitalism which define the economic interest that government must serve by securing markets or subventing a declining rate of profit. Less grandiosely and more particularly, most radical interpretations of British economic decline place great emphasis on the subordination of British government policy to the interests of finance and the City of London.

These interpretations, however, raise major problems. To begin with, it is clear that economic interests cannot be directly expressed in politics: they must be represented by agents in finance or industry before they can be articulated by political agents for mass consumption. The process of representation and articulation depends on various kinds of calculation of interest made by the relevant agents. The premises, processes and results of such calculations of interest are not predetermined by any kind of economic logic. There is scope for identification of interests which will often appear perverse and, thus, for the advocacy of policies which often appear to be harmful. Consider, for example, the way in which representatives of British manufacturing consistently supported British entry into the Common Market in the early 1970s. British manufacturers seem to have been so bemused by the alluring prospect of a market with hundreds of millions of consumers that they failed to notice that this market would be a free trade area dominated by our strongest European competitor, West Germany. The unanticipated but predictable result has been a large and growing deficit in our manufacturing trade with West Germany.

Moreover, it is clearly unacceptable to suppose that government policy has exclusively ideal conditions of existence in the representations of agents such as politicians and lobbyists. In the political sphere, there are material conditions of government calculation, just as there are conditions of enterprise calculation in the manufacturing sector. The conditions of existence of economic policies are often as varied and heterogeneous as the conditions of existence of enterprise strategies. As Tomlinson (1981) has demonstrated, the fiscal Keynesianism of the 1950s did not simply arise from this practice's intellectual force, or from its appeal to the economic interests of capital. The practice of Keynesianism had specific conditions in the demise of the gold standard, a domestic fiscal system which could be used for regulatory purposes, the development of national income accounting and the practical exigencies of the Second World War. The general implication is that government economic policies are practices with specific institutional and material conditions of existence.

Although our alternative view of national economic policies may be preferable to the synoptic orthodoxies, it does immediately complicate matters for us. The basic problem here is that our analysis resolves different policies into so many particularities and it is difficult to ascend from this level towards generalisation. It can, however, be noted that our analysis does generally open up the possibility of disengagement or disjuncture between government economic policies and the conditions of enterprise calculation. Our analysis denies the supposition that any national manufacturing sector has unproblematic interests which must be served and promoted by government policies. More specifically, given heterogeneous conditions of existence of policies, there is no *a priori* reason why the peculiarly British problems discussed in this essay should ever have been identified, or resolved, by contemporary policymakers. Furthermore, we would argue that, in the case of British privately owned segments of capital, post-war government policies *did* consistently fail to engage the conditions of enterprise calculation and modify them in a positive way. The field of economic policies is large and there have been many policy changes over the past thirty years. Therefore, our conclusion can hardly be established in a few pages. We shall, however, review some policies and develop a general illustrative argument about British disengagement. In the case of the increasingly important state-owned nationalised manufacturing sector, it is possible to be more definite; in these areas, government itself set the conditions of enterprise calculation and failed to do so constructively.

If we survey the whole field of government economic policies since the early 1950s, perhaps the most immediately striking peculiarity is the dominance of macro-economic policies concerned with the manipulation of aggregates like consumer demand or the money supply. The 1950s and 1960s were the decades of fiscal Keynesianism, while the 1970s was the decade of monetarism; the dividing line between the two periods comes in 1972 with the Barber boom, which was the last attempt at reflation using the then orthodox fiscal measures. Such policies were privileged for a variety of reasons; practically, for example, they were attractive because at the outset the available fiscal and monetary tools appeared adequate to the task of controlling the relevant aggregates. In this respect, Keynesianism and its successors were timid 'practical' alternatives to the radical policy Keynes (1936) advocated in the *General Theory* where he proposed a 'socialisation of investment' or, at least, occasional large pushes towards full employment by means of state concerted investment projects. Intellectually, both Keynesianism and monetarism were justified with the argument that they would help manufacturing industry by producing the 'right' economic climate. In the 1950s and 1960s, politicians argued that manufacturing would benefit from a high and stable level of demand, just as they have recently argued that manufacturing would benefit from lower levels of inflation.

These rhetorical justifications have always been rather dubious; there is no good reason to suppose that macro-economic policy is a powerful instrument which could create the right conditions of enterprise calculation. Keynesians of the 1950s and 1960s assumed uncritically that, if the macro demand climate could be got right, then the micro managers of manufacturing enterprises would respond smoothly and effectively to the opportunities facing them. This was always implausible when the secular deterioration in the balance of payments and worsening payments crises before 1967 provided a clear indication that British manufacturing enterprises were unable to exploit an unprecentedly favourable demand situation at home and abroad. The monetarist belief that lower inflation rates and the pressure of low or contracting demand can reactivate a lost manufacturing efficiency is equally implausible. The central assumption here is that British manufacturers will benefit in so far as they become low-cost producers. This assumption is highly questionable because, as we have already argued, some of the key problems of British manufacturing are problems of non-price competitiveness. In this situation, the elimination of high-cost British producers may simply produce a permanent decline in the size of the domestic manufacturing base and a rise in the import ratio without securing any sizeable improvement in the capability of the remaining producers to make exports and resist imports.

If post-war macro policies could not help British manufacturing, they may have harmed manufacturing by reinforcing already adverse conditions of enterprise calculation. At the time of writing, in mid-1982, it is not possible to assess the outcome of the Thatcherite policy experiment which is being undertaken in the middle of a world recession. We will, therefore, concentrate our attention on the fiscal Keynesianism of the 1950s and 1960s. These practices of economic management aimed to maintain a high level of capacity utilisation in the economy by regulating home consumer demand through changes in income tax, purchase tax and hire purchase controls. Some 1960s commentators, notably Dow (1964) and Brittan (1969) alleged that Keynesianism was actually destabilising in that it produced worse economic fluctuations than would otherwise have occurred. In our terminology, the question is whether Keynesianism unintentionally and harmfully changed the level and composition of demand facing firms.

In retrospect, the debate about Keynesianism's destabilising effects seems to have been much ado about nothing. Fiscal policy adjustments were of relatively minor importance in determining the path of the economy. The long international boom worked autonomously to keep the British economy near full employment. Fiscal policy changes were usually relatively small; Dow (1964) shows that between 1946 and 1960, the average budget changed consumer purchasing power by only £100 million. Furthermore, Dow's and Brittan's impressionistic arguments about chancellors responding inappropriately are flatly contradicted by the results of econometric tests which have compared 'policy on' fluctuations with a simulated 'policy off' path; after undertaking such tests, Bristow (1968) and Artis (1972) concluded independently that fiscal policy made little difference.

If government fiscal policy did not create the fluctuations, our next point must be that the economic fluctuations of the 1950s and 1960s were very gentle and no worse than those experienced in other capitalist national economies. Capacity utilisation in manufacturing must always have remained high when unemployment never rose above 2·5 per cent in the 1950s and 1960s. While the recessions which did occur were very mild indeed: manufacturing output never dropped significantly in any of the British recessions of the 1950s and 1960s. There were problems about periodic collapses of demand in some sectors of manufacturing industry; the emphasis on changes in hire purchase regulations caused severe fluctuations in demand for many consumer durable manufacturers. But in some of these industries, such as motor cars, producers in other national economies such as West Germany coped successfully with equally severe fluctuations. The underlying British problem was that many consumer durable manufacturers were constrained by problems about industrial structure, composition of demand and supply of capital. Even if all the demand fluctuations had been ironed out, such conditions of enterprise calculation would have been persistent and intractable. Much the same arguments apply in the case of the reflationary booms which exposed a more general latent weakness. Import penetration rose upwards in a step with each reflationary boom. But, as we have noted, this happened because the income elasticity of demand for manufacturers was unusually high in Britain. The macro managers can hardly be blamed for that or for the underlying conditions which explain it.

It could be argued that the overall maintenance of a high level of demand through the 1950s and 1960s had unfavourable effects on the conditions of enterprise calculation, especially on control of the labour process. Sustained labour shortage made management reluctant to shed any reasonably skilled labour when there was a temporary decline in demand for the products of a particular firm or industry. The interaction between labour shortage and a high level of demand probably also had its effects; these circumstances encouraged firms to accept restrictive labour practices and limited their resistance to wage increases which could be passed on to consumers. If there is some substance in such speculations, they miss the basic point that the practices of fiscal Keynesianism were generally irrelevant to most of the problems of manufacturing industry analysed earlier in this essay. This irrelevance was built upon an oversight. In the problematics of Keynesianism, the manipulation of the quantity of aggregate demand was seen as *the* problem and *the* opportunity. Problems about the quality (or composition) of demand and the range of institutional problems on the supply side were simply unseen.

The obverse of the dominance of macropolicies was the underdevelopment of effective micro policies which involved a detailed piecemeal intervention in the problems of specific industries and enterprises. Interestingly enough, however, from the early 1960s onwards, if successive governments failed to develop an effective micro policy, it was not for want of trying. The 1960s saw a variety of new micro initiatives including, for example, the creation of the Industrial Reorganisation Corporation and schemes for supporting research and development under the 1965 Science and Technology Act. The 1970s saw similar efforts including, for example, sectoral support schemes for encouraging investment under the 1972 Industry Act.

Much of this policy effort seems to have been misdirected and ineffective for one of two reasons. Firstly, many of these initiatives were short-lived and had unfortunate effects because they reflected only the fashions of the moment. The IRC, for example, naively aimed to encourage mergers which would give a leading industrial role to good management; it provided official sponsorship for merger mania which, as we have seen, generated problems of size without scale. Secondly, many of the initiatives turned out to be much less specific than they appeared to be since they were administered under general non-discriminatory rules. The 1972 Industry Act, for example, aimed to encourage modernisation, new product development, and so forth. But the act was administered by laying down general guide lines; if a company satisfied general criteria, it received the grant and no attempt was made to select either the projects or the manufacturing enterprises which were supported.

These criticisms of micro policy may be correct, but they do not immediately explain the failure of the 'little Neddies' which were the most enduring and significant of the 1960s micro policy initiatives. The National Economic Development Council ('Neddy') was originally set up by the Conservative government during its flirtation with French-style ideas of 'indicative planning'. From this sprang the 'little Neddies' or sector working parties which were established for particular industries. Most of manufacturing industry was covered by about sixty working parties which included senior company executives, trade unionists and government officials. Each working party aimed to collect and exchange information, to present analyses of the problems of its industry, and to formulate targets of performance. The little Neddies could have played a key role in an effective micro strategy; in each industry they could have identified and dealt with the concrete problems created by the conditions of enterprise calculation.

Why therefore did the little Neddies fail to perform these functions? Imberg and Northcott's (1981) recent study of the operation of little Neddies in four industries suggests some reasons. Outright opposition by firms has not been a problem; on the contrary, the sector working parties commanded much goodwill and were regarded as useful bodies which could communicate industrial needs to government. The central problem was that the analyses, targets and proposals of the little Neddies were all made at the industry level. There was no mechanism for converting any of this into targets for the individual enterprise and, crucially, there was no means at all of securing implementation of working party proposals at the enterprise level. The Imberg and Northcott (1981) investigation surveyed thirty-five companies over a number of years; the authors could not find a single case where a specific investment decision had been taken as a result of a recommendation from one of the sector working parties. Even in the case of the little Neddies, government policy has never firmly engaged the conditions of enterprise calculation because there has been no mechanism for intervening so as to modify the given processes of calculation at an enterprise level.

Our argument so far about the disengagement of government policy from the conditions of enterprise calculation establishes one more national peculiarity. In other advanced capitalist countries, especially France and Japan, there is a general tendency for administrations to push economic policies to operational levels which are more closely specified. The irrelevance of macro policy and the ineffectiveness of micro policy ensured that the British government played a much more indirect role. Much of its conditioning impact on enterprise calculation depended on middle-range policies which usually applied to all firms and either set one aspect of the conditioning environment or aimed to affect one aspect of business behaviour. Environment-setting policies would include the commitment to an over-valued currency before 1967, British entrance into the Common Market in 1973, or the acceptance of high interest rates at the start of the 1980s. As the list shows, these policies were generally unfortunate in that they exposed British manufacturing to a harsher environment which tested latent weakness; the secular national conditions of enterprise calculation have been so unfavourable that British manufacturing cannot really afford to pay the price for our national government's political delusions of grandeur which have determined many of the environmental policies. Behaviour-modifying policies would include competition policy, regional policy and corporate taxation. Both competition and regional policy were undiscriminating and jointly reinforced the adverse conditioning effects which were spontaneously established by other non-policy conditions. As we have already noted, competition policy directly encouraged mergers which were freely allowed by the government while it penalised collusion between independent firms. Regional policy aggravated the 'size without scale' problems which merger produced in the big business segment since it encouraged or compelled many large firms to open branch factories in the north and west. Corporate taxation policy had a special role because it partially and unsatisfactorily compensated for the ill-effects produced by other policies and it is therefore sufficiently important to merit separate treatment.

Corporate taxation is a modern innovation; only since 1947 has the tax on companies been a permanent feature of British fiscal policy. The subsequent history of corporate taxation is complicated because there were significant changes in the British system in 1958, 1965 and 1973. In the capitalist economy in general, the existence of corporation tax will condition enterprise calculation because managements will attempt to minimise its burden. Indeed, for the manufacturing enterprise, effort which is expended to save a given amount of tax is as worthwhile as effort expended to earn a similar sum by producing manufactures. As long as enterprises seek to avoid paying tax, the corporate taxation rules can be used to change the overall amount, composition and sources of investment in manufacturing. But all this is a matter of abstract general possibilities. Over the past thirty years in Britain, corporate taxation has played a conservative and passive role in so far as it has reinforced the tendency of manufacturing enterprises to finance investment out of their own retained earnings.

In 1965, for example, when corporation tax was introduced, enterprises paid a flat rate on taxable profits and shareholders separately paid income tax on dividends. The result was that companies were encouraged to raise finance for investment by retaining profits rather than by raising new capital. If profits were retained and applied to investment, a substantial benefit accrued to the firm because the company used gross profits minus corporation tax; if profits were distributed, a much smaller benefit accrued to the shareholder because the shareholder received gross profits minus corporation tax and income tax. The main object of the company tax reform of 1973 was to change this discrimination in favour of retentions which were subsequently less favoured as a source of company finance. Corporation tax was imposed at the high rate of 52 per cent, but shareholders receiving dividends were credited with tax paid at the standard rate; for standard rate taxpayers, the taxman no longer took two bites from the cherry of distributed profits. The 1973 reform did not change the way in which the system favoured finance of investment by issue of fixed interest securities; interest changes were exempt from tax and could be deducted before profits were declared.

Nevertheless, the influence of corporation tax on sources of finance was secondary. The primary conditioning effect of corporate taxation was exerted through its effect on the apparent accounting rate of return when an increasingly generous corporate tax system propped up the dismal pre-tax rate of return. On King's (1975) calculations, average tax rates on manufacturing company income fell dramatically in the twenty years up to the early 1970s.

TABLE 16   *Effective tax rate in manufacturing industry*

	1956	*1960*	*1965*	*1970*	*1973*
Tax as percentage of gross trading profit	31·0	24·8	15·7	13·0	11·6
Tax as percentage of gross trading profit minus stock appreciation and capital consumption	41·4	31·6	21·4	24·6	24·4

Source: King (1975).

It must be admitted that other studies of effective tax rates by Price, Glyn and Sutcliffe, Walker, Panić and Close, concede that the effective average rate of tax on company profits was always low and below 50 per cent, but they do not show a declining rate (Martin and O'Connor, 1981). Nevertheless, we would accept King's results which do show a declining rate since his study is the only one which focuses on manufacturing, which shows the post-tax rate of return to the company rather than the dividend recipient, and which makes full current replacement cost depreciation and stock appreciation allowances. All the other available studies can be faulted on one or more of these counts.

It is certain that the trend towards a more generous corporate tax system was not reversed in the 1970s. Concern over investment levels led to increasingly generous depreciation allowances so that by the end of the 1970s manufacturing investment in plant and machinery could immediately be fully (100 per cent) depreciated against profits of the three previous years. Moreover, when problems arose with accelerated inflation after the huge increases in oil prices, companies were allowed from 1974 onwards to deduct the appreciation in the value of stocks of raw materials and finished goods. In the big business segment it has thus become possible for many companies to adjust their affairs so that they do not need to pay corporation tax. It was recently demonstrated that of twenty top British firms, only seven actually paid any corporation tax in 1976–7 and only three (GEC, Marks and Spencer, Bass Charrington) paid a significant amount (Kay and King, 1980).

A chorus of right-wing 'pro-business' journalists and academics often complains about high taxation levels in Britain. But, as we have now demonstrated, the corporate tax system has become a vast and undiscriminating system of outdoor relief for British manufacturers; the increasingly severe problems of most segments of manufacturing capital were reflected in poor accounting profits, and this pressing constraint was eased by successive governments' decisions to forgo tax revenue raised from corporate profits. In a situation where micro policy never engaged the conditions of enterprise calculation, we would interpret the wholesale remission of corporate taxes as an unconstructive palliative expedient. This expedient would, of course, only work where companies were earning some kind of profit which they could be allowed to retain. A cynic might observe that where enterprises and whole industries were chronically unable or unlikely to earn a profit, the British solution was nationalisation. We must now, therefore, consider the impact of nationalisation on British manufacturing.

There have been two waves of nationalisation in the British economy. The first wave in the later 1940s under the Attlee Labour government nationalised utilities and public services in the transport and energy sectors; coal, rail, gas and electricity were all nationalised at this time. This was relevant to manufacturing because the nationalised utility and service industries were often the most important purchasers of particular types of capital equipment (such as heavy electrical generating equipment or coal cutting gear) from private sector manufacturers. Nevertheless, in the 1950s and 1960s, the nationalised sector did not itself include many large manufacturing enterprises. One major manufacturing industry (steel), was nationalised by the post-war Labour government; but steel was then denationalised by the Tories before being re-nationalised by Labour in 1967.

The second wave of nationalisation under Labour and Tory governments, in the first half of the 1970s, involved the takeover of several manufacturing industries and of major manufacturing enterprises in other industries where private capital remained predominant. All the major independent firms in shipbuilding and airframe manufacture were nationalised. In aero engines, government took over Rolls Royce which was the only British producer of large jet engines. In cars and machine tools, when government nationalised BL and Alfred Herbert, it took over the largest independent enterprises in the relevant British industries. Most of these enterprises were making losses when they were nationalised; the official receiver was the only alternative to nationalisation for many shipbuilders, for BLMC, for Alfred Herbert and for Rolls Royce. Even where profits were being made, as in airframe manufacture, prospects were poor, given the marginal status of British producers in world terms. But from a broader viewpoint, nationalisation of these manufacturing enterprises represented a major opportunity; from the mid-1970s, government could directly set the conditions of calculation in a significant sector of British manufacturing by making funds available for strategic plans which were officially scrutinised and approved.

Whatever the ideologues of the Institute of Economic Affairs may pretend, the failure to exploit this opportunity proves nothing about the relative merits of 'state ownership' and 'free enterprise'. The fact of government ownership in the manufacturing sector does not have any invariant universal consequences for enterprise conduct or performance. The specifically British problems in state-owned manufacturing are attributable to the particular national forms of organisation, control and direction imposed on nationalised industries; these forms of organisation and control in Britain have not provided beneficial conditions of enterprise calculation. To begin with, therefore, we must examine the evolution of the characteristically British structures and controls.

When the public utilities were nationalised in the late 1940s, they were subjected to few formal controls and directions. Their quasi-independence was partly guaranteed by the institutional form of the Morrisonian public corporation; government only exercised indirect control through political appointment of board members and the provision of finance. The financial and economic objectives of the utilities were never clearly defined; generally, the newly nationalised utilities were enjoined only 'to pay their way', taking one year with another. Since the 1950s, there has been surprisingly little experiment with institutional form. The major innovation came in 1976 with the formation of the National Enterprise Board which has since acted as a state holding company; state shareholdings in BL and Rolls Royce were vested in the NEB which also subsequently provided large loans to these enterprises. Official effort in Britain has concentrated on elaborating strategic principles which might define the aims of nationalised industries and the means by which those aims could be achieved.

There were major statements of official policy in three White Papers (Treasury, 1961, 1967 and 1978). The master objective was to be profit or, more exactly, a positive accounting rate of return on assets. Both the 1961 and 1978 White Papers put their faith in target overall rates of return; the 1978 Paper suggested that an overall (pre-tax) rate of return of 5 per cent on new investment would be appropriate in a framework of financial targets fixed over a three- to five-year period. On the means to this end, the 1967 White Paper suggested return on investment criteria should be applied to the appraisal of individual projects; a test discount rate of 8 per cent was proposed and in 1969 this was raised to 10 per cent. The 1978 White Paper rejected such universalistic criteria for individual projects; test discount rates had been found to be inapplicable in many cases where low-yield investment projects were necessary to the attainment of an overall enterprise strategy. Nevertheless, the 1978 White Paper did support strategic planning in the nationalised industries where return on investment was the standard criterion used in appraising and selecting strategic options.

It is well known that these increasingly elaborate official principles were in practice ignored by successive governments. Through the 1950s and 1960s, there was a long tradition of *ad hoc* political interference in the affairs of the nationalised industries; power station orders, for example, were brought forward or held back according to short-run political considerations, and there was never an overall programme for ordering different types of station (nuclear, oil-, or coal-fired) in the context of a national energy policy. On a wider front, short-run political interference culminated in the early 1970s when pricing and wage bargaining decisions in the nationalised industries were generally subordinated to the requirements of Labour and Tory governments' anti-inflation policies; prices were held down to restrain cost-of-living increases and wage rises were resisted so that government *qua* employer could be seen to be setting an example. The disastrous results were an aggregate annual deficit of 1 billion pounds in the nationalised sector and a miners' strike which brought down the Heath government. From November 1974, government formally renounced such manipulations and promised that nationalised industries would be allowed economic pricing. But the nationalised industries never obtained their freedom since they were by the mid-1970s increasingly enmeshed in the government's restrictive monetary policies; from 1976 onwards, cash limits were applied to the nationalised industries.

The conventional interpretation of this experience was summed up by NEDO (1976) in its influential report on the nationalised industries: 'there is an absence of declared, long term policies, particularly in the energy and transport sectors, but a surfeit of short term interventions which are seldom made in the context of an industry's strategic plans.' The implication drawn by NEDO and others was that the problems of British nationalised industries could be solved if *ad hoc* interference was minimised, while Parliament and the sponsoring ministries exerted effective control at the strategic level. Reform on these lines would certainly have helped private sector manufacturers of telecommunication or electricity generating equipment who wanted stable, or at least predictable, demand. We would, however, question whether such a reform could solve the problems of nationalised industries or, more specifically, the problems of nationalised manufacturing enterprises. There were fundamental defects in the forms of rationality embodied in the strategic principles which the government was notionally committed to imposing on the nationalised sector. Strategic planning on this basis could not, and did not, engage with the realities of the position of nationalised manufacturing enterprises and government could not therefore by these means constructively set conditions of enterprise calculation in the nationalised manufacturing sector.

To begin with, strategic planning which evaluates alternatives in ROI terms can only provide a rational basis for choice between strategies if the enterprise makes realistic market forecasts. As the experience of the electricity supply industry shows, in practice, it is very difficult to make accurate medium-term projections of demand. Furthermore, the experience of nationalised cars and steel suggests that, if demand forecasts are sufficiently optimistic, expansive options requiring huge investments could be justified by management. After 1971, BSC's management bid for £3000 million of public money on the basis that it could by 1980 make and sell 43 million tons of steel, a quantity which was almost twice as large as then current output. In 1975, BL's management persuaded Ryder to recommend the injection of £2000 million of public money into the enterprise on the basis that BL could maintain its existing share of the home market and dramatically increase exports to the EEC countries three- or four-fold. In both steel and cars, corporate planning was a means by which management justified what it already wanted to do by producing an appropriate set of supporting figures. The key piece of obfuscation here was the presentation of market forecasts in an aggregated form. On a disaggregated market-by-market basis, the market forecasts and, more especially, the export projections would have appeared thoroughly implausible. The 1973 development strategy in steel and the 1975 Ryder report were never fully implemented. Nevertheless, managements in steel and cars did obtain large investment funds which were largely wasted since the market would not absorb final product in anything like the projected quantity when home market shares collapsed and increased export volume never materialised.

The argument so far may suggest that the problem was only that government was insufficiently critical of management proposals and

allowed management to choose the wrong option. This is the conclusion that has already been drawn by Bryer et al. (1982) in their
book on British Steel. We would argue, however, that the problem
was more deep-seated because all the newly nationalised manufacturing enterprises were in weak strategic positions which compromised their ability to obtain a decent rate of return on any option
which involved large-scale investment. Gale's (1980) recent work
examines the variability in return on investment in 1,700 American
businesses. He concludes that, for the average business, ROI falls
with increased investment; a normal return on sales combined with
a greater than normal amount of investment per dollar of sales yields
a lower return on investment. Businesses where new investment is
rewarded with particularly low rates of return commonly share
certain strategic characteristics – low market share, high rate of
new product introduction, low capacity utilisation and strong union-
isation. If similar relations exist in the British economy, it is unlikely
that investment in nationalised manufacturing enterprises will be
rewarded with a decent rate of return; the exact problems differed
from industry to industry, but most of the enterprises nationalised
in the 1970s were burdened with at least four of Gale's five adverse
characteristics. Furthermore, it seems likely that American type
relations do exist in some of these manufacturing industries because,
in activities like steel and cars, private and state capital in many
West European countries cannot find a reasonable rate of return.

It was always unreal to suppose that, if state funds were injected
into newly nationalised manufacturing enterprises, they could be
turned round into accounting profit; such strategies never recognised the market-defined conditions of enterprise calculation which
were likely to keep the accounting rate of return negative or very
low. We would not accept the argument that low or negative
accounting rates of return necessarily justify British abandonment
of a particular type of manufacturing activity. Nevertheless, the
reasons for maintaining a British manufacturing capability in cars,
shipbuilding, steel or aero-engines would have to be demonstrated.
Employment benefits, import savings and other considerations must
be examined before an enterprise or government ministry can decide
how much manufacturing capability to preserve and in what form
this capability should be maintained and developed. Rowthorn and
Ward's (1979) article on the Corby steel closure shows how this
might be done. But the accounting practices of nationalised indus-

tries are narrowly concerned with accounting profit and do not encourage or enforce such broader calculations, while government has conspicuously failed to take a broader view. In the case of utilities, like rail or bus transport, government has been unable to provide a coherent framework within which the provision of a level of 'social' service and financial compensation for social obligations could be determined. In the state-owned manufacturing sector, the questions about state manufacturing's social obligations have yet to be posed in any official document and clearly will not be posed as long as the Thatcher government remains in power.

At present we are in a reactive rather than a constructive phase in state manufacturing. Naive expectations of profit have not been realised and where large accounting losses are reported, it is the workers who must pay the price for managerial miscalculation and governmental non-calculation. Enterprises like British Steel and BL have been allowed, and even encouraged, to solve their self-created over-capacity problems by sacking masses of workers. At the beginning of the 1970s, BSC employed just over 200,000 workers, but by 1982 the workforce was reduced to just 83,000 workers. In BL, it is a similar story, although the major redundancies started later and may well not yet be over. In both industries, the redundancies were achieved most dramatically by the closure of branch plants and smaller plants; Consett, Corby and Shotton in steel, and Speke, Canley and Solihull in cars. The rationale was the same in both industries. Major investments in the modernisation of large-scale production had been made in the central plants and, if accounting losses were to be contained, the new facilities at the central plants had to be loaded; throughput was therefore concentrated in the large plants while smaller plants were closed. The gratifying effect of such closures on labour productivity allowed management to make a virtue of redundancy. This was just as well because it distracted attention from the central point; many of the men who were made redundant would not in the foreseeable future ever work again.

We must, therefore, conclude that in nationalised manufacturing, government failed to set its own constructive conditions of enterprise calculation. Elsewhere, government economic policies were at best irrelevant to the problems we have analysed and at worst counter-productive. As government economic policies did not modify the conditions of enterprise calculation for privately owned manufacturing capital, these government policies themselves established a further and final constraint on enterprise calculation.

At this point it is possible to summarise the whole argument about the national conditions of enterprise calculation. In Britain the major segments of manufacturing capital have performed badly and have failed to surmount problems about the composition of demand. The workers and their unions are scapegoats rather than villains. There is no evidence that the workforce has done more than encourage multi-nationals to switch production. There are other more fundamental constraints affecting most segments of manufacturing which have not been helped by government, while big and small businesses have in different ways been positively hindered by the operations of the financial sector.

Appendix A
British trade in manufactures

TABLE 1   *Share of UK manufactured^a imports by source, 1951–1980*

	Value of total manufactured imports^b £ m	Source of manufactured imports as a percentage of total manufactured imports					Included in previous columns			Manufactures as % of total imports
		EEC^d	Rest of W. Europe^c	N. America	Japan	Rest of world	W. Germany	France	Sterling Area^f	
	(i)	(ii)	(iii)	(iv)	(v)	(vi)	(vii)	(viii)	(ix)	(x)
1951	758	34·6	15·6	22·4	1·4	26·0	6·6	8·5	22·4	19·4
1952	768	33·4	13·0	30·9	3·2	19·5	9·1	5·9	18·0	22·1
1953	643	30·1	13·8	30·8	1·0	24·3	9·2	6·4	21·8	19·2
1954	679	28·8	15·1	27·5	1·0	27·6	9·0	6·0	23·3	20·1
1955	893	27·9	14·6	30·1	1·4	26·0	8·7	6·1	20·2	23·0
1956	906	31·1	14·4	27·3	0·8	26·4	10·7	6·2	20·5	23·3
1957	927	33·6	15·5	27·6	1·1	22·2	11·9	5·9	18·4	22·8
1958	909	34·4	15·4	26·7	1·0	22·5	13·3	5·0	17·3	24·1
1959	1,051	34·8	15·0	25·3	1·0	23·9	12·3	5·6	19·2	26·4
1960	1,445	31·7	14·4	32·4	0·9	20·6	11·2	5·6	16·1	31·8
1961	1,428	32·9	15·1	29·2	1·1	21·7	12·1	5·2	16·2	32·5
1962	1,467	33·4	15·1	28·3	1·2	22·0	11·9	5·0	16·4	32·7
1963	1,568	34·0	15·6	26·7	1·6	22·1	11·8	5·5	16·9	32·6
1964	2,009	32·8	15·9	29·5	1·9	19·9	11·9	5·2	15·9	36·5

1965	2,253	31·6	15·2	27·3	2·0	23·9	10·7	5·1	18·4	39·2
1966	2,471	33·0	15·8	25·9	2·1	23·2	11·1	5·2	18·4	41·5
1967	2,844	32·6	17·3	26·1	2·2	21·8	10·7	5·4	16·9	44·2
1968	3,772	31·6	16·8	26·9	2·1	22·6	10·5	5·0	18·0	47·8
1969	4,137	27·4	17·4	24·5	1·9	28·8	9·1	4·8	17·6	49·8
1970	4,572	32·7	18·2	26·5	2·3	20·3	10·9	5·0	15·4	50·6
1971	5,003	37·3	19·5	21·5	3·3	18·4	11·8	5·8	16·7	50·9
1972	6,093	38·5	21·2	18·5	4·7	17·1	12·7	6·9	13·8	54·7
1973	8,908	39·1	21·5	17·2	4·6	17·6	14·1	7·1	13·1	56·2
1974	11,913	41·5	20·2	17·8	4·5	16·0	14·3	7·2	12·0	51·6
1975	12,528	43·3	28·9	27·0	5·0	15·8	13·9	8·4	12·2	52·2
1976	16,933	44·7	18·9	16·2	4·4	15·8	14·5	8·8	11·9	54·2
1977	21,310	45·8	18·8	15·2	4·8	15·4	15·0	9·0	11·7	58·4
1978	26,079	46·4	21·0	13·7	4·8	14·1	15·7	9·2	10·3	63·7
1979	31,441	49·0	19·2	13·3	4·6	13·9	16·9	9·7	9·4	64·9
1980	33,205	46·6	18·0	16·3	5·0	14·1	15·6	9·2	10·0	64·3

Sources: 1951–62, Annual Statement of Trade of the UK., vol. 1, 1954, 1958 and 1962.
1963–75, Annual Statement of Overseas Trade of the UK, vol. 1, 1963 to 1975.
1976–80, Overseas Trade Statistics of the UK, December, 1976–80.

TABLE 2   *Share of UK manufactured^a exports by destination, 1951–1980*

	Value of total manufactured exports^c £ m	Destination of UK manufactured exports as a percentage of total manufactured exports					Included in previous columns				Manufactures as % of total exports
		EEC^d	Rest of Europe^e	N. America	Japan	Rest of world	W. Germany	France	Sterling area^f	Oil exporters^g	
	(i)	(ii)	(iii)	(iv)	(v)	(vi)	(vii)	(viii)	(ix)	(x)	(xi)
1951	2,212	14·6	12·4	9·7	0·3	63·0	1·0	2·1	51·8		81·7
1952	2,168	14·8	12·4	10·6	0·3	61·9	1·2	2·2	49·3		79·5
1953	2,122	15·6	11·1	12·0	0·6	60·7	1·8	2·6	48·3		79·0
1954	2,195	17·8	11·6	10·0	0·4	60·2	2·2	2·4	49·9		79·1
1955	2,416	17·1	10·2	10·5	0·4	61·8	2·2	2·5	49·3		79·9
1956	2,655	16·8	11·4	13·3	0·6	57·9	2·6	2·6	45·6		80·8
1957	2,795	17·1	10·6	13·3	0·7	58·3	2·8	2·5	45·1		80·8
1958	2,735	16·8	10·6	14·4	0·5	57·7	3·7	2·1	45·2		81·5
1959	3,860	17·8	10·9	17·2	0·7	53·4	4·0	2·0	40·9		82·6
1960	3,047	18·7	13·3	15·0	0·7	52·3	4·3	2·4	40·9		82·4
1961	3,176	21·6	13·3	13·0	1·0	51·1	4·5	3·1	38·2		82·7
1962	3,248	24·0	14·0	13·0	1·1	47·9	5·0	3·8	35·6		82·3
1963	3,438	24·9	14·3	12·1	1·1	47·6	4·9	4·4	38·8		81·2
1964	3,615	25·2	14·9	12·3	1·4	46·2	5·1	4·4	36·3		82·0

1965	4,095	24·5	14·7	14·3	1·1	45·4	5·1	3·8	34·5		83·6
1966	4,390	24·6	15·4	16·4	1·3	42·3	4·9	4·0	31·5		83·8
1967	4,386	25·2	15·7	16·1	1·7	41·3	4·9	4·2	30·5		84·1
1968	5,413	25·9	14·7	17·8	1·5	40·1	5·3	4·0	28·3		84·5
1969	6,256	27·1	15·8	16·3	1·8	39·0	5·3	4·3	27·6		85·7
1970	6,806	28·2	17·0	14·7	1·8	38·3	5·9	4·2	27·8		84·4
1971	7,824	28·0	16·4	15·3	1·7	38·6	5·4	4·3	29·8		85·2
1972	8,257	28·7	17·9	16·4	1·7	35·3	5·7	5·1	24·8		84·7
1973	10,455	30·7	18·2	15·7	2·1	33·3	6·0	5·2	23·6		83·9
1974	13,685	31·5	17·3	13·9	1·9	35·4	5·8	5·5	24·5		83·0
1975	16,459	29·9	16·4	11·8	1·5	40·4	6·1	5·7	26·2		83·3
1976	21,347	33·3	16·5	12·1	1·3	36·8	6·7	6·4	24·2	13·0	82·8
1977	26,796	34·1	17·4	11·2	1·4	35·9	7·0	6·1	24·1	14·1	81·3
1978	30,004	35·0	15·7	11·4	1·5	36·4	7·4	6·3	24·9	14·0	80·3
1979	33,095	38·3	16·4	11·3	1·5	32·5	8·4	7·0	23·1	10·1	77·3
1980	36,990	37·2	17·2	10·8	1·3	33·5	8·6	5·0	23·9	11·6	74·7

Sources: 1951–62, *Annual Statement of Trade of the UK*, vol.I, 1954, 1958 and 1962.
1963–75, *Annual Statement of Overseas Trade of the UK*, vol.1, 1963 to 1975.
1976–80, *Overseas Trade Statistics of the UK*, December 1976–80.

TABLE 3 *Percentage shares in the value of world[h] exports of manufactures, 1950–1980*

	USA[i]	UK	W. Germany	France	Japan	Italy	Others
	(i)	(ii)	(iii)	(iv)	(v)	(vi)	(vii)
1950	27·3	25·5	7·3	9·9	3·4		26·6
1951	26·6	21·9	10·0	10·0	4·3		27·2
1952j	26·2	21·5	12·0	9·2	3·8	3·2	24·1
1953	26·2	20·9	13·4	9·1	3·8	3·3	23·4
1954	25·2	20·5	14·9	9·1	4·7	3·1	22·5
1955	24·5	19·8	15·5	9·3	5·1	3·4	22·4
1956	25·2	19·2	16·4	7·8	5·7	3·5	22·1
1957	25·4	18·2	17·5	8·0	5·9	3·8	21·1
1958	23·3	18·1	18·5	8·6	6·0	4·1	21·4
1959	21·1	18·0[k]	19·0	9·2	6·7	4·4	21·6
1960	21·6	16·5	19·3	9·6	6·9	5·1	21·0
1961	20·5	16·4	20·2	9·4	6·8	5·7	21·0
1962l	21·9	15·5	19·5	9·0	7·2	5·9	21·0
1963	21·4	15·3	19·8	9·0	7·5	5·9	21·1

1964	21·5	14·4	19·3	8·7	8·1	6·3	21·8
1965	20·3	13·9	19·1	8·8	9·4	6·7	21·8
1966	20·1	13·4	19·3	8·6	9·7	6·9	22·0
1967	20·4	12·3	19·5	8·5	9·8	7·0	22·5
1968	20·1	11·6	19·4	8·2	10·6	7·3	22·8
1969	19·3	11·3	19·5	8·2	11·2	7·3	23·2
1970	18·5	10·8	19·8	8·7	11·7	7·2	23·3
1971	17·0	10·9	20·0	8·8	13·0	7·2	23·1
1972	16·1	10·0	20·2	9·3	13·2	7·6	23·5
1973	16·1	9·4	22·1	9·5	12·8	6·8	23·3
1974	17·2	8·8	21·7	9·3	14·5	6·7	21·8
1975	17·7	9·3	20·3	10·2	13·6	7·5	21·4
1976	17·2	8·8	20·5	9·7	14·6	7·1	22·0
1977	15·5	9·4	20·7	9·9	15·4	7·6	21·4
1978	15·1	9·5	20·7	9·8	15·6	7·9	21·4
1979	15·9	9·7	20·7	10·4	13·6	8·4	21·3
1980	16·9	10·2	19·8	10·0	14·8	7·8	20·5

Sources: 1950–75, Brown and Sheriff (1978), table 10.
1975–80, *National Institute Economic Review*, no.96, May 1981, table 23.

TABLE 4   *Import penetration and export/sales ratios for products of manufacturing industry in the UK*[m]

	UK manufacturing Sales[n] £ m	Manufactured imports[o] £ m	Manufactured exports[o] £ m	Ratio (a)[p] Imports as % home demand	Ratio (b)[q] Imports as % home demand + exports	Ratio (c)[r] Exports as % manufacturing sales	Ratio (d)[s] Exports as % manufacturing sales + imports
	(i)	(ii)	(iii)	(iv)	(v)	(vi)	(vii)
1955	12,816	893	2,416	8	7	19	18
1956	13,549	906	2,655	8	6	20	18
1957	14,239	927	2,795	7	6	20	18
1958	14,838	909	2,735	7	6	18	17
1959	15,661	1,051	2,860	8	6	18	17
1960	17,194	1,445	3,047	9	8	18	16
1961	(17,730	1,428	3,176	(9	7	18	17
	(18,300			(9		18	16
1962	18,563	1,467	3,248	9	7	17	16
1963	18,962	1,568	3,438	9	8	18	17
1964	21,427	2,009	3,615	10	9	17	15
1965	23,099	2,253	4,095	11	9	18	16
1966	23,923	2,471	4,390	11	9	18	17
1967	24,338	2,844	4,386	12	10	18	16
1968	26,113	3,772	5,413	15	13	21	18
1969	28,469	4,137	6,256	16	13	22	19

	col. i	col. ii	col. iii				
1970	32,084	4,572	6,806	15	12	21	19
1971	34,027	5,003	7,824	16	13	23	20
1972	36,863	6,093	8,257	18	14	22	19
1973	43,821	8,908	10,455	21	17	24	20
1974	55,375	11,918	13,685	22	18	25	20
1975	62,054	12,528	16,459	22	17	27	22
1976	75,942	16,933	21,347	24	18	28	23
1977	88,669	21,310	26,796	26	19	30	24
1978	96,518	26,079	30,004	28	21	31	24
1979	110,202	31,441	33,095	29	22	30	23
1980	114,101	33,205	36,990	30	22	32	25

Sources:

(a) col. i
  1955–69, *Census of Production* (PA 1002) and *Historical Record of the Census of Production* (with sales totals adjusted and estimated as explained in Addendum B).
  1970–80, Statistics supplied by the Department of Trade and Industry.

(b) cols ii, iii
  1955–62, *Annual Statement of the Trade of the UK*, vol.1, 1954, 1958, 1962.
  1963–75, *Annual Statement of Overseas Trade of the UK*, vol.1, 1963–75.
  1976–80, *Overseas Trade Statistics of the UK*, December.

(c) cols iv–vii
  1955–80, calculated from totals given in cols i–iii.

Totals for GNP and GDP used in interpolation calculations (see addendum B) are the most recent estimates given in CSO *Annual Abstract of Statistics.*

Notes to appendix A

a Manufactures are officially defined as those goods classified in sections 5–8 of the Standard International Trade Classification. They include chemicals, manufactured goods classified chiefly by material, machinery and transport equipment and miscellaneous manufactured articles. They exclude manufactured food and drink.

b This column gives the current value of imports on the standard cif (cost, insurance and freight) basis. This value is obtained by adjusting the actual or estimated contract price of imported goods to include cost, insurance and freight charges up to the landed point. This value excludes import duties, purchase or value added tax, etc. Where imports are paid for in foreign currency, this is converted to its sterling equivalent at the rate of exchange appropriate at the time of lodgment of the customs import duty.

c This column gives the current value of exports on the standard fob (free on board) basis. This value represents the cost of goods to the purchaser abroad including packing and transport costs up to the point where goods are deposited on an exporting ship or aircraft. This value excludes purchase or value added tax. The current value total of exports excludes re-exports before 1963 but includes re-exports in all subsequent years. This inconsistency is not a major problem because re-exports have always accounted for a small proportion of total exports. In 1951 4·5% of total exports were re-exports and by 1963 the percentage had fallen to 3·6%.

d European Economic Community here includes France, West Germany, Italy, Belgium, Netherlands, Luxembourg, Denmark and the Irish Republic. This is the Common Market as constituted in 1973 after enlargement.

   The percentages in these columns do not therefore measure British trading commitment to the political club and customs union whose membership has grown since it was founded in 1959. The percentages measure British trading commitment to a group of countries whose composition does not change and which usefully includes all the senior members of the Common Market, which Britain joined in 1973. By holding the 'EEC' group of countries constant from 1951–80, we ensure that the increasing relative importance of the EEC as a trading partner is not exaggerated by the growth of the community with the entrance of new members.

e 'The rest of Western Europe' is a residual category that includes all West European Territories and countries which were not EEC members after the 1973 enlargement. This group includes the Faroe Islands, Finland, Iceland, Norway and Sweden in northern Europe; Austria, Liechtenstein and Switzerland in central Europe; and Andorra, Gibraltar, Greece, Malta, Portugal, Spain, Turkey and Yugoslavia in southern

Europe. The composition of this group is held constant between 1951 and 1980 for reasons explained in note d.

f 'Sterling Area' here includes all countries and territories in the 1975 Sterling Area. In this case, the composition of the group is, as far as possible, held constant for the thirty years after 1951, so that long-run trends are not obscured by the effects of the departure of countries from the Sterling Area. Membership of the Sterling Area overlaps, but is not coincident with, membership of the Commonwealth. Two Commonwealth countries, Canada and Rhodesia, were outside the 1975 Sterling Area. Rhodesia (formerly S. Rhodesia) has been excluded only from 1965 because separate trade figures for S. Rhodesia are not given in the sources for the years 1955–64.

g This group includes all countries classified as 'oil exporting' in the 1981 UK trade statistics – Algeria, Libya, Nigeria, Gabon, Saudi Arabia, Kuwait, Bahrain, Qatar, Abu Dhabi, Sharjah, etc., Oman, Iraq, Iran, Brunei, Indonesia, Trinidad and Tobago, Venezuela and Ecuador.

h The world here consists of developed Western countries with a significant manufacturing capability. The countries listed individually are France, West Germany, Japan, Italy, UK and USA. The 'others' category in column vii includes Belgium-Luxembourg, Canada, Netherlands, Sweden, Switzerland.

i American exports of manufactures exclude 'special category' exports.

j Post-1952 figures exclude arms.

k From 1959 onwards, UK figures include re-exports. On the importance of re-exports see note c above.

l The UK and USA figures from 1962 to 1977 were adjusted by the National Institute so as to allow for under-recording in the official trade statistics of the two countries.

m This series is not constructed on the same classificatory basis as the official Central Statistical Office series on import penetration and exports in relation to sales. The official series begins in 1970 and is based on the census of production SIC definition of manufactured products (SIC Orders III–XIX). Our own long-run series is based on the International Trade SITC definition of manufactured products (SITC, sections 5–8). The same definition of manufactured products is used in all our other tables.

A new long-run series had to be constructed because it is difficult to extend the official CSO series back before 1970, and because Brown and Sherriff's earlier National Institute attempt to construct a long-run series is open to criticism. These points are explained in Addendum A which also reproduces the CSO and National Institute series for purposes of comparison.

n These are UK manufacturers' sales with manufactures defined as SIC orders IV–XIX. This excludes manufactured food and drink (SIC order III) and therefore ensures that the sales totals are directly comparable with the import and export totals in columns (ii) and (iii). Sales totals are on an ex-works or delivered basis and exclude 'work done.' For the years 1970–80, totals on this basis were directly supplied by the

Department of Trade and Industry. For earlier years estimates on this basis were obtained by adjusting census of production 'sales and work done' totals. The procedures used to obtain estimates are explained in detail in Addendum B.

o Manufactured imports and exports here exclude manufactured food and drink. This is the conventional (SITC sections 5–8) definition of manufactures which is used for example, in the trade figures in the Annual Statement of Overseas Trade of the UK. The resulting import and export totals are directly comparable with the sales totals in column (i).

p Imports: home demand (= UK manufacturers' sales + imports − exports). This is ratio (a) which is most often used to measure import penetration.

q Imports: home demand + exports. This is ratio (b) which registers UK manufacturers' commitment to exports whereas ratio (a) does not. As a high or increasing level of exports by United Kingdom manufacturers could offset increasing import penetration, ratio (b) is a generally preferable measure. See also footnote s for the important point that ratio (b) and ratio (d) share a common denominator.

r Exports: UK manufacturers' sales. This is ratio (c) which is most often used to measure the export commitment of UK manufacturing.

s Exports: manufacturers' sales + imports. This is ratio (d) which registers import penetration of the home market whereas ratio (c) does not. As a high or increasing level of import penetration on the home market could offset UK manufacturers' commitment to exports, then ratio (d) is a generally preferable measure to ratio (c). Import ratio (b) and export ratio (d) have the same denominator because home demand plus exports equals manufacturers' sales plus imports.

Addendum A: The CSO and National Institute series on import penetration and export/sales ratios

The official Central Statistical Office series on import penetration and export/sales ratios for manufactured products begins in 1970 and the results are given below in columns i, iii, v and vii. We could not extend the official series back before 1970 because of various problems about obtaining pre-1970 totals for manufacturing sales and manufactured imports and exports on the appropriate basis.

One minor problem is that the post-1970 series uses manufacturing sales figures which exclude 'work done', that is, they exclude payments for certain kinds of jobbing and contracting work undertaken by a manufacturer who, for example, might supervise the installation of equipment which he manufactured. The pre-1970 census of production sales totals include work done. More seriously, the official post-1970 series is based on the SIC definition of manufactures, but the pre-1970 trade statistics on imports and exports are only available on an SITC basis. The major problem with extending the official series backwards before 1970 is that the pre-1970 trade figures are not available in the necessary SIC categories.

In any case, given the SIC basis of the post-1970 official series, we would not wish to extend it backwards. All the other tables on manufacturing and trade in this statistical appendix are based on the SITC classification. For purposes of comparability we would therefore prefer to work out import penetration and export/sales ratios inside an SITC framework.

TABLE 5   *Official (CSO) and National Institute series on import penetration and export/sales ratios*

	Ratio (a)		Ratio (b)		Ratio (c)		Ratio (d)	
	Imports as % home demand		Imports as % home demand + exports		Exports as % manufacturing sales		Exports as % manufacturing sales + imports	
	(i) CSO	(ii) NI	(iii) CSO	(iv) NI	(v) CSO	(vi) NI	(vii) CSO	(viii) NI
1955		6		5		15		14
1956		6		5		16		15
1957		6		5		16		15
1958		6		5		15		15
1959		7		5		15		15
1960		8		7		15		14
1961		8		7		15		14
1962		8		7		15		14
1963		8		7		16		14
1964		9		8		15		14
1965		9		8		15		14
1966		9		8		15		14
1967		10		9		15		14
1968		12		10		17		15
1969		12		11		18		16
1970	16·6	13	14·1	11	18·1	18	15·6	16
1971	17·2	13	14·3	11	19·3	19	16·6	17
1972	18·2	15	15·4	12	18·5	19	15·7	16
1973	21·4	18	18·0	15	19·6	20	16·1	17
1974	23·3	19	19·3	16	21·4	22	17·2	18

TABLE 5   *Continued*

	Ratio (a)		Ratio (b)		Ratio (c)		Ratio (d)	
	Imports as % home demand		Imports as % home demand + exports		Exports as % manufacturing sales		Exports as % manufacturing sales + imports	
1975	22·0	18	17·9	15	22·6	23	18·5	19
1976	23·1	21	18·6	16	23·7	25	19·3	21
1977	24·1		19·2		25·0		20·2	
1978	24·8		19·8		25·2		20·2	
1979	25·8		20·8		24·3		19·2	
1980	25·4		20·1		26·1		20·8	

Sources: (a)   cols i, iii, v, vii.
                    1970–9, Central Statistical Office, *Economic Trends*, June
                    1980.
                    1980, Central Statistical Office, *Monthly Digest of Statistics*,
                    July 1981.
              (b)   cols ii, iv, vi, viii – Brown and Sherriff (1978), table 9.

Brown and Sherriff of the National Institute attempted to construct
a long-run series on import penetration and export/sales ratios for
the years 1955–76. Their results are given above in columns ii, iv,
vi, and viii. This attempt is unsuccessful because of problems about
the sales totals used by Brown and Sherriff in calculating the various
ratios. First, in all years their sales totals do not define manufactures
in the same way as do their trade totals for imports and exports.
Second, for the years 1955–69, these sales totals are obtained by
over-complicated estimation procedures.

On the question of definition, sales totals in the National Institute
series (SIC total manufacturing, orders III–XIX) include manufactured food and drink, whereas their import and export totals (SITC
total manufacturing, sections 5–8) exclude manufactured food and
drink. This is significant because, according to figures supplied by
the Department of Trade and Industry, manufactured food and
drink on a SIC basis accounted for 16·6 per cent of sales and 10·4
per cent of imports in 1980. Brown and Sherriff's inconsistency in
the definition of manufactures explains the obvious discrepancy
between the National Institute and CSO series on import penetration. The CSO series consistently shows higher levels of import
penetration because it includes manufactured food and drink in
totals of imports and exports as well as in sales.

The problems about estimation procedures arise because before 1970 Brown and Sherriff could not obtain a suitable sales estimate which excluded 'work done'. They therefore estimated pre-1970 sales in constant 1970 prices by reducing the first official sales total for 1970 with the aid of an output volume index.

$$\frac{\text{estimated sales in}}{\text{constant 1970 prices}} = \frac{\text{1970 officially calculated sales}}{\substack{\text{manufacturing output volume} \\ \text{index 1950--70}}}$$

In a second computation they then converted their estimated constant price sales totals into current prices using a wholesale price index.

$$\frac{\text{estimated sales in}}{\text{current prices}} = \frac{\text{estimated sales in 1970 prices}}{\text{wholesale price index 1955--70}}$$

These estimation procedures are so indirect that there must be some doubt about the reliability of the sales totals for the earlier years.

We have therefore calculated our own long-run series (in table 4) which consistently excludes manufactured food and drink from sales, imports and exports and which uses more direct procedures for estimating pre-1970 sales.

Addendum B: Estimation procedures used in calculating UK manufacturing sales 1955–69

To begin with, manufactured food and drink had to be excluded from the sales totals and this was generally done by subtracting the relevant SIC order III sub-total from the all manufactures total in SIC orders III–XIX. The years 1955–7 posed special problems because the census of production for these years does not give a separate sub-total for manufactured food and drink in order III. For these years, sales of manufactured food and drink have been estimated on the basis of their contribution to total manufacturing in 1954 (0·200) and 1958 (0·208).

The next step was to exclude 'work done' from the pre-1970 sales totals. This problem arises because Department of Trade post-1970 sales totals 'as far as possible' exclude work done while census of production pre-1970 sales totals include work done. Work done was generally excluded from pre-1970 sales totals by applying a deflator of 0·849. This deflator for pre-1970 sales totals was obtained by averaging the 1970–80 ratio between Department of Trade sales (excluding work done) and census of production sales (including work done).

The final problem was the gaps in the pre-1970 series of sales totals. The census of production does not record any sales and work done total for some years (1959–62, 1964–7, 1969). For these years, sales totals were interpolated. It was assumed that manufacturing sales in current prices increased year by year in line with the annual increase of the national product generated in manufacturing industry. On this assumption, estimated sales figures could be obtained by applying an 'inflator' to manufacturing GNP or GDP.

Because of the availability of official series, gross national product was used for filling gaps between 1959 and 1961, while gross domestic product was used for filling gaps between 1961 and 1970. The two sales figures for 1961 were obtained by using first gross national product and then gross domestic product. Sales between 1959 and 1962 were estimated using an inflator of 2·084 which averages the sales to GNP relation of 1955–8. Later estimated sales figures were obtained by applying an inflator of 2·174 which averages the sales to GDP relation of 1963, 1968 and 1970–3.

This method of estimating sales totals is accurate and reliable because the manufacturing product to sales ratio is very stable until the later 1970s. Cross-checks for years when we do have recorded sales totals, show that the estimation method produces estimated sales totals which only vary by up to ± 3 per cent from recorded sales totals. Errors of this magnitude in estimated sales totals would only bias the ratios by ± 1 per cent.

References

Aaronovitch, S. and Sawyer, M. C. (1975), *Big Business: Theoretical and Empirical aspects of Concentration and Mergers in the UK*, London, Macmillan.

Artis, M. J. (1972), 'Fiscal policy for stabilisation', in Beckerman, W. (ed.), *The Labour Government's Economic Record 1964–70*, London, Duckworth, pp. 262–99.

Bacon, R. and Eltis, W. A. (1978), *Britain's Economic Problem*, London, Macmillan.

Bannock, G. (1981), *The Economics of Small Firms: Return from the Wilderness*, Oxford, Blackwell.

Blackaby, F. T. (1979), *De-industrialisation*, London, Heinemann.

Bolton Report (1971), (Report of the Committee of Inquiry on Small Firms), Cmnd 4811, London, HMSO.

Boston Consulting Groups Ltd (1975), *Strategy Alternatives for the British Motorcycle Industry*, London, HMSO.

Bristow, J. A. (1968), 'Taxation and income stabilisation', *Economic Journal*, June, pp. 299–311.

British Overseas Trade Board (1977), *Fifteen Export Case Studies*, London, BOTB.

Brittan, S. (1969), *Steering the Economy: The Role of the Treasury*, London, Secker & Warburg.

Brown, C. J. F. and Sherriff, T. D. (1978), *De-industrialisation in the UK: Background Statistics*, National Institute of Economic and Social Research, Discussion paper no. 23.

Bryer, R. et al. (1982), *Accounting for British Steel*, London, Gower Press.

Carrington, J. C. and Edwards, G. T. (1979), *Financing Industrial Investment*, London, Macmillan.

Central Policy Review Staff (1975), *The Future of the British Car Industry*, London, HMSO.

Chandler, A. D. (1962), *Strategy and Structure: Chapters in the History of the American Industrial Enterprise*, Cambridge, Mass., MIT Press.

Chandler, A. D. (1977), *The Visible Hand: Managerial Revolution in American Business*, Cambridge, Mass., Harvard University Press.

Channon, D. F. (1973), *The Strategy and Structure of British Enterprise*, London, Macmillan.

Clark, T. A. and Williams, N. P. (1978), 'Measures of real profitability,' *Bank of England Quarterly Bulletin*, vol. 18, no. 4, December 1978, pp. 513–22.

Connell, D. (1979), *The UK's Performance in Export Markets: Some Evidence from International Trade Data*, London, NEDO.

Cowling, K. et al. (1980), *Mergers and Economic Performance*, Cambridge, Cambridge University Press.

Cutler, A. J. et al. (1978), *Marx's 'Capital' and Capitalism Today*, vol. 2, London, Routledge & Kegan Paul.

Denison, E. F. (1968), *Why Growth Rates Differ: Postwar Experience in Nine Western Countries*, Washington D.C., Brookings Institution.

Department of Employment (1978), 'Concentration of industrial stoppages in Great Britain: 1971–1975', *Department of Employment Gazette*, vol. 86, no. 1, January 1978, pp. 9–10.

Dornbusch, R. and Fischer, S. (1980), 'Sterling and the external balance', in Caves, R. E. and Krause, L. B. (eds), *Britain's Economic Performance*, Washington D.C., Brookings Institution, pp. 21–80.

Dow, J. C. R. (1964), *The Management of the British Economy, 1945–60*, Cambridge, Cambridge University Press.

Dunning, J. H. (1973), *U.S. Industry in Britain; an Economists Advisory Group business research study*, London, Financial Times.

Economic Progress Report (January 1982), 'Recent trends in labour productivity', *Economic Progress Report*, no. 141, January, pp. 1–4.

Economic Progress Report (June 1982), 'Measures of competitiveness in British manufacturing industry', *Economic Progress Report*, no. 146, June, pp. 6–8.

Elliott, D. C. and Gribbin, J. D. (1977), 'The abolition of cartels and structural change in the UK', in Jacquemin, A. P. and De Jong, H. W. (eds), *Welfare Aspects of Industrial Markets*, Leider, Martinus Nijhoff.

Fetherston, M., Moore, B. and Rhodes, J. (1977), 'Manufacturing export shares and cost competitiveness of advanced industrial countries', *Economic Policy Review*, no. 3, pp. 62–70, Cambridge Department of Applied Economics.

Flemming, J. S. et al. (1976), 'The cost of capital, finance and investment', *Bank of England Quarterly Bulletin*, vol. 16, no. 2, June, pp. 193–202.

Gale, B. T. (1980), 'Can more capital buy higher productivity?', *Harvard Business Review*, July-August, pp. 78–86.

Hannah, L. (1979), *The Rise of the Corporate Economy*, London, Methuen.

Hannah, L. and Kay, J. A. (1977), *Concentration in Modern Industry: Theory, Measurement and the UK Experience*, London, Macmillan.

Hart, P. E. and Clarke, R. (1980), *Concentration in British Industry 1935–75*, Cambridge, Cambridge University Press.

Hayes, R. H. and Abernathy, W. J. (1980), 'Managing our way to economic decline', *Harvard Business Review*, vol. 58, no. 4, July-August, pp. 67–77.

Hayes, R. H. and Garvin, D. A. (1982), 'Managing as if tomorrow mattered', *Harvard Business Review*, vol. 60, no. 3, May–June, pp. 70–79.

Hill, T. P. (1979), *Profits and Rates of Return*, Paris, OECD.

Hood, N. and Young, S. (1979), *The Economics of Multinational Enterprise*, London, Longman.

Hu, Y. S. (1975), *National Attitudes and the financing of industry*, Political and Economic Planning, Broadsheet no. 559, December 1975.

Imberg, D. and Northcott, J. (1981), *Industrial Policy and Investment Decisions*, London, Policy Studies Institute.

Johnson, P. S. (ed.) (1980), *The Structure of British Industry*, London, Granada.

Jones, D. T. (1976), 'Output, employment and labour productivity in Europe since 1955', *National Institute Economic Review*, no. 77, August, pp. 72–85.

Kanter, R. M. (1982), 'The middle manager as innovator', *Harvard Business Review*, vol. 60, no. 4, July–August, pp. 95–105.

Kay, J. A. and King, M. A. (1980), *The British Tax System*, London, Oxford University Press.

Kennedy, C. and Thirlwall, A. P. (1979), 'Import penetration, export performance and Harrod's trade multiplier', *Oxford Economic Papers*, vol. 31, no. 2, July, pp. 303–23.

Keynes, J. M. (1936), *The General Theory of Employment, Interest and Money*, Macmillan, London.

Kilpatrick, A. and Lawson, T. (1980), 'On the nature of industrial decline in the UK', *Cambridge Journal of Economics*, vol. 4, no. 1, March, pp. 85–100.

King, M. A. (1975), 'The UK profits crisis: myth or reality?', *Economic Journal*, vol. 85, no. 337, March, pp. 33–47.

Kuehn, D. (1975), *Takeovers and the Theory of the Firm: An Empirical Analysis for the UK 1957–1969*, London, Macmillan.

Maddison, A. (1977), 'Phases of capitalist development', *Banca Nazionale del Lavoro Quarterly Review*, vol. 30, no. 121, June, pp. 103–37.

Martin, W. E. and O'Connor, M. (1981), 'Profitability: a background paper', in Martin, W. E. (ed.), *The Economics of the Profits Crisis*, London, HMSO, pp. 7–89.

Meeks, G. (1977), *Disappointing Marriage: A Study of the Gains from Merger*, Cambridge, Cambridge University Press.

Meeks, G. (1981), 'Cash flow and investments', in Martin, W. E. (ed.), *The Economics of the Profits Crisis*, London, HMSO, pp. 115–42.

Meeks, G. and Whittington G. (1976), *The Financing of Quoted Companies in the UK: the significance of equity capital and dividends for companies of different sizes, sectors and rates of growth* (Royal Commission on the Distribution of Income and Wealth, Background paper no. 1), London, HMSO.

National Institute Economic Review (1961), 'Britain's falling share of sterling area imports', *National Institute Economic Review*, no. 14, March, pp. 18–54.

Newbould, G. D. (1970), *Management and Merger Activity*, Liverpool, Guthstead.

Panić, M. (1975), 'Why the UK's propensity to import is high', *Lloyds Bank Review*, no. 115, January, pp. 1–12.

Panić, M. and Rajan, A. H. (1971), *Product changes in industrial countries' trade*: 1955–68, Monograph 2, London, NEDO.

Prais, S. J. (1976), *The Evolution of Giant Firms in Britain 1909–70*, Cambridge, Cambridge University Press.

Prais, S. J. (1981), *Productivity and Industrial Structure: A Statistical Study of Manufacturing Industry in Britain, Germany and the US*, Cambridge, Cambridge University Press.

Pratten, C. F. (1976a), *A Comparison of the Performance of Swedish and UK Companies*, Cambridge, Cambridge University Press.

Pratten, C. F. (1976b), *Labour Productivity Differentials within International Companies*, Cambridge, Cambridge University Press.

Prest, A. R. and Coppock, D. J. (eds) (1980), *The UK Economy: A Manual of Applied Economics*, 8th edition, London, Weidenfeld & Nicolson.

Rowthorn, R. E. and Ward, T. (1979), 'How to run down a company and run down an economy: the effects of closing down steel-making in Corby', *Cambridge Journal of Economics*, vol. 3, no. 4, December, pp. 327–40.

Singh, A. (1977), 'UK industry and the world economy: a case of de-industrialisation?', *Cambridge Journal of Economics*, vol. 1, no. 2, June, pp. 113–36.

Smith, D. C. (1980), 'Trade Union growth and industrial disputes', in

Caves, R. E. and Krause, L. B. (eds), *Britain's Economic Performance*, Washington DC, Brookings Institution.

Solomon, R. F. and Ingham, K. P. D. (1977), 'Discriminating between MNC subsidiaries and indigenous companies: a comparative analysis of the British mechanical engineering industry', *Oxford Bulletin of Economics and Statistics*, vol. 39, no. 2, May, pp. 127–38.

Stout, D. K. (1977), *International Price Competitiveness, Non-price Factors and Export Performance*, London, NEDO.

Thirlwall, A. P. (1978), 'The UK's economic problem: a balance of payments constraint?', *National Westminster Bank Quarterly Review*, February, pp. 24–32.

Thirlwall, A. P. (1982), 'De-industrialisation in the UK', *Lloyds Bank Review*, no. 144, April, pp. 22–37.

Thomas, W. A. (1978), *The Finance of British Industry, 1918–1976*, London, Methuen.

Tomlinson, J. (1981), *Problems of British Economic Policy 1870–1945*, London, Methuen.

Treasury (1961), *Financial and Economic Obligations of the Nationalised Industries*, Cmnd 1337, London, HMSO.

Treasury (1967), *Nationalised Industries: A Review of Economic and Financial Objectives*, Cmnd 3437, London, HMSO.

Treasury (1978), *The Nationalised Industries*, Cmnd 7131, London, HMSO.

United Nations (1978), *Transnational Corporations in World Development*, New York, UN Department of Economic and Social Affairs.

Wenban-Smith, G. (1981), 'A study of the movements of productivity in individual industries in the UK 1968–79', *National Institute Economic Review*, no. 97, August, pp. 57–61.

Williams, K. (1975), 'Facing reality – a critique of Karl Popper's empiricism', *Economy and Society*, vol. 4, no. 3, August, pp. 309–58.

Williamson, O. E. (1981), 'The modern corporation: origins, evolution, attributes', *Journal of Economic Literature*, vol. 19, no. 4, December, pp. 1537–68.

Wilson Committee (1977), Committee to Review the Functioning of Financial Institutions (Chairman Sir H. Wilson), Evidence vol. 1 (Treasury, Department of Industry), vol. 2 (CBI, TUC, AIB), Progress report on the financing of industry and trade, London, HMSO.

Winter, S. G. (1964), 'Economic natural selection and the theory of the firm', *Yale Economic Essays*, vol. 4, Spring, pp. 225–72.

Wood, A. (1975), *Theory of Profit*, Cambridge, Cambridge University Press.

Wragg, R. and Robertson, J. (1978), 'Britain's industrial performance since the war', *Department of Employment Gazette*, vol. 86, May, pp. 512–19.

CASE STUDIES

1 GEC: An Outstanding Success?

John Williams

There is widespread agreement that the GEC has been one of the most, perhaps *the* most, consistently successful major British manufacturing company over the last two decades. It would be generally accepted, too, that great significance attaches to the fact that these were the years during which Arnold Weinstock (now Lord Weinstock) has effectively controlled the company.

Headlines like 'GEC Keeps on Sparking' or 'GEC steam-rollers through recession' (*Investors' Chronicle*, 14 December 1973, 12 December 1979) are common enough in the financial press. The tendency for the company's profits to do even better than forecast usually ensures a suitably rapturous reception for its annual reports. All this reflects, as we shall see, the real achievements of GEC and, indeed, the initial expectation of the present essay was that it would be mostly concerned with explaining the company's success. So general an acceptance of GEC's attainments does, however, create an atmosphere in which it is more difficult to examine that experience in rather more depth. Most of this is understandable enough: successful companies escape scrutiny. It is the failures, like BL, which are subjected to probing, sick-bed examination and forced to answer deeply embarrassing questions about their structures and habits. Even so, in GEC's case, the situation is compounded because the company's style is unforthcoming. It has released little information for the present study. Much reliance has, therefore, had to be placed on the public reports and accounts and on bringing together a good deal of scattered material. As a result, the argument is often indirect and the essay is an unavoidably speculative attempt to understand a major enterprise.

1   A flying start

The present GEC was formed by the merging together in the late 1960s of the three leading British electrical engineering firms, Associated Electrical Industries, English Electric, and General Electric Company (hereafter AEI, EE and GEC). In one sense these major rapid-fire mergers were events which were as startling as they were significant: yet in another sense they represented a logical, almost a natural development of the industry. To appreciate these dual aspects we need to make a brief historical survey of electrical engineering in Britain. (The following account draws heavily on the excellent work of Robert Jones and Oliver Marriott, *Anatomy of a Merger*, 1970.)

From the view-point of neo-classical economics, the electrical engineering industry was deformed at birth since it was strongly monopolistic from its earliest days. The reasons for this need not detain us, but one of its results was that on a world-wide scale the industry before 1914 was dominated by two American firms (General Electric and Westinghouse) and two German (Siemens and AEG). In this period electrical manufacturing in Britain largely took the form of offshoots from these companies.

It was the First World War which provided the opportunities which led to the emergence by the 1920s of more specifically British firms, and especially EE, AEI and GEC. Despite this all three were (or soon became) dominated by American capital: EE fell into serious financial difficulties in the late 1920s and was surreptitiously reconstructed and financially underpinned by the American Westinghouse company; the merger (of British Thompson Houston and Metropolitan Vickers) which created AEI was clandestinely arranged by GE of America; and although attempts to swallow GEC were beaten off by Hugo (later Lord) Hirst, GE of America owned the largest (though non-voting) block of its shares.

It was thus easy to fit the British companies into the international cartel arrangements which were a normal part of the industry's inter-war structure. Even so, none of these British-based firms was very profitable especially in heavy electrical engineering. This led Gerard Swope, as president of General Electric of America, towards still tighter control by attempting to secure a merger of AEI, EE and GEC in the 1930s. The attempt was abortive, but it was a pre-run of what happened in the late 1960s. In the inter-war years some of the advantages of merger were instead obtained through the close co-operation of the major British firms over prices and tendering in the home and Commonwealth markets which were their tacit territory under the international cartel arrangements.

The Second World War led to substantial expansion and improved profitability. Partly as a result, the post-war situation was significantly changed, although there were many other influences besides the increased strength of the main British firms. The war had also disrupted the cartel arrangements especially so far as European (and particularly German) producers were concerned. The loosening was further encouraged by anti-trust pressure on the US firms in the late 1940s, a factor which also induced the US companies to sell out their financial interests in the British firms. (In 1946, for example, GE of America still held 40 per cent of AEI shares.)

The potential competitive effects of these developments were, however, not felt for some time. The European manufacturers did not re-establish themselves for a decade or so; the British firms continued to run co-operative arrangements in the British markets; and they continued to have a more or less free hand in the Commonwealth. The big shift came in the late 1950s and forms an essential preliminary to the mergers of the 1960s, which in an important sense represented a means of ending this brief period of unwonted (and unwanted) home competition.

The 1957 report of the Monopolies Commission on Electrical and Allied Machinery and Plant directly condemned the common price system as being against the public interest. The industry – especially the heavy engineering end – strongly opposed the findings and feared the instability they thought it was bound to produce. The feelings of instability were compounded when, at much the same time, competition from Germany and Japan re-emerged. Indeed, such competition now took a more serious form since the ending of the cartels meant that the home market itself was exposed. 'What have previously been regarded primarily as British markets are now scenes of international competition' (Lord Nelson, Chairman of EE, 1961).

The move towards merger in the 1960s was thus partly a natural attempt to limit competition between the major British firms. It was also an equally natural response to create a firm or firms large enough to compete internationally. At the time it must have seemed

that the most likely victim would be GEC. It had borrowed heavily
for expansion in the 1950s, much being spent on developing nuclear
power which was not profitable. For much of the decade this was
disguised because of the big boom in electrical goods, but it became
increasingly clear that GEC was faring less well than AEI or EE,
especially AEI. It was thus not surprising that the initial move was
a suggestion from EE that it should merge with GEC. The former
was mostly engaged in heavy engineering and in airplanes, both of
which were suffering from lack of home orders and severe foreign
competition; the latter was mostly concerned with lighter electrical
goods where conditions were better but where the management
was singularly unsuccessful. GEC turned down the proposal and,
surprisingly, EE did not press through to a takeover.

During the course of the 1960s the relative fortunes of the various
companies underwent substantial change. Almost at the time of the
abortive 1960 merger, GEC took over Radio and Allied Industries
and with it acquired Arnold Weinstock (or perhaps it was really
the other way round). R and A was a television firm run by Michael
Sobell and his son-in-law, Weinstock. It was enormously profitable
through the TV boom of the 1950s and this success was widely
attributed to Weinstock's management skill. So when it was taken
over by GEC it brought an exceptional management talent at just
the time when this was GEC's greatest need. By 1963 Weinstock
was managing director of GEC as well as being a major shareholder.
He soon accelerated the growing profitability of GEC, partly by
concentrating increasingly on the lighter end of the business. GEC,
the smallest and in some respects the least successful of the big
three firms in the 1950s, became stronger and stronger in the 1960s.

AEI's progress was almost the reverse. The switch was partly
caused because in the mid-1950s AEI (under Lord Chandos) had
embarked on a vast programme of expansion including a huge new
works at Larne in Northern Ireland. The growth was concentrated
on the heavy side and was aimed at a poorly specified but rosy future
for electricity based on nuclear power, electric railway traction and
automated equipment. The lighter side, which might have been
more immediately profitable, was relatively neglected – indeed AEI
shed much of its interest in valves, lamps and domestic appliances
during the 1960s. AEI did, however, undertake a serious exercise
to integrate the company into a series of product divisions instead
of continuing, as it had for three decades, as a loose union of

separate and often antagonistic companies (BTH, Metrovick and, later, Siemens). This often disruptive exercise was completed just in time to be inherited by GEC.

English Electric, the biggest of the three, was an in-between case. It was generally accepted that its management – unlike that of AEI – was capable. But in the crucial years of the mid-1960s its profitability was suffering from a period of general over-capacity in the heavy electrical engineering industry, and the need to service a substantial weight of debt. It was an essentially sound but temporarily vulnerable firm.

In the space of a couple of years in 1967 and 1968 the position was dramatically transformed. GEC first took over AEI, and then was clearly the dominant partner in a merger with EE. The smallest of the three leading British electrical engineering firms had become, in domestic terms, a giant, and the new enlarged GEC had become of some significance on an international scale. It was, indeed, a flying start. How was it attained?

2   The stock market

As we have argued in the introductory essay, mergers were attractive in Britain in the 1960s because they could be largely financed with company paper. The stock market mechanism facilitated this process which was also fostered by the propensity for the market's valuation to give great weight to short-run profitability performance. In the late 1960s the market placed a high valuation on GEC: after a bad period it had become increasingly profitable; it had Arnold Weinstock who had produced this financial result; it was more concentrated at the lighter end of the industry which financial comment at the time regarded as less risky and more profitable. The market, however, placed a low valuation on AEI and EE: they had a poor recent profit record; they had expanded capacity too fast; they were more concentrated at the heavy end of the industry.

It was within this institutional context that GEC was able to emerge as the dominating concern[1] and it was certainly shrewd enough not to pay out large sums of cash. Moreover the company paper which was issued as part of the deals was carefully limited. As a result the financial terms, both for the takeover of AEI and the merger with EE, placed no great burden on profitability. All this represented two brilliant financial coups in quick succession, especially in face of the relative sizes of the companies. In 1967 GEC had a turnover of £180 million; AEI had a turnover of £260 million; and EE a turnover of more than £400 million. The GEC final bid for AEI valued its assets at £160 million, and the merger terms valued EE's assets at £300 million. Yet less than £16 million in cash was spent on the acquisition of these two major firms.

The bulk of the financial cost was provided in paper, either in the form of loan stock or as equity in GEC. The loan stock, with inflation, was no great burden especially as the amount was not large. More significantly, the high market valuation given to GEC because of its success in the 1960s and the market's faith that Arnold Weinstock could continue the trend, meant that the nominal increase in GEC's equity was modest in relation to the assets acquired. It rose only from £57 million to £136 million. Thus the enlarged company would not have to be wildly successful before it could hope to achieve financial profitability.

The fusion of the GEC-AEI-EE trinity was not, however, solely achieved through the working of the stock exchange. We have already seen that the reduction of national and international cartel arrangements led many in the industry to look for other means of restraining competition. More importantly, the government of the day wanted, and so facilitated, the mergers. The Labour administrations of 1964 to 1970 put much stress on improving the international competitiveness of British industry in general; and in particular believed that Britain needed an electrical engineering enterprise which could look the American, European and Japanese giants in the eye.

In 1966 the government had set up the Industrial Reorganisation Corporation (IRC) to implement rationalisation in the private sector of industry. In 1967 the IRC positively initiated the process which led to the takeover of AEI by GEC and actually gave its public support to the GEC whilst the takeover battle was in process in the market. Weinstock, moreover, was careful to cultivate the support of both ministers and civil servants.

In 1968 the IRC more discreetly, but not less decisively, supported the merger between GEC and EE in preference to various other possibilities which were then available (i.e. allowing Plessey to take over EE, or allowing EE to form a new group with BICC, Plessey, Thorn and Reyrolle-Parsons). The government was also more directly involved. The Ministry of Technology (Tony Benn) saw the merger as a means of creating, in an area of growth and technical progress, a British firm which would be large even by international standards. The Board of Trade (Anthony Crosland) co-operated by not referring the largest merger in British history to the Monopolies Commission, a decision which was confirmed by the Cabinet.

The government gave support, then, when the merger was suggested, but in this case it was not the initiator. Neither was GEC. The action which set events in motion was, in this sense, fortuitous. It was a bid to take over the giant EE by the much smaller Plessey company. EE was incensed not just by the 'impudence' of this move but by the fact that Plessey had no experience at all in the heavy electrical industry. But EE's poor profitability and heavy debt at the time made the company very vulnerable, so the prospect of merging as an equal with GEC, which it might in most circumstances have treated with some disdain, became much more attractive.

The possibilities of success were, indeed, created by the mergers. The recognition of this was implicit in Weinstock's comment, after the AEI takeover but before the EE merger: 'It's just like playing with a one-armed bandit. Getting one or two lemons in the window is not too difficult, but you need three in a line before all the money comes pouring out.' And once Weinstock had found his third lemon, the possibility of substantial savings certainly opened up. All three companies, although the balance of their activities had been different, had engaged on a wide range of activities in the field of electric engineering. There were thus substantial overlaps offering immediate savings through rationalisation – which, as usual, mostly served as a euphemism for closing plants to concentrate the production of particular lines. The possibilities were especially enticing in the heavy engineering sector because this was the area in which both AEI and EE had invested heavily from the late 1950s. The resultant over-capacity, especially as CEGB orders fell in the mid-60s, reduced their profits, increasing the weight of this debt and making them vulnerable to outside bids. But once they were all under a single control, acquired under terms which had written down much of this capital expenditure, excess capacity could be more easily shed. Even where excess capacity continued, it was no longer a basis for desperate price-cutting competition between rival companies.

The prospects were also favourable in the longer term because many of the company's operations were in areas of industry which were growing fast. This seemed to be true of domestic electrical appliances, especially TV, which had carried GEC so far forward in the 1960s. A colour TV boom was imminent. It was even more obviously the case in telecommunications and electronics. If the company could master changing technologies the market prospects were glittering.

Finally, GEC had the management and the organisational structure. Many of AEI's problems were imputed to poor and indecisive top management. EE, on the other hand, was universally credited with a highly competent management team. Perhaps this contrast contributed to the solution of what some commentators in the 1960s had seen as a major shortcoming of GEC as it moved to expand: its managers were lacking in experience of heavy electrical engineering. Such minor misgivings were, however, engulfed by the general confidence placed in Arnold Weinstock. The City, industry and government all agreed on his rain-making infallibility.

The creation of GEC by takeover and merger in 1967 and 1968 had, therefore, a solid base for success. It was thus not a typical 1960s merger operation. As one contemporary observer noted (*Investors' Chronicle*, 18 October 1968), it seemed set for a period of 'spectacular growth.'

Was this attained?

3 Financial success

The favourable immediate prospects which seemed to confront the enlarged GEC at the end of 1968 did actually materialise. By 1972 it was possible to point out that in the previous three years profit had risen by one-third, and there had been a favourable turnround of £100 million in the firm's cash position (*Investors' Chronicle*, 24 November 1972). Clearly this particular merger was not one of Meeks's 'disappointing marriages', where profits in the years immediately after merger are below the combined pre-merger levels of the separate companies. A recent study has indicated that GEC profitability certainly increased from at least 1971 onwards

(Cowling et al., 1980, pp. 198–201). The financial results have always been good and this both explains and justifies the enthusiasm of the media.

It is not difficult to illustrate a financial success which has been so consistent and well-based. In what follows attention will be concentrated on the period starting with the report and account for the year ending March 1970, the first year in which the takeover of AEI and the merger with EE were fully assimilated. The general growth during this period is indicated by the rise in the value of the company's turnover by 331 per cent in the decade after 1970 (total sales, a somewhat different measure, showed a similar increase of 337 per cent). In the same period the value of exports rose almost exactly four-fold and pre-tax profits increased more than seven times from £58 million in 1970 to £415 million in 1980.

The last two measures also suggest that the overall efficiency of the firm was improving since both exports and profits were increasing more rapidly than turnover. In 1970 exports were 26·3 per cent of UK turnover: in 1980 they were 32·1 per cent. (UK turnover is calculated by deducting overseas turnover from the total. It is a more appropriate measure for some purposes.) The behaviour of profits is a more appropriate and persuasive indicator of efficiency, and it gives a still more decisive and positive result. Between 1970 and 1980 profit more than doubled as a proportion of total turnover (from 6 to 13 per cent), and profit as a proportion of capital employed nearly trebled (from 8·4 to 23·7 per cent).

There are similar indications if attention is turned to the company's use of labour. Turnover per UK employee rose four-and-a-half times during the decade (from £3,700 to £16,400). The profit figures already suggest that these productivity gains were not absorbed by the labour force, and this is confirmed by the fact that employees' remuneration (effectively, wages and salaries) fell slightly as a proportion of UK turnover from 31·8 per cent (in 1971) to 28·6 per cent in 1980 (30·1 in 1981).

All these figures seem strongly to suggest that GEC was, throughout the difficult decade of the 1970s, a company which was steadily growing, and that this growth was being accompanied by a more efficient use of its capital and of its labour force. Growth and a more efficient use of inputs thus seem to be essential aspects of the nature of the success of GEC. At least one other feature of the success emerges with even more clarity: shareholders seem to have consistently and substantially gained. Earnings per share rose seven times (from 7·25p in 1970–1 to 54·5p in 1980–1) and dividend per share rose four-fold in the same period (from 3·3p to 14·6p). There were some complaints about the company's tendency to retain profits over a long period without putting such funds to the direct use of the company. But such murmurings were drowned in the acclamation accorded to the steady enhancement of the stock market value of the shares and the increase in the value of the real assets of the company.

GEC is thus a substantial financial success and this, sustained through the usually unfavourable climate of the post-1970 British economy, represents a major achievement. From the point of view of society as a whole, however, it is still necessary to ask whether this is enough. In terms of economic theory such a question might seem to be otiose. At least, in the simplified public presentation of that theory, the pursuit of profitability, especially when conducted as singlemindedly and successfully as at GEC, should be enough. A general pursuit of profit maximisation should ensure that society's resources are being used to produce the 'right' amount of the 'right' output with everyone getting their 'correct' reward. Such a harmonious outcome, however, depends on rather strong assumptions (such as that the prices of all goods and services reflect their real scarcities; that all producers and consumers know the full range of prices and costs, etc.). Such objections might seem excessively abstract but so too are the arguments for profitability and a full market economy which provoke them, and which are used to justify Thatcher-type economic policies.

From our viewpoint, which emphasises variable and specifically national conditions, it is certain that the individual firm cannot be taken to be operating in an environment which is just as the general theory assumes. Profitability cannot, therefore, be enough to silence all doubts. If the individual firm operates from a base in the British national economy, some specific questions can reasonably be raised about the sufficiency of the financial success outlined above. The profitability which GEC pursues and achieves is not coincident with the profit of economic theory. GEC is unavoidably concerned with accounting profit (see the introduction for comments on the distinction). Therefore, it is simply not possible to draw implications about optimal output or welfare from the maximisation of accounting profit. More fundamentally, against the background of the general decline in British manufacturing, it could reasonably be argued that a 'successful' British manufacturing firm should meet several broad criteria. Such a firm should certainly be a financial success; but it should also be expected to show a substantial increase in the level of physical output, make a marked and growing contribution to manufacturing exports, and provide more employment.

The following section attempts, therefore, to put alongside GEC's financial success some assessment of its performance in terms of these additional criteria.

4 Manufacturing – a growing concern?

(a) Output

The level of physical output provides an obvious yardstick against which the success of the group as a manufacturing concern could be measured. GEC, however, does not readily lend itself to such an exercise. There are half-a-dozen major operating divisions, whose products are quite different, even though they nearly all fall within the general field of electronics and electrical engineering. Moreover, within any particular division, a quite extensive and diverse range of products may be manufactured. The Power Engineering Division, for example, produces turbine generators, gas turbines, turbo-chargers for diesels, high voltage switchgear, distribution switchgear, power transformers, distribution transformers, rectifiers and insulators. Some of these products might be separately amenable to some sort of physical aggregation but it is not easy to see how heterogeneous goods could be added together. Beyond that difficulty, however, is also the fact that in several of the major areas merely counting the physical product may not be meaningful, or even possible. Generators for electric power stations, for example, are always to some extent custom-built and the individual requirements of each purchaser become even more inescapable at the installation stage. Similarly, the telecommunication division might be involved in providing, say, a complete system of telephone exchanges for a country or region or city or company. At all levels basic designs need to be modified to meet particular customer requirements.

The difficulties are formidable, but it would be a mistake completely to discount the utility of physical output measures. Certainly for any particular product it is often, or usually, possible to find a reasonable proxy for output. In the case of turbine generators for power stations, for example, a crude, but for some purposes useful, means of aggregating generators of very different sizes is simply to give their total capacity of Mega-watts (Mws). None the less it is clear enough that no plausible single measure of physical output for GEC as a whole is possible, nor could the growth experience be reliably captured by using a small range of measures (or proxy measures) for selected products.

The basic problem is that physical output measures can reasonably be applied only where a minimal homogeneity of output exists and GEC's output lacks such homogeneity. The absence of homogeneity does not, of course, imply any shortcoming on the part of the company: on the contrary, the diversity of output has been a major strength. It does mean that overall growth can only be indicated by reducing the heterogeneous bundle of output to the common denominator of its value in money terms. The annual value of company turnover is thus taken as proxy for annual output. (The value of sales could also be used and our rough calculations show that it would give much the same results.)

The results are startling. Or, at least, they appear so against the widespread assumption that GEC's undoubted success has implied significant growth in the company's real output. On the surface this interpretation does seem to be vindicated. It has already been seen that turnover in 1981 (£3,683 million) showed an increase of 382 per cent over that of 1970 (£965 million). That measure is, however, calculated simply on current prices and makes no allowance for inflation and the extent to which the apparent increase in output (measured in monetary terms) reflects instead a general rise in prices. Before the true increase in output is obtained the figures need to be corrected to remove changes in the value of money. The result is shown in table 17.

Before any conclusions are drawn from the table, however, it needs to be mentioned that there is, of course, no single simple way of adjusting for price changes. For many purposes the retail price index is the most useful guide (it is used below, p. 151, for trying to convert money wages into real wage changes at different dates). But it is not particularly appropriate for the present purpose: if we used the retail price index, then we would be assuming that the manufacturers' prices for electrical goods altered to the same extent as the retail prices of general consumer goods. Fortunately it is not necessary to make so strong an assumption: a separate index exists purporting to give the average changes in the wholesale prices of goods produced in electrical engineering. It is obviously a more appropriate measure for our purposes, but it still contains several difficulties, the most obvious of which is that electrical engineering does not cover the full range of products made by GEC. Nevertheless, this index is the best available for our present purposes. It should also be added that it makes GEC's performance look better than if we had used the retail price index. If the retail price index were applied to the GEC figures, the implication would be that turnover (output) in 1981 would be less than in 1970.

The table indicates that total GEC output from 1970 to 1981 rose by only 13 per cent. Moreover, even this modest increase seems only to have occurred at the end of the period: up until 1978 the real value of turnover was very little above its 1970 level. At the aggregate level financial success was not matched by any commensurate increase in real output.

TABLE 17   *Real value of GEC's UK turnover, 1970–81*

Date	Wholesale price index (elect.eng.) (1970=100)	Value of UK Turnover (in current prices)[a] (£m)	Value of UK Turnover adjusted for price changes	
			(£m)	(As % of 1970)
1970	100	789	789	
1971	108·1	831	769	97·5
1972	113·3	854	754	95·6
1973	119·5	937	784	99·4
1974	142·8	1153	807	102·2
1975	173·2	1399	808	102·4
1976	202·6	1641	810	102·7
1977	234·7	1902	810	102·7
1978	256·6	2196	856	108·5
1979	284·8	2503	879	111·4
1980	324·0	2886	891	113·0
1981	344·5	3085	896	113·6

Sources: GEC *Reports and accounts*; CSO *Monthly Digest of Statistics*.
[a] Figures relate to the company's financial year ending the following March. This gives greatest degree of comparability with index for calendar years.

TABLE 18   *Value of turnover by division, 1970 and 1981*

	1970[a]	Turnover £m 1981[a]	1981 in 1970 prices	(iii) as a % of (i)
	(i)	(ii)	(iii)	(iv)
Power Engineering	134[b]	589	171	127·6
Industrial	124	359	104	83·9
Electronics, Automation and Telecoms.	308	1419	412	133·8
Components, Cables & Wire	129	441	128	99·2
Consumer Products	94	277	80	85·1
Overseas Subsidiaries	227	1333[c]	387	170·5

Sources: GEC *Reports and accounts*; CSO *Monthly Digest of Statistics*.
[a] Figure relates to company financial year ending in following March.
[b] The figure for 1970–1 happens to be exceptionally low (1969–70 was 164, and 1971–2 was 159), and hence exaggerates the growth in this division.
[c] Two conflicting aspects need to be considered. On the one hand the figure for 1981–2 shows a huge jump of £536m (current prices) in the Overseas division over 1980–1, mostly reflecting the acquisitions of companies in the US. Otherwise the real increase in output in this division would be nearer 10 per cent. On the other hand, to increase comparability with early years the turnover from associated (as opposed to subsidiary) companies overseas has been excluded. Its inclusion would tend to push up the growth rate.

If the figures are disaggregated to show the experience of the different Divisions of GEC, there is, naturally, a substantial variation (table 18). Roughly speaking,[2] change in the real value of turnover ranged from a decrease of nearly one-fifth for Industrial Products (diesels, electric motors, lifts, etc.) to an increase of one-third for Electronics, Automation and Telecommunications, for UK production. The largest increase was for the output of Overseas Subsidiaries.

The more interesting point is that in three of the Divisions (Consumer Products, Components, and Industrial) real output seems to have declined. There were definite increases in output in Power Engineering and in Electronics. Even these, however, could be considered as relatively modest in manufacturing terms. The growth in Power Engineering is, in any event, partly exaggerated by the accident that output for 1970–1 was exceptionally low. On the other hand, the components output seems under-stated because the 1981–2 turnover seems exceptionally low. Any reasonable correction for this would, however, be unlikely to result in an output increase for components over the decade of much more than 10 per cent. This is not impressive when it is realised that the output of this division for the latest years includes the output for Avery, the largest UK acquisition made by GEC since the merger with EE. Even the rise of over one-third in Electronics might seem a comparatively modest output achievement for a leading company in one of the major growth areas of contemporary manufacturing industry.

Output produced overseas is the other growth area. It is clear that GEC's overseas production has been increasing more rapidly than that of its UK divisions. The point will be developed later, but against everything else that has been stated about real measures of turnover, the fact is obviously relevant to assessments of GEC's success as a *British* manufacturing concern.

At all events the indicators strongly suggest that GEC's manufacturing output rose only slowly during the 1970s. It was not an easy decade, of course, and this point needs to be emphasised in any final judgment. For the moment, however, it is not unreasonable to stress the bare, unqualified facts to make one general point: if the output achievement of our most successful manufacturing company seems so modest, the prospects for British manufacturing as a whole must, perhaps, seem bleak.

Output, however, is only one consideration. It is time now to look at exports and the labour force.

(b)   Exports

In 1970 GEC exports were just over one-quarter (26·3 per cent) of its UK turnover: in 1982 they were just over one-third (35·5 per cent). The picture thus presented seems to suggest a company which had always exported on a significant scale but which nevertheless continued to increase exports not only absolutely but also as a proportion of its total output. The figures thus indicate a real improvement in GEC's ability to export and demonstrate that it is an internationally competitive concern. Against the broad background of exports by British manufacturing generally, however, the GEC performance is seen to be sound rather than spectacular. Indeed, it is about the average for manufacturing as a whole, where the export/sales ratio rose from 21 per cent in 1970 to 32 per cent in 1980. (In the nearest comparable years GEC's export ratio rose from 27·1 per cent to 33·4 per cent.)

The growing proportion of exports perhaps indicates that the company (and British manufacturing industry in general) was responding to the emergence of more difficult sales conditions at home by putting more effort into exporting. The overall growth rate of the UK economy, and hence of home demand, was lower than in the earlier post-war decades and, indeed, was actually negative by the closing years of the 1970s. For several important sectors of electrical engineering the impact was still more direct: the virtual halt in CEGB orders for power stations, coupled with investment constraints on the Post Office and British Rail, greatly reduced the secure platform of home orders. The situation was rather different in the case of Consumer Products. Here, the difficulties at home did not arise out of the fickleness of government orders, nor, indeed, is the general downturn in the economy a sufficient explanation. GEC's share in the home market declined in the face of competition from Japanese television sets and audio systems, and continental washing machines and refrigerators.

To some degree the influence of such factors is reflected in the disaggregated (or less aggregated) figures which show a very variable success in switching to exports. In two of the product divisions – Components, Cable and Wire; and the largest division of Electronics, Automation and Telecommunications – exports were in 1981 rather below the average at 28 and 31 per cent respectively. But in Power Engineering (concerned particularly with power station equipment like turbine generators, gas turbines and switchgear) exports were 60 per cent of turnover; and in the Industrial division (concerned largely with diesels and electrical machines), 44 per cent was exported. The last of the broad product divisions – Consumer Products (consisting of lamps, television sets, fans, washing machines, furniture, etc.) – exported only 7 per cent. The example of Consumer Products also shows the limitation of any claim that GEC recoups through overseas sales when it faces pressure at home and is efficient enough to do so. In this sector, at least, the company's competitiveness and efficiency would, by international standards, be questioned. It must be admitted, however, that if the ability to withstand a Japanese onslaught in the markets for radios and television sets is made the criterion of efficiency, not many of the leading international firms would satisfy it unaided.

Some of the main points can be defined and focused if attention is directed to the experience of one particular sector of the company's activities – the export of heavy electrical plant where the UK share in world exports fell sharply from the 1950s to the 1970s. In 1955 the UK accounted for 22 per cent of all world exports of electrical power equipment; in 1975 this had fallen to less than 9 per cent. The decline was, however, almost entirely a phenomenon of the 1960s: by 1964 the share had already dropped to 13 per cent, and by 1969 to 9½ per cent (Surrey et al., 1980, p. 240). The initial loss of share had thus already taken place by the time of the 1960s mergers. Some relative decline – the chief gainers were Japan, France and Germany – was probably unavoidable, particularly when home demand from the CEGB was exceptionally high in the 1960s.

None of the ground lost then was, however, regained in the following decade, the era of GEC's 'success'. The problem does not appear to have been one of price: in heavy electrical plant UK labour costs expressed in US dollars actually rose more slowly than in other countries between 1974 and 1976, largely because of currency movements (Surrey et al., 1980, p. 247). It *was* partly a problem of home demand. In the 1960s home demand was so high that output was perhaps diverted from exports: in the 1970s it was so low that it probably weakened GEC's product base in a profitable domestic market. All the major international producers in this area consider it is essential to have a strong home market because it allows a company to demonstrate reliability to overseas buyers, to spread overhead costs and to gain manufacturing experience in new designs. GEC was one of the two UK producers in the field of steam turbines. The other was the Reyrolle-Parsons combine which also emerged from the takeovers of the 1960s. Both British firms faced great difficulties in exporting in this field. Even so, it has to be noted that their export orders were largely confined to the traditional markets. Canada (where Parsons had a special connection), Australia, South Africa and Hong Kong accounted for three-quarters of UK exports of heavy electrical plant; Europe and Latin America remained insignificant.

The record of resistance to imports on the British home market raises further reservations. For the electrical engineering industry as a whole, import penetration rose from 14·3 per cent in 1970 to 26·1 per cent in 1980. This is quite high considering that in several major product areas, government policy ensures the home market is virtually reserved for home producers. For telephone and telegraph apparatus (MLH 362), for example, the ratio was normally well below 10 per cent. In other product areas where the industry was not sheltered there were very high import penetration ratios: in 1980 the import penetration ratio was nearly 50 per cent for broadcast receiving and sound reproducing equipment and the position was much the same in electronic computers. In British electrical engineering generally import penetration was growing faster than the ratio for manufacturing industry as a whole.

A final comment concerns the geographical spread of GEC exports. In terms of exports from the UK there was a slight tendency for the share going to Europe and the Americas to decline and for that of Asia and Africa to increase. Exports to Australia were always small and tended to fall. GEC has, until very recently, continued to do best in a number of Commonwealth countries and former British zones of influence, which used to be the allotted territories for British firms in the old days of the international cartel. Against this the export sales of, especially, the early 1980s show a greater activity in non-Commonwealth Asia, the Middle East and Latin America. This does not change the basic point that the company has apparently made no significant breakthrough in either of the two major markets of Europe and the United States. Given the strength of the indigenous firms, the relatively slow progress in the United States is not surprising; but in the case of Europe the major institutional change of Britain's joining the Common Market might have been expected to produce a greater impact.

As a UK exporter, GEC has done reasonably well. In some sectors like power stations and railway equipment favourable export results have, in difficult circumstances, countered the effects of a low level of home demand. The overall achievement, however, is not remarkable. GEC just matches the average attainment of British manufacturing industry: it seems to have had no greater success in repelling import penetration especially in consumer goods; and, though there are more encouraging recent signs, in the 1970s it had only limited success in breaking into the toughest new markets.

(c)   Labour

If we are considering labour's share in GEC's financial success, two considerations are immediately relevant – the aggregate share of the company's growing income which went to the labour force and the average level of labour remuneration.

On the face of it the labour force did quite well in aggregate terms. Total UK employee remuneration increased by three-and-a-half times (353 per cent) in the decade after 1971 when the total expenditure increased from £253 million to £919 million.[3] But two major qualifications must be noted. In the first place, the increase in the general price level during the same period was just as rapid since the retail price index shows a rise of 369 per cent. Thus in real terms aggregate employee remuneration was unchanged. Secondly, and more significantly, labour's remuneration as a proportion of total UK turnover was more or less static and even showed a slight fall from 31·8 per cent in 1971 to 30·0 per cent in 1981. In the same period the share of profits doubled.

The aggregate level of wages does, however, under-state the gains made by the individual worker since, during this period, the total amount was being shared amongst a dwindling body of UK workers. While total remuneration increased only three-and-a-half times, the average amount per employee rose just over four-and-a-half times from £1,398 p.a. in 1971 to £6,338 p.a. in 1981.[3] Since prices increased by 370 per cent, real average wages per employee rose during the decade. But the increase was hardly dramatic, when at 1971 retail prices the average remuneration in 1981 was equivalent to £1,719, or a real increase of just over 20 per cent (22·9). Still less does it appear that the workers in this outstandingly successful company in a major growth sector of the economy did dramatically better than manufacturing workers generally. Average weekly earnings for full-time manual workers in manufacturing industry rose by four times between 1971 and 1981. GEC's rate of increase was faster than average, but this was barely sufficient to reverse the 1971 situation where average GEC remuneration was less than that for manufacturing industry as a whole. In 1971 earnings in GEC were £1,398 against an average of £1,570 in manufacturing as a whole. By 1981 the relevant figures were £6,338 against £6,203.

The point remains that the labour force shared to only a limited extent in GEC's brilliant financial success. Nevertheless, it could be argued that this is a secondary consideration, if the company created jobs. The importance of this consideration in GEC's case is reinforced because the company presents itself as Britain's largest employer. What does the evidence show?

In the middle of 1967, just before the merger activity began, the three companies in total employed 268,000 at home and abroad; the individual company totals were: GEC 63,000, AEI 85,000, and EE 120,000 (see Jones and Marriott, 1970, p. 322). In 1982 the comparable figure for the GEC combine was 189,000. In relation to our argument about British manufacturing, the more relevant figure is perhaps that of the number of UK employees: in 1970 there were 206,000 and in 1981 only 145,000. It is clear that GEC gives employment to substantially fewer people than at the time of the merger. Indeed, the decline has been one of over 25 per cent. The basic fact, therefore, is that GEC went into the 1980s employing substantially fewer people in the UK than it had employed in 1970. Some of the fall can be attributed to the 'inevitable' demands of post-merger rationalisation. That process did give rise to major redundancies. The most widely publicised of these was the closure of the AEI telecommunications plant at Woolwich, which had already been substantially completed by 1970 and where more than 5,000 workers lost their jobs. Woolwich was simply the largest and most dramatic of a series of redundancies arising out of the mergers. Thus Woolwich and Harlow and a few others in 1968 were followed by redundancies at nineteen different places in 1969 and the process rolled on into the 1970s. The decline in employment did level off after 1973. But, significantly, there was a further marked fall of 15,000 in the UK labour force from 1975 to 1977 and another sharp dip of 10,000 from 1981 to 1982, long after the phase of rationalisation.

Lord Weinstock has claimed that the removal of 'a number of our operations which either did not fit into a sensible business structure or could not be made viable', made for greater security for those who remained (GEC 79, *Britain's Largest Private Employer*, p. 7). But this claim is contradicted by the aggregate evidence on GEC after the mid-1970s. Furthermore, relative stability in employment in the 1970s was sustained only at the aggregate level. It disguised quite large changes within the group. Even at a very minimal level of disaggregation, for example, the fact that turnover in the Telecommunications division rose from £278 million in 1970 to £1,235 million in 1981 whilst that of the Consumer Products division rose only from £88 million to £290 million must have required some changes in divisional employment. Most employees were not interchangeable as between one activity and another, either on grounds of skill or location.

In the British context, the most worrying single aspect of GEC's performance is the decline in the overall size of the labour force. In our 'most successful' manufacturing company employment actually declined faster than in the manufacturing sector as a whole, which seems to contradict the doctrines of Thatcherism as an economic faith. The industrial cut-backs and lay-offs which accompanied Conservative economic policies at the beginning of the 1980s naturally caused disruption and encountered opposition. One line of defence was to argue that the cuts, especially in employment, were unavoidable if there was to be a secure basis for future growth. The creation of short-run unemployment was presented as the essential prelude to a long-run recovery of employment: the abolition of over-manning and the elimination of 'unfit' firms would create a new industrial base which could in the long run generate employment opportunities. Our analysis of GEC provides little support for this view. Sharp cut-backs had, indeed, been made by GEC in the face of much union opposition and substantial public concern, in the late 1960s and early 1970s; but they have not proved to be simply the harsh-but-necessary prelude to a later sound and successful growth in employment. If GEC as an enterprise has not managed to establish a manufacturing base for employment growth in the course of more than a decade, the prospects for employment in British manufacturing as a whole must be dismal.

5 The cash reserve and acquisitions

The story so far is one of soaring financial success and more leaden productive attainment. It is in this context that GEC's huge build-up of cash reserves becomes intelligible. The company was by skilful management making large profits out of its existing manufacturing business but was not expanding its manufacturing activities dramatically. Therefore the cash piled up.

The turn-round from debtor to creditor has been quite remarkable. It represents a sound and substantial managerial accomplishment. The company inherited significant bank overdrafts from both AEI and English Electric: indeed the over-extension of these two companies was one of the reasons why the smaller GEC was able to swallow them. One of the major achievements of the merger was the rapidity with which this situation was turned round: from 1971 onwards there was always a net cash balance. Sales of assets initially helped: the vast AEI headquarters in Grosvenor Place was sold as was GEC's holding in C. A. Parsons, its link with heavy turbo-generators. In the early years also, reductions in staff and plant were possible by the overlapping activities of the three companies. Later on, skilful and purposive financial management was crucial because the trend continued well after the initial load of debt had been removed. Indeed, the accumulation of cash seemed to accelerate through the 1970s. By March 1972 the net cash balance, or cash minus bank overdrafts, was £51 million: a decade later the net cash balance amounted to £1,036 million. The progressive build-up of cash reserves was almost continuous.

Indeed, the increases in the cash reserves were so large that GEC ceased to be simply a manufacturing company. By the end of the 1970s its earnings were no longer just a reflection of its manufacturing success because the cash hoard began to make a significant contribution to earnings. From 1977 onwards the net income[4] from, mainly, GEC's cash reserve has normally amounted to over 10 per cent of the company's total profits before taxation and has tended to rise: in 1979 it was over 13 per cent and in 1982 nearly 15 per cent.

The company has argued that, in the prevailing circumstances this was the most efficient use that could be made of its cash reserves. But this argument is dubious. One of Lord Weinstock's major successes has been to boost the rate of return on capital employed from 8 per cent in 1970 to a massive 27 per cent in 1982. The cash mountain has not been earning anything like this. Of course, in the late 1970s and early 1980s the economic climate hardly favoured new investment, but opportunities cannot have entirely dried up for a major company like GEC which was operating in an industry which still had recognisable growth points.

It may be that the cash is being conserved to meet some decisive strategic plan requiring a big move into a new product or a new geographic area. Such possibilities threaten any interim judgments, but the company's decade-long record on acquisitions does not suggest that there is any clear long-run strategic design.

GEC has followed the path of growth through acquisitions. But pursuit of growth by this means has not been pressed too hard. In the UK, indeed, the company has since 1970 disposed of rather more firms than it has acquired. Such a result could have been expected in the early years where the sale of surplus and overlapping capacity and assets offered the obvious quick fruits of merger. But it continued as a marked characteristic throughout the 1970s, even when the cash was available for a vigorous acquisitions policy. A few substantial buys were enough to outweigh the more numerous but generally smaller disposals. The two major purchases were: Schreiber furniture which was bought in 1974 in a bid to halt the general decline in the domestic appliance sector, and of Avery, the weighing and testing machines firm which was bought in 1980 in a bid to put GEC electronics into Avery machines. More surprisingly of the fifteen or so UK businesses acquired in the 1970s over one-third had already been disposed of by 1982. If GEC can be thought of as a train, then as many carriages have been uncoupled as have been coupled.

There was more persistent expansion by acquisition overseas. The purchases were, however, concentrated in the United States. In the four years from 1977 nine overseas holdings were purchased, all of them in the US. Both the major purchases were of companies with product lines undergoing electronic revolutions: A. B. Dick in office equipment and Picker, the medical suppliers. The other firms were mostly producers of electronic control equipment and software. The American activity therefore seems to represent an attempt to establish a strong base in that market which would ensure for GEC access to electronics developments. Despite this most of the principal overseas subsidiaries and associated companies were still concentrated in the old Commonwealth: India, Pakistan, Bangladesh, Malaysia, Singapore, Hong Kong, Australia, New Zealand, South Africa, Zambia, Zimbabwe and Canada. These, however, were mostly long-standing associations: in almost none of these territories were there any additional acquisitions.

It is also striking that there was no sustained attempt to expand European activities through acquisition. In a brief burst of activity in 1973–5 three French businesses were acquired (one of which was later re-sold). Otherwise, Europe was not a target for acquisitions.

The possible exception when it came was on the heroic scale. The German electrical firm AEG-Telefunken was in increasing financial difficulty through the 1970s. In the summer of 1982 GEC made a strong bid to purchase a substantial part (40 per cent) of a new company AEG-Technik formed essentially by shedding the German company's unprofitable operations in consumer electronics and domestic appliances. The producer-good side of the business would have a turnover of £2·5 billion, or about half that of GEC itself. GEC was prepared to buy AEG for cash; it seemed that a relatively modest sum of around £200 million would have made GEC a major shareholder in a firm with large connections in Europe and South America. The deal, however, foundered on the fears of German workers that GEC involvement would mean heavy redundancies, and on the unwillingness of many German industrialists to see so strategic a concern pass into foreign control.

Surveying the acquisitions record as a whole, no grand strategic plan is immediately apparent. The individual moves, of course, generally made a lot of obvious sense. The acquisition of Schreiber's, for example, bought the company expertise in the marketing of domestic 'white goods' and also gave an entry into the market for fitted kitchens which seemed to offer the best outlet for GEC's more expensive domestic appliances. Avery's offered an entry into important manufacturing sectors in weighing, testing, measuring and dispensing machines which were about to go electronic; at the same time the purchase secured a good servicing and distribution network for these markets. The American purchases gave footholds in that important market as well as some access to American technology. The AEG deal offered a leap forward in Europe – and perhaps a means of limiting some competition in other areas. These particular moves in America and Europe would be consistent with a strategy aimed at enhancing GEC as a multi-national concern but they do not seem adequate enough for that purpose.

Furthermore, at the time of writing none of these approaches has been conspicuously successful. Schreiber's in a difficult market became a loss-maker: the effect of the American assault was muted: and AEG seems to be the big fish that got away. The impression thus persists that the company has made no positive decision to go for growth by acquisition. Possibly it subjected potential acquisitions to financial tests which were too stringent and/or too short-term. Certainly such a strategy would not have been blocked through lack of cash. Indeed, the money hoard made GEC unique in the extent to which its strategic calculations could be independent of the stock market and the banks. New issues and borrowings were otiose: the company was free if it chose to take a long view.

If it chose: the next section suggests that the enthusiasm to do so was limited.

6 Innovation and the long view

The combination of a company having a billion pounds of free cash with a manufacturing output which has not expanded strongly seems curious. At the least it provokes the suggestion that the company has not been successful in finding and seizing strategic investment opportunities in new processes, new products and new marketing arrangements where resources could be profitably and productively used. The whole industry of electrical engineering is one of persistent flux and change. It follows that no company could stay as strong and prominent as GEC has done without substantial adaptability. Even so it is not unreasonable to observe that the company seems occasionally to have missed an important bus. We will try to establish this point with case studies in two producer goods: (a) semi-conductors and (b) telephone equipment.

Related to the question of innovation is that of time horizons. The company's financial position would certainly have allowed it to support activities which were making short-run losses in the hope of long-run profits. Indeed, to some extent its financial resources were so large as to make such an outcome reasonably probable. At the least, it gave the company some leeway – especially in its home market – in deciding the product areas which it wished to nurture with the aim of long-run success. As with the issue of strategic innovations, it is difficult to judge and generalise from the outside about the time horizons governing the company's calculations. None the less there is evidence of short-run defensive behaviour when the company is pressed by competitors. We will try to establish this point by examining the ailing consumer products division.

(a) Innovation and some producer goods

The semi-conductor industry is a division of the electronic components industry. It is the sector concerned with the provision of active devices for electronic systems used in a wide range of uses. These devices include transistors, integrated circuits, opto-electronic systems and micro-processors. It is the area in which the development of micro-chips has taken place. And the semi-conductor industry is, like the micro-chip which lies at its centre, small but highly strategic for the electrical engineering industry as a whole.

Both AEI and GEC had been actively involved in the industry since the mid-1950s. (Much of what follows is based on Sciberras, 1977.) GEC, through its association with Mullard in Associated Semi-conductor Manufacturers, was the leading firm in the British industry. It was then deposed by Texas Instruments, a development which was probably unavoidable given the enormous US lead, fostered by defence and space expenditure, in the industry. It was by no means so obvious, however, that by the mid-1970s foreign multi-nationals (led by Texas Instruments and Philips) should have captured 85 per cent of the UK market, the second largest in Europe. It was even less obvious that GEC should have been ranked as a 'little League' firm and, in 1973, was small even in that company, ranking twelfth in its share of the UK market for semi-conductors.

It was reasonable to expect that GEC's position in semi-conductors would have been much strengthened in the late 1960s with the acquisition of AEI which had long been involved in this field. In effect, however, GEC seems to have withdrawn (or, at least, substantially contracted its involvement) when the industry was about to undergo a substantial expansion. The semi-conductor market in Europe almost doubled in size in the five years after 1968 (Sciberras, 1977, p. 49). During these years GEC became, indeed, Texas Instruments' largest UK customer displacing the British government on the basis of whose defence expenditure TI had initially established its UK position. In addition, GEC sold off the computer interests which had come with the merger with English Electric (Sciberras, 1977, p. 177). In 1968, before the sudden Plessey bid which precipitated the merger with GEC, English Electric was described as holding the 'dominating position outside the US' in automation, computers and electronics (*Investors' Chronicle*, 8 March 1968).

From the mid-1970s, GEC became more actively involved, and more resources were directed into its two companies AEI Semi-conductors and GEC Semi-conductors. Even so, GEC sales accounted for only 5·5 per cent of the UK market in 1977, and GEC failed to appear at all in a list of the 15 leading world producers (Sciberras, 1977, ch. 16, pp. 285, 287, in Pavitt, 1980). In addition, a link was forged in 1978 with the American firm Fairchild Camera to produce semi-conductors, and in 1979 government assistance expected to be of nearly £7 million was arranged for GEC-Fairchild Ltd to set up a new manufacturing plant for micro-electronic devices in the Merseyside Development Area at Neston, Cheshire (*Trade and Industry*, 1979, vol. 34, p. 561). The link did not, however, last, being ended in July 1980 perhaps because Fairchild saw the arrangement more as a means of increasing distribution of its products in the UK and could always control the extent to which it shared technology with GEC. The factory, intended for the production of micro-chips, was switched by GEC to manufacture of the Sting Ray torpedo, a major defence contract (*Financial Times*, 2 July 1980). At all events, it has been a continuing complaint (see e.g. *Guardian*, 5 February 1981) that GEC has not involved itself in mainstream computer development, backing out – as has been seen – of the mass production of micro-chips and selling its large stake in ICL in 1975.

Of course, the picture is more complex than that. The US firms had, for example, vital initial assistance from large Federal orders for defence and space research. But it could be said that – although not on an American scale – GEC was relatively favourably placed as the largest recipient of the relatively high British defence expenditure on electronics. Defence (because of its specialised custom-made requirements) has become less important both as a market and as a source of innovative change than the commercial market. But, with or without defence orders, four European firms (Philips of Holland, Siemens of Germany, Sys Ates of Italy and Thomson of France) had managed by the end of the 1970s to secure a place in the world's top fifteen (Sciberras in Pavitt, 1980). It is difficult not to feel that GEC could and should have done better. With its widespread activities in the production of a diversified range of end-equipment GEC was in a strong position to integrate the design and development of components for these final products. GEC was certainly in a stronger position to do what several European producers have done: acquire technical and managerial skills by buying one of the smaller American firms.[5]

The case of the semi-conductors is significant because it raises questions about the appropriateness of GEC's financial controls for some important sectors of the industry. Some of the American firms, more open about their management techniques and motives, have made it clear that they have pursued long-run strategies based on sharply reducing costs, firstly through the big-scale economies available if large numbers of standard devices are manufactured, and secondly through the learning process which is involved in mass production in this technologically developing area. The strategic *potential* of cost-reduction was relied upon to extend the market – a process clearly seen in the rapid march of, for example, pocket calculators and desk computers. Such strategies are not readily compatible with a system of management control which, like GEC, relies heavily on tests of short-run financial return.

The story of technical development in telephone exchanges is quite different. In this case there has been a great deal of innovative effort, which has not at the time of writing (1982) led to the commercial sales which might reasonably have been expected. A bald statement of the sweep of technical development since the 1950s could reduce it to a progression from electro-mechanical systems (Strowger exchanges) to semi-electric systems (Crossbar) to semi-electronic (TXE-4) to an entirely electronic, digital computer-controlled system (System X). The Post Office stuck to Strowger up to the 1970s although Crossbar was already being widely introduced in other countries. The result severely constrained the export activities of the main British producers (Plessey, GEC and STC). Plessey developed its own Crossbar system which GEC also marketed abroad under licence, and some Crossbar exchanges were bought by the Post Office in the 1970s (*Investors' Chronicle*, 24 November 1972, 16 February 1973). The Post Office basically decided, however, to make the jump from Strowger to an all-electronic system (TXE-4 and then System X).

All this bristles with complications and interest. It raises, for example, large questions about the part state institutions like the Post Office play in encouraging (or retarding) technical development in national enterprises. The simpler point suggested here, however, relates to the development of System X. Initially, British firms, and especially GEC, seemed to be in a favourable situation. The start was early: AEI was already developing the all-electronic System X before it was taken over by GEC. In the early 1970s it became a joint project of GEC, Plessey and STC. Yet by the end of 1981 nothing had been sold abroad and only two Systems X exchanges (City of London and Woodbridge, Sussex) had been introduced at home. Foreign companies (like Ericsson of Sweden and Philips of Holland) had started early but had been selling overseas from 1978 onwards. By the late 1980s the British consortium had slipped further behind: French and German competitors had now joined those selling electronic telephone systems abroad (*Sunday Times*, 22 November 1981). In the autumn of 1982, STC withdrew from the tripartite arrangements over Systems X, leaving Plessey and GEC as the two companies to compete for an accelerated programme for British Telecom and to secure overseas orders (*Financial Times*, 5 October 1982).

The lack of export sales, no doubt, has many causes. It is, however, surprising to find lack of cash being suggested even if GEC is understandably reluctant to invest for the benefit of other firms in a consortium. It is also suggested that GEC had opposed giving tenders until the actual costs were known: seed-corn tendering clashed with GEC's cautious or prudent style of wanting to see a good return (*Sunday Times*, 22 November 1981). At all events it is difficult to avoid the conclusion that part of the difficulty of bringing System X to a rapid fruition has stemmed from the problem of reconciling its needs with those of GEC's methods of short-run financial scrutiny. Indeed, some reports suggested that Plessey particularly welcomed the arrangements introduced in October 1982 partly as a way of freeing them for more aggressive sales of the system (*Guardian*, 5 October and *Observer* 12 October 1982).

It is important to keep these criticisms in perspective. Over a large part of its widespread activities the company maintains a sound enough technological position: this indeed is a condition for survival in electrical engineering. The company's reports and the financial and technical press provide numerous examples of new development brought to a successful commercial fruition. In addition, GEC also expands occasionally into entirely new fields. In 1980, for example, GEC bought the controls division when Alfred Herbert collapsed and moved into the production of computer-controlled machine tools like Microset (*New Scientist*, 26 February 1981). None the less, the case studies establish that there have been lapses in significant growth sectors of the electrical engineering industry. The implications of the case studies are, moreover, supported by more general evidence on Research and Development expenditure. It is difficult to be specific about individual firms, but GEC is a major part of an industrial grouping which has a poor record in this respect. A recent study found that in the period from 1967 to 1975 there had been a decline in innovative activity, as measured by proportions spent on Research and Development in electrical and electronic products in Britain (Pavitt, 1980, p. 6). The same study (pp. 41–2) showed British Research and Development expenditure in this sector to be half that of Japan and Germany and only two-thirds that of France.

(b)   Time horizons in consumer products

For consumer products, which had been the strong point of the pre-merger GEC, the 1970s began auspiciously enough. There was the rapid growth of colour television breathing new life into the demand for sets. During the Barber boom, there was a government-induced expansion in consumer demand which boosted sales of other domestic products. Conditions then became progressively worse. There was sharp competition from, especially, the Italians in laundry appliances and refrigerators (white goods) and from the Japanese for televisions and related products (brown goods). The problem of competition was, moreover, compounded by market saturation in many areas and, much more significant and pervasive, by the slow growth of British real income.

Even so, GEC's production performance in these areas has not been good. In part the evidence for this is to be seen in the High Street electrical shops. But the judgment is not simply impression-istic. It is also reflected in, for example, the company's turnover figures. Even in current value terms, the Consumer Product division only grew three-fold from 1970 to 1982: when turnover is adjusted for price changes, output in 1981 was substantially less (85 per cent) than it had been in 1970. The relative failure also emerges from the import penetration and export sales ratios. For broadcast receiving and sound reproducing equipment (MLH 365) the import penetration ratio increased from 14 to 46 per cent between 1970 and 1980 while the export ratio rose only from 8 to 16 per cent: for electrical appliances primarily for domestic use (MLH 368) the import ratio rose from 10 to 26 per cent, while the export ratio *fell* from 18 to 16 per cent. Finally, there was a dramatic drop in the contribution which Consumer Products made to the company's earnings. Consumer Products accounted for around 10 per cent in 1970 and subsequently peaked at 18 per cent: by 1982 they were down to a meagre 2 per cent of earnings.

Was this market failure avoidable? It will be argued that it could at least have been mitigated. In white goods the Italian competition was towards the bottom end of the market and perhaps not much could have been done directly about that. What the company did immediately was to import and brand Italian appliances: but that could not solve the home production problems. At the more expensive end of the market there were clearer opportunities and it did look as if the company moved shrewdly to exploit them. The opportunities arose from the difficulties of the British market leader (Hoover) and from the development of the market for complete kitchens.

Hoover was vulnerable because it did not produce a full integrated range of appliances for a complete kitchen, the designs of its washing machines and vacuum cleaners became more dated, and it ran into increasing financial problems. The formation of GEC-Schreiber in 1974 quickly put GEC in a position where it could take advantage of this vulnerability. It offered the complete kitchen package of cabinets plus appliances, and some of the problems of Hotpoint were successfully resolved. The standard of Hotpoint servicing was transformed, largely by persuading the unions to abandon piece-rates which led to skimping, while factory productivity and product reliability were increased by similar changes which accompanied reductions in the labour force (*Investors' Chronicle*, 21 January 1977).

The problems, however, persisted. The company's market share and reputation still fell. Apart from the general economic climate, part of the trouble seemed to be the slowness of the shift to new models. In washing machines, for example, most Hotpoint production until the late 1970s was of an expensive, difficult-to-service top-loading machine. This had served the company well for over a decade but was sold in a market which was increasingly dominated by front-loaders. By the early 1980s, GEC's home laundry sector was reviving and a new factory was being built at Rhyl to supplement the one at Llandudno. But the division as a whole was still troublesome: by the early 1980s Schreiber furniture was making

losses which threatened to bring down the Hotpoint appliance business and, meanwhile, the company had retreated from the field of
smaller domestic appliances by selling off Morphy Richards.

If the company was doing badly in the home market for white
goods, a recently published article (*Financial Times*, 29 October
1982) suggests that its export performance in this area was even
worse. Comparisons of national industrial performance in the white
goods field suggest the real failure of the British industry is in the
export field. The French, West German and Italian producers have
not all successfully resisted import penetration; but they have all
managed a substantially higher level of exports to near West European countries than Britain has achieved. Hotpoint constitutes a
significant part of the British white goods industry, and thus must
take its share of the blame. Because of the failure of British firms
like Hotpoint to make export sales, they have been sidelined as
weak marginal producers. In a long article discussing possible
remedies by major European producers, no UK firm received a
specific mention, and the only general reference was the laconic:
'the British manufacturers are regarded as too small and weak to
figure' (*Financial Times*, 29 October 1982).

The relative losses in the television market were much more
remarkable. It was, after all, on the basis of producing highly cost-
effective black and white sets that the Weinstock reputation was
first made with Sobell in the 1950s. It was his drive in this area
that had been a significant part of turning round GEC in the
following decade. And the newly enlarged firm gained significantly
from the new boom in colour television which began after the first
colour commercials in 1969. In 1973, on this wave, the Consumer
Products division was the most successful part of the group and
Weinstock himself was talking confidently of maintaining the
momentum for colour television sales in Europe (*Investors' Chronicle*,
27 July 1973). But by 1977 television production was one of the
company's major problems.

Why? The deterioration, and especially its pace, was partly
implicit in the nature of the response made to the Japanese challenge. Effectively this was one of retreat. In television itself this took
the form of seeking secure outlets by extending into the rental
business: Spectra Rentals was bought for this purpose in 1974
(*Investors' Chronicle*, 9 August 1974). This was sensible but on its
own hardly sufficient.

The retreat was also seen in the failure to establish a manufacturing capacity in the areas of audio-cassettes and video-recorders. In market terms buying in from Far Eastern producers and putting a European brand name on the product was reasonable in the short-run and the bottom end of the market. In production terms, however, this was suicidal for European firms unless it was backed by long-run development of their own products. Firms such as Philips of Holland and Grundig of West Germany were more positive in this respect. They have maintained a market presence and a significant productive capability by offering a range of video-recorders which technically can match the Japanese products. Philips and Grundig video-machines may now only have 10 per cent of the European market; but these companies have maintained a technical capability and market presence in this area. If nothing else, they are now in a position to make co-operative deals with the Japanese majors on terms of reasonable equality.

GEC's own co-operative deal made with Hitachi in 1978 for the joint production of television sets in Britain could be represented as a further retreat, or as the start of an advance. It was not, however, encouraging to find that when virtually identical sets came off the same assembly line, the set with an Hitachi label could command a substantial retail premium over one with the GEC badge. Further discouragement came with the announcement in 1982, when production was only just under way, that job losses were already necessary because of lack of sales. GEC's joint ventures – with System X (Plessey and STC), micro-processors (Fairchild), and television (Hitachi) – seem not to run smoothly, and perhaps – as will now be suggested – this is partly because GEC is unusually preoccupied with short-run returns and finds it difficult to co-operate with firms whose calculations are more geared to establishing a long-run market presence. The pace and scale of the mid-1970s decline in television and related products, long an area of strength, suggests a failure to fight. The company certainly had the means to sustain substantial short-run losses to protect its position in the home market. Such a policy would, however, not have met the usual stringent financial requirements. At all events it is mildly surprising and depressingly instructive to see that a company as strong and successful as GEC was in this area no more able to hold its share of its home market than BL was in cars.

What has been attempted is a brief survey of the GEC experience in part of its Consumer Products division. The exercise suggests some conclusions, which cannot be established conclusively by outsiders without access to company records. We would claim, however, that the conclusions are not only plausible but are also consistent with what is known about the financial controls operated by top management. There does seem to have been a reluctance to develop new products especially if initially they are only expected to sell in small segments of the market. The neglect of the video-recorder, despite its complementary importance for 'traditional' television sets, would be a prime example. The company seems to be reluctant to spend heavily and early on developing and re-packaging established lines in order to snatch market advantage and technical superiority; this is epitomised by the company's persistence with the top-loader washing machine.[6] The company seems reluctant to buy a market share by supporting loss-making lines in areas where it wishes to be represented in the long run. The retreat from High Street retail sales of GEC colour television sets would make the point – which is not that the company does not and has not supported losses in some consumer products, but rather that there is little sign of this being undertaken as part of a strategy.

These characteristics, when they emerge, stem chiefly from enterprise calculations being determined by time horizons which are relatively short. The innovative lapses discussed earlier can in part be similarly explained. But why – in apparent contrast to Japanese electronic firms – should decision-making at GEC seem to give more weight to short time horizons? The essential point is that such a tendency is inherent in the company's basic management techniques and style.

Fundamental to GEC organisation is a small headquarters staff. The underlying philosophy is to give a great deal of autonomy to the individual producing units. The only way in which these two aspects can be reconciled with the obvious fact that GEC is a very tight-run ship, is through applying stringent and largely standardised financial controls to the production centres. If a small head office is to maintain a tight grip over a large diversified organisation, the logic of the situation demands close financial control. In the case of GEC the existence and effectiveness of financial controls have become legendary.

Arnold Weinstock, as he then was, indicated the nature of the controls in an interview he gave at the time of the mergers of the late-1960s (Vice, 1971, p. 24 and *Times Business News*, 29 November 1968). He then identified seven key criteria on which he relied to exercise the crucial financial control over the performance of the various divisions within the group and of the individual profit centres within the divisions. The ratios used as yardsticks were: profit on capital employed; profits on sales; sales as a multiple of capital employed; sales as a multiple of fixed assets; sales as a multiple of stocks; sales per employee; and profit per employee. The detailed list of ratios is not, however, as important as their functions. They were precisely geared to the purpose of operating a major combine with a small central staff so that operating autonomy could be allowed whilst head office retained tight overall financial control. The ratios were explicitly described as danger signals, an early-warning system for existing operations and they have performed these functions effectively as the financial results testify.

But there are costs to be paid because financial ratios cannot positively guide enterprise strategy. It has already been argued in our introduction that modern management methods using return on investment criteria are flawed in their assumptions and are therefore a poor guide to strategic investment. They may inhibit strategic decision-making, especially that geared to productive growth. Financial controls, moreover, do not allow the company to assess whether losses should be accepted to protect and sustain a market presence. It is certain that the financial criteria listed above are in their nature essentially short-term, and hence less useful when the company has to assess new areas and growth sectors.

Arnold Weinstock once stated that 'except between the twenty-first and the end of the month, when I'm going through the monthly reports, I'm not very busy really. I browse around a bit' (Vice, 1971, p. 12). Such a picture of effortless efficiency was no doubt a very effective piece of public relations, but it would be foolish to suppose that Lord Weinstock and Sir Kenneth Bond simply sit in the centre mechanically operating financial switches. None the less, the financial controls have played a crucial part in producing the financial success: they provide a framework for decision-making which is well-geared to the identification of areas of worsening trade and profit, allowing prompt action to stem losses. They can also highlight the areas of greatest immediate profit and encourage resources to flow towards them. But, since the ratios are less efficient at defining and guiding enterprise strategy, they may well lead towards policies of risk-aversion and the pursuit of short-term profit. In this respect it is significant that the company has recently shown greater awareness of the limitations of financial controls. Sir Robert Clayton, the company's technical director, and Derek Roberts, its director of research, have ready access to Lord Weinstock. They also sit in at GEC's annual budget exercise at which each operating unit has its record and its requests scrutinised (*Financial Times*, 4 June 1981). These innovations can be seen as an attempt to redress the balance and to give weight to factors other than short-run financial returns.

In making these comments, sight must not be lost of the fact that persistent profitability is in itself immensely important. Apart from other considerations it naturally makes the company less vulnerable to critical attack. Two possible sources of such attack are the labour force and the government. The next sections will argue that in dealing with these two groups the company (or, perhaps Lord Weinstock himself) has largely been able to persuade them to acquiesce in the management plans.

7   Labour and the workforce

Given the way in which the company is organised, top management cannot know much about the detailed control of the labour process. It is implausible, however, to expect that GEC has been unaffected by the lax working practices which are common in British industry: over-manning, machinery operated below capacity and with frequent breakdowns. And there have been scattered industrial stoppages. Such considerations, however, are given very little attention in the company's *Reports* and *Reviews*, nor do they figure much in the coverage of a press generally hungry for such tit-bits.

Management, it is reasonable to conclude, does not see poor working practices as constituting a major problem or obstacle. Of course, this attitude can arise because a complacent management prefers not to consider the unfavourable consequences of lack of control over the labour process. Such an interpretation hardly fits the GEC case. It would, at the least, be difficult to reconcile with the five-fold increase in turnover per UK employee between 1970 and 1981, growing a lot faster than prices. Furthermore it is not readily compatible with the stable ratio of wages to turnover at a time when profits doubled in proportion to turnover. It seems more reasonable to accept that the GEC top management attitude to labour control simply reflects basic philosophy: in this, as in other matters, top management believes that, provided the financial ratios come out right, operating details can safely and efficiently be delegated to lower management echelons in the productive units.

Nevertheless, top management has crucially contributed to the control of labour costs. It is initially surprising that in this hugely profitable concern, wages, as we have seen, rose only a little faster than in manufacturing industry generally, despite large increases in output per worker. Management did much to create the conditions which made such a result possible.

After the merger, management started off with the advantage that there was no real tradition of company-wide labour activity in electrical engineering. The heterogeneous nature of the industry discouraged united action and this tendency was intensified by the existence of several unions. But the company has successfully pressed forward with the logic of this. In wage-bargaining terms it is hardly too much to say that GEC simply does not exist as a national entity. (The contrast with firms in many other industries is marked. In a company like Ford, for example, national negotiations over wage rates are normal and large profits inevitably trigger wage claims.) GEC's whole management structure, based on the premise of giving maximum autonomy to the numerous individual companies has always encouraged the workforce to accept that labour problems are handled at the level of the individual profit centre. More recently GEC decided to leave the Engineering Employers' Federation (although a number of its constituent companies continued as members). The aim seems to be to contain difficulties and disputes. The policy makes sense for management, especially as it maximises some of the company's advantages. GEC is able to use the large cash reserve as a weapon in overcoming resistance at particular points in operating divisions. Furthermore it can appeal to the loyalty of the whole workforce. Much attention has been given to these representational issues: Lord Weinstock himself is said to have pressed through the production of a popular synopsis of the financial accounts which emphasised the dependence of employment on essentially precarious sales.

More specifically, top management early established the right of management to fire workers from loss-making operations (subject, of course, to statutory compensation). This was a prerogative which private-sector management as a whole only clearly obtained in the industrial slump under the Thatcher administration at the end of the decade. Weinstock established the right to fire workers a whole decade earlier during the second Wilson administration. This indeed is the real significance of the confrontation with the unions over the Woolwich closure of the 1960s.

In the early post-merger days the major source of improved performance and higher profit was rationalisation: essentially the clearing away of whatever was considered excess capacity and the closing of the oldest, least efficient plant. Woolwich was the most dramatic example of the process. A single plant employing over 5,000 workers had its total closure announced on 1 February 1968. There was a great deal of local and national criticism, as well as demonstrations and parliamentary questions. The company was clearly taken aback at the force of some of the reaction, but much of this was easily deflected because it reflected unease at the bluntness of the announcement and the apparent unconcern of the company. It could be met, and was, by showing a more human and caring face, for example, by setting up a company advisory service to help place redundant workers. The two possible sources of tangible support for the Woolwich workers' protest represented no real threat. The government was a Labour government but was in no position to act. A government which had positively encouraged and facilitated the mergers to raise efficiency could hardly effectively protest at the consequences. The unions were equally impotent: there was much rhetoric and bombast but no serious attempt to organise a company-wide stoppage which was the one action which might have been effective.

Thereafter the company did not have to confront any major head-on opposition when dismissals were found to be necessary. This was so despite, or perhaps because of, the setting up of a National Joint Consultative Council to improve communications between the management and those unions with substantial membership amongst GEC staff and workers. The NJCC was largely concerned with redundancies and, although the council may have succeeded in improving the terms for redundant workers, it does not seem to have altered any of the company's basic decisions about closures. The unions thus tended to be associated with the redundancies and the NJCC became known as 'the burial party' (Cowling et al., 1980, pp. 251–6). Redundancy is of course a notoriously difficult issue for unions and few unions have successfully fought closures. But in GEC the decisive management action over the Woolwich closures seems to have produced an atmosphere which made it unusually difficult to resist further closures. At all events in the period from January 1968 to January 1972 over seventy redundancy operations were effected involving over 40,000 persons (CIS, 1973; Cowling et al., 1980). These could be seen merely as the result of post-merger reorganisation, but in later years the right to impose dismissals has remained especially important to GEC because of the extent to which its corporate strategy has been guided by financial signals. The solutions suggested by financial criteria often pointed towards the closure or reduction of particular plants, the abandonment of a given market, or the divestment of unwanted subsidiaries.

Most of these factors are seen in operation in the changes introduced after the take-over of Avery, the weighing and measurement specialists, in November 1979. The workforce was substantially reduced. A two-year no-redundancy agreement was part of the takeover terms: none the less 1,600 employees voluntarily left the company. Several small establishments were closed down. The remaining workforce was by 1982, in the words of Keith Hodgkinson, the manager introduced by GEC, 'more understanding and committed to change' (*Financial Times*, 28 July 1982). The takeover obviously entailed a radical change but there is little indication that opposition from the labour force had been, or was expected to be, a major problem.

As already indicated, GEC has proceeded like a train to which carriages are regularly being coupled and uncoupled. The process must have been unfortunate for those who happened to be in an uncoupled carriage, but their ticket did plainly say that 'management reserved the right . . .'

8 Government

The enterprise, and Lord Weinstock himself, go to some trouble to cultivate links with government – more perhaps with officials than with politicians. It is helpful to the company that successive governments have wanted, and want, to sustain an internationally significant British firm in this area. It provides the company with a small lever in its natural desire to manipulate its relations with the government to its own advantage. As a major customer in some areas – like defence – where commercial considerations may not be either over-riding or easy to define, the government is necessarily subject to national, not to say nationalist, needs. On the other hand, the relation to government is not simply a source of advantage: GEC is also more than usually susceptible to the vagaries of government policies.

The first point to notice in examining the relation of GEC to government is that the government gave significant positive encouragement to the formation of a major British enterprise in the electrical engineering industry. The industry's private monopoly and cartel arrangements at home and abroad were removed or reduced in the 1950s and 1960s and might have been expected to produce a more competitive atmosphere with a number of more or less equal-sized firms in each sector of the electrical engineering industry. At just this time, however, the government and particularly the Labour administrations of 1964-70 made the establishment of large-sized enterprises in the technologically advanced sectors of the economy into a corner-stone of government industrial strategy. Electrical engineering obviously fitted into this policy. Hence, as was demonstrated earlier, the government greatly encouraged GEC's takeover of AEI and its merger with English Electric. Neither of these clear concentrations of manufacturing industry was referred to the Monopolies Commission for investigation. GEC's privileged status was moreover maintained well beyond this. In the battle to acquire Avery it was difficult to avoid a reference to the Commission; the takeover was being pressed in face of Avery's protests and would clearly result in an increase in market power in measurement instruments. The Monopolies Commission did indeed investigate: but its studiously unenthusiastic report was widely seen to reflect the Monopolies Commission's reluctant acquiescence under political pressure.

Naturally enough these are not the aspects to which top management gives public expression when referring to the company's relationship with government. Such public company statements concentrate on the drawbacks. In the 1970s the annual statements of the Chairman (Lord Nelson) and other pronouncements, made reference to the inability of government to curtail inflation (especially of wages) and there were complaints about rising public expenditure. Lord Weinstock (*Guardian*, 19 November 1980) also stressed the general problem that employment opportunities in the public sector diverted the most talented of the young from industrial employment. At this rhetorical and ideological level there were also frequent complaints about high taxation; but these were usually diplomatically made on behalf of skilled workers rather than of managers and directors.

Much of this grumbling was routine and probably of no great significance. At the same time it must be stressed that the relation of GEC to government did also create sharp problems. The government certainly made life difficult through its effect upon demand, both at a general and at a more specific level. As governments often switched between policies of curbing and policies of encouraging aggregate demand, there were problems of adjustment for the company. These adjustments, moreover, were the more complicated for an enterprise like GEC because of the wide range of its production. The speed and extent of the effects of government demand policies fell quite differently, for example, on capital goods and on consumer goods. Even more traumatic, however, was the effect when government seemed to forgo these relatively short-run fluctuations. From 1979, perhaps even from the time of the restrictions imposed to meet IMF requirements in 1976, there was a prolonged period of deflationary pressure on the British economy, and a substantial recession in the international economy.

Curbs on public expenditure also encouraged cut-backs in nationalised industries like electricity supply and postal services. Indeed, the public sector demand for several key products of GEC was subject to even larger fluctuations. For a substantial part of the 1970s there was, as already indicated, an additional problem of a persistent absolute decline in CEGB orders for power stations, Post Office orders for exchanges, and British Rail orders for track and rolling stock. In some cases there were problems about underlying trends in market demand; in power stations it was increasingly clear from the late 1960s that the demand for electricity was not going to grow at anything like the rate envisaged in earlier forecasts. Elsewhere state bodies could not be persuaded to act more decisively: in telephones the Post Office having been late to shift from the Strowger (electro-mechanical) system, dithered about whether and how to make the leap to an all-electronic system.

Recognition of such disruptive aspects, however, should not

obscure the point that the extent and scale of government demand greatly benefited GEC. Even in the areas just quoted orders never completely dried up and, much more important, whole sectors of the electrical engineering industry – power generating, diesels and electronics – had largely been nurtured and developed by public patronage. Moreover, even with the cutbacks in public expenditure in the 1970s the industry, as a whole, and GEC in particular, was still a major beneficiary of government demand. Defence requirements remained high and, in any event, the nature of military needs was shifting in ways favourable to GEC. Of the private sector industries which gained most from the government's orders for military purposes the electrical industry ranked second only to aerospace, and within the electrical industry GEC was the largest beneficiary (Angus, 1979). Most of the defence-related activity was concentrated in GEC's electronic subsidiaries – Elliotts, Marconi Avionics, Marconi Radar Systems, and Marconi Defence and Space Systems. These produced such things as communications equipment, radar and sonar equipment, surveillance and missile systems, electronic counter-measures and fire control systems. In all it was estimated that the UK defence electronics sector had a turnover, in 1976, of £800 million and gave employment to 90,000. A sizeable share of the money and the jobs must have gone to GEC.

It is not simply the case that GEC benefited from large contracts in defence and related spheres. Despite much hard bargaining the terms of these contracts were almost unavoidably generally favourable to the supplying company (*Economist*, 3 July 1982). Much defence equipment is necessarily supplied with development costs largely charged to government, and production frequently undertaken on a cost-plus basis. It is difficult to see how else major weapons systems can be developed. Of course, the government can, and does, buy in technology from abroad – American weapons systems or nuclear reactors. But even here, as a privileged national supplier, GEC can often negotiate second-best arrangements. Consider, for example, the decision about whether to develop a new British torpedo. If the government had decided against developing a British (GEC) torpedo, Lord Weinstock had already negotiated a fall-back arrangement for GEC factories to make (under licence) a significant part of the 'American' missile. Even if the development teams were not fully occupied, the production lines would be busy. In the event, however, the decision went in favour of GEC's Sting

Ray underwater missile so GEC obtained its first best solution and the chance to produce a weapons system with considerable export potential. Where GEC is exporting defence equipment the company usually benefits because the British government has normally borne a significant part of the development costs.

9 Conclusion

We came to praise Caesar, not to bury him. In fact, the essay has turned out to be more critical than was expected. That, however, is neither the main point nor the main purpose. The starting point was quite simply the observation that GEC was widely regarded as a brilliant success. The intention, then, was to examine how far the success was related to the company's ability to overcome the constraints on enterprise calculation which we identified in our introduction. Much of this has, indeed, emerged in the sections on GEC's handling of the labour process and of its relations with government. Above all, financial success obviously freed GEC's strategic planning from the particular restraints of financial institutions like the stock market and the British banking system. GEC could develop as it wished without needing to raise capital or borrowing from the banks.

It was the use made of this freedom which initially provoked our criticism. The central concern of this study is that of UK manufacturing. From this standpoint the GEC story looks decidedly less triumphant. Although it had the means, the company has not pursued aggressive manufacturing growth through UK acquisition. It has made more acquisitions overseas, but this is an inefficient and oblique way of boosting British manufacturing. It has lost some innovative opportunities and limited the extent to which it pursued its own expansion through direct new investment. It has ceded market ground at home in several important sectors. Even these considerations, however, are not in themselves the basic issue. They are, after all, well within the company's prerogative and could – though it seems unlikely – simply reflect the company's considered and legitimate strategy. The more crucial observation is that the missed opportunities in new markets and retreats in old ones both stem more or less directly from GEC's methods of enterprise calculation, grounded in financial criteria which favour relatively short-run profitability. The paradox of GEC is that the same controls which produced the financial success also account for the more modest productive achievement in manufacturing. The story of GEC can thus be seen in part as a cautionary tale. It should, at the least, cast doubt on the proposition that the simple pursuit of 'profit' will necessarily lead to 'beneficial' results for society as a whole. It should also be considered carefully by those politicians who believe that industrial rationalisation involving the elimination of loss-making activities and enterprises will lead to a revival of British manufacturing.

Notes

1 It is interesting to speculate as to what might have happened to an unchanged GEC in the 1970s when much of its strength in the lighter end of the industry faltered in the face of Japanese and European competition. Whatever the results of such speculation it might serve to emphasise the particularly fortuitous conjunction of circumstances for GEC in the late 1960s.

2 It has already been indicated (see p. 144, para. 4) that adjusting for price changes is tricky and no single deflator can accurately reflect trends over such a wide-ranging field. The cautionary comments need reinforcing when the same indicator is applied separately to each of the broad divisions. Everyone who uses pocket calculators, for example, will know that their prices (for what they can do) have actually fallen over the last decade. None the less the broad picture presented here is a reasonable approximation. It will be obvious that the degree of disaggregation indicated here is inadequate. It is however, all that is available from the published accounts and it has not proved possible to obtain a greater breakdown on a continuous basis.

3 To get the greatest comparability with the price index based on calendar years, the company figures for the year ending March 1972 and March 1982 have been taken for 1971 and 1981 respectively.

4 Net income is income from interest and investment *minus* interest paid on bank overdrafts and loan capital *minus* interests on convertible loan stock.

5 The escalating costs of R and D make it increasingly difficult for all European companies to keep pace in this industry. The Japanese have tackled the problem by combining substantial government assistance with the pooling of research effort by the leading companies. A similar approach is proposed for Europe: the EEC together with twelve major firms will jointly provide funds for co-operative research effort (*Financial Times*, 3 August 1982). Whether the scheme, named Esprit, will work across both company organisations and national boundaries must be

doubtful. But it offers GEC, one of the three British firms with Plessey and ICL, a possible way to secure both standardised production in components and of integrating these into its own wide range of end-products.

6 Household appliances, radio and television have been explicitly identified as areas where Britain has been comparatively weak in technical innovation (Pavitt, 1980, p. 56).

References

Alberts, W. W. and Segall, J. E. (eds) (1974), *The Corporate Merger*, London, University of Chicago Press.

Angus, R. (1979), *Organisation of Defence Procurement and Production in the UK*, Aberdeen Studies in Defence Economics (ASIDES), paper no. 13, University of Aberdeen.

Counter Information Services (CIS) (1973), *The General Electric Company Ltd, An Anti-report*.

Cowling, K. et al. (1980), *Mergers and Economic Performance*, Cambridge, Cambridge University Press.

Daniel, W. W. (1972), *Whatever Happened to the Workers in Woolwich? A Survey of Redundancy in South-east London*, London, Political and Economic Planning.

Dutton, P. A. (1978), *A Case Study of the GEC-AEI-English Electric Mergers*, University of Warwick.

Jones, R. and Marriott, O. (1970), *The Anatomy of a Merger: a History of GEC, AEI and English Electric*, London, Cape.

Latham, Sir Joseph (1969), *Take-over: The Facts and Myths of the GEC-AEI Battle*, London, Iliffe.

Monopolies and Restrictive Practices Commission: (Chairman: Sir David Cairns QC) (1957), *Report on the Supply and Export of Electrical and Allied Machinery and Plant*, London, HMSO.

Monopolies and Restrictive Practices Commission: (Chairman Sir David Cairns QC) (1957), *Report on the Supply of Electronic Valves and Cathode Ray Tubes*, London, HMSO.

Pavitt, K. (ed.) (1980), *Technical Innovation and British Economic Performance*, London, Macmillan.

Pratten, C. F. (1971), *Economies of Scale in Manufacturing Industry*, Cambridge, Cambridge University Press.

Samuels, J. M. (ed.) (1972), *Readings on Mergers and Takeovers*, London, Elek Books.

Sciberras, E. (1977), *Multinational Electronics Companies and National Economic Policies*, Connecticut, JAI Press.

Sciberras, E. (1980), 'The UK Semiconductor Industry', in Pavitt, K. (ed.), *Technical Innovation and British Economic Performance*, pp. 282–96.

Surrey, A. J. et al. (1980), 'Heavy electrical plant', in Pavitt, K. (ed.), *Technical Innovation and British Economic Performance*, pp. 235–51.

Vice, A. (1971), *The Strategy of Takeovers: A Casebook of International Practice*, London, McGraw-Hill.

GEC, annual *Reports* and *Reviews*, including editions of *Britain's Largest Private Employer*, 1978–

The Economist
Financial Times
Guardian
Investors' Chronicle
New Scientist
Observer
Sunday Times
Times Business News
Trade and Industry

2 Shipbuilding – Demand Linkage and Industrial Decline

Dennis Thomas

Two of the case studies in this book, those concerned with BL and GEC, concentrate on a single enterprise. In the present essay, dealing with merchant shipbuilding in the period up to nationalisation, the approach is somewhat different. The emphasis will be placed first on the conditions which have affected calculations for the industry as a whole before the analysis turns to examine how these have been reflected at the level of the individual enterprise.

The different approach has been adopted for a variety of reasons such as the absence, in this industry, of a single dominating firm, and the more obvious importance of general international considerations in shipbuilding. It also, however, developed quite naturally from the analysis of the problems of shipbuilding. It became increasingly clear that a central reason for the decline of the industry was the changing pattern of the world demand for shipping and the peculiar institutional reasons which inhibited the British industry as a whole from making prompt and suitable adjustments. The industry, of course, faced many other problems such as prolonged under-investment, bad working practices, poor industrial relations and inadequate management. It will be contended, however, that a resolution of these problems would have done little to have halted the general decline of the industry unless it had been accompanied by a solution to the basic market problem. In this respect, these other problems, despite their importance, were secondary.

The essay will thus aim to indicate the circumstances which impeded the response of British shipbuilders to the general market situation. These partly arose out of the long-standing relationship between the industry and the UK shipping fleet. The demand for British yards was based first on the needs of British shipowners whose requirements had several peculiarities to meet which the builders had substantially moulded their practices and equipment. Such a demand linkage between shipbuilders and shipowners natur- ally carried mutual benefits. It was, however, a linkage based for the most part only on custom and convention and was, for example, not much formalised through common ownership by vertical integ- ration. The crucial point was that the link was a firm attachment for the shipbuilders, but only a loose connection for the owners. Thus when the changing needs of world shipping required it, British shipowners removed their custom, creating formidable problems for a shipbuilding industry adapted to a demand which had been taken elsewhere. The problems were exacerbated because the government, despite several official and semi-official inquiries, failed to identify the nature of the demand problem. The government might have acted to enforce or encourage a resumption of the linkage between these two, apparently complementary, British industries, but such actions as it took were mainly directed towards the secondary problems mentioned above.

Before developing these themes, however, it is first necessary to establish the nature and extent of the relative decline of British shipbuilding in the post-war period.

1   Relative decline

The most direct and straightforward measure of the relative decline in British shipbuilding is provided by the trend in the UK share of world shipbuilding output. In 1930, just over half of the additions to the world's merchant fleet had been built in Britain, and even in 1950, Britain still remained easily the world's largest producer, accounting for nearly 40 per cent of world output. The succeeding quarter-century saw a dramatic decline which, from 1955 onwards, is recorded in table 19. From being the leading producer, the UK industry declined to such an extent that it occupied a marginal position. As the table shows, by the mid-1970s the UK's share in world tonnage had dropped to less than 4 per cent. (*Lloyd's Register* is the source for many of the figures and calculations which appear in the text.)

The decline did not, however, represent a collapse in British output. In absolute terms, the annual production of UK yards in the 1970s was much the same as it had been in the 1950s – a little over 1·2m tons gross compared to a little over 1·3m tons gross in the earlier period. The UK's dramatic relative decline resulted from the fact that whilst its own output was static, that of the rest of the world was rising sharply. The long world trading boom from the 1950s until the early 1970s necessarily required an expanded world fleet. Between 1955 and 1975, the annual world shipbuilding output rose from about 5m gross tons to 36m gross tons, an average rate of increase of about 10 per cent per annum.

TABLE 19   *UK and world output 1955–1977*

Year	UK launchings		World launchings		UK as % of world launchings	
	No.	Tons gross	No.	Tons gross	No.	Tons gross
					%	%
1955	276	1,473,937	1,437	5,314,850	19·2	27·7
1956	275	1,383,387	1,815	6,670,218	15·2	20·7
1957	260	1,413,701	1,950	8,501,404	13·3	16·6
1958	282	1,401,980	1,936	9,269,983	14·6	15·1
1959	274	1,372,595	1,808	8,745,704	15·2	15·7
1960	253	1,331,491	2,020	8,356,444	12·5	15·9
1961	247	1,191,758	1,990	7,940,005	12·4	15·0
1962	187	1,072,513	1,901	8,374,754	9·8	12·8
1963	160	927,649	2,001	8,538,513	8·0	10·9
1964	179	1,042,576	2,147	10,263,803	8·3	10·2
1965	158	1,073,074	2,280	12,215,817	6·9	8·8
1966	166	1,084,299	2,561	14,307,202	6·5	7·6
1967	149	1,297,678	2,778	15,780,111	5·4	8·2
1968	134	898,159	2,798	16,907,743	4·8	5·3
1969	136	1,039,516	2,819	19,315,290	4·8	5·4
1970	130	1,237,134	2,700	21,689,513	4·8	5·7
1971	126	1,238,692	2,645	24,859,701	4·8	5·0
1972	125	1,233,412	2,561	26,714,386	4·9	4·6
1973	125	1,017,665	2,884	31,520,373	4·3	3·2
1974	113	1,281,214	2,854	34,624,410	4·0	3·7
1975	128	1,304,097	2,632	35,897,515	4·9	3·6
1976	120	1,341,274	2,471	31,046,859	4·9	4·3
1977	89	1,119,222	2,549	24,167,025	3·5	4·6

Source: *Lloyd's Register Annual Summary of Merchant Ships Launched.*

For a time in the 1950s it could be claimed that Britain's relative decline was not obvious. The sellers' market concealed any weaknesses and full order books encouraged complacency: as late as

1957, UK order books stood at 4·4m tons, or more than three years' normal output. The apparent security of the order books was, as was soon to be shown, deceptive. But there were already other warning signals. The continental yards were being rebuilt and expanded. During the 1950s, indeed, a whole series of countries – Sweden, Holland, France, the USA, Denmark, Belgium and Norway – all more or less doubled their output (DSIR Report, 1960, p. 3). At the same time West Germany and Japan also re-entered the industry.

The effects of these developments on the British industry were soon evident. There was a substantial recession in world shipbuilding from 1958 to about 1963. The UK shipbuilding industry suffered disproportionately. The orders melted away and the decline in output was more prolonged for British yards. In 1963, for the first time since the war, output fell below 1m gross tons. Shipbuilding was a capital goods industry which was everywhere more susceptible than most other industries to fluctuations in trade, but the British industry was clearly particularly susceptible.

The context within which this failing performance was taking place was one which saw vast shifts in the location of world shipbuilding activity. From 1950 to 1980, the centres of major production moved, first, away from Western Europe and towards Japan, and then tended to be attracted towards newly developing countries such as Brazil and South Korea. These changes help to explain part of the UK experience.

During the early 1950s, the industry was mostly concentrated in Western Europe whose yards accounted for some 80 per cent of world output. At that time the main challenge to British shipbuilders came from Sweden and West Germany. Japan, however, experienced a growth which was characteristically meteoric. Already by 1956, it was the first country to surpass the UK in terms of absolute output. In 1950, the Japanese had produced 350,000 gross tons: by 1975, this had reached nearly 18m gross tons, an average rate of increase of over 16 per cent per annum. By the mid-1970s, the Japanese, as the British had done four decades earlier, accounted for about half of the world's annual output.

The 1970s saw signs of a further modification in the locational structure of world shipbuilding with the emergence of developing and East European (COMECON) countries as significant ship producers (BS Report, 1977, p. 8). These countries doubled their output between 1971 and 1976 from 2½m to 5m gross tons, and this accounted for 14 per cent of world production. About 40 per cent of this growth came from Brazil and South Korea. The latter country, which had built virtually nothing before 1970, launched nearly 700,000 gross tons of merchant shipping in 1976. In this context, the relative decline of the British industry can be seen as unavoidable and readily understandable. Any comfort which might be contained in such a conclusion is, however, largely dissipated when the British experience is compared to that of other Western European producers. In face of the broad locational shifts, all the countries of Western Europe were losers in proportional terms, but in making accommodation to the changes the British industry did especially badly.

Such a judgment is not difficult to demonstrate. It emerges clearly from a comparison between Britain and the individual performance of two of her major European competitors, Sweden and West Germany. Sweden's market share fell from nearly 10 per cent in 1955 to 7·7 per cent in 1976 but between the same years, launchings increased from 526,000 gross tons to nearly 2·4m gross tons. Similarly, West Germany's fall in market share from 17·5 per cent to 5·8 per cent in the same period disguised an increase in launchings from 900,000 gross tons to 1·8m gross tons (calculated from figures in Lloyds). Each of these countries had, like Britain, suffered a loss in overall market share: but each of them had, unlike Britain, managed to increase the absolute volume of their output in an expanding world market.

It is still more instructive to compare Britain with Western Europe as a whole. The output of the EEC countries declined during the recession of the early 1960s and did not surpass its 1958 level until 1969, but there was then quite rapid growth in the early 1970s in Germany, France, Denmark and the Netherlands. At the same time the progression of the non-EEC countries – principally Norway, Sweden and Spain – was much smoother, growing from 1·2m gross tons in 1959 to 5m gross tons in 1975. For Western Europe as a whole (excluding the UK) market share between 1950 and 1976 fell only from 40 to 35 per cent, whilst output during the same period quadrupled to 12m gross tons (BS Report, 1977, p. 8).

The striking fact which emerges is that no other major ship-building nation failed to increase its absolute output. In an overall market which expanded seven-fold in the two decades after 1955, the British industry was unique in that it not only lost its market share but it also failed to expand its absolute level of output.

2   Changing patterns of demand

Britain fared so badly partly because there were enormous changes in the types of ships which were demanded. More precisely, the problem was the relative inability of British builders to accommodate to these changes. To some extent the fortunes of the major shipbuilding nations varied with the degree to which they adapted their industry to the dramatic alterations in the type of product being demanded. This section will outline the major demand shifts as a prelude to an attempt, in the following sections, to explain why the adjustments in the British industry were so little and so late.

The most spectacular changes were dictated by the needs of world trade. In 1950, seaborne trade totalled just 50m tonnes; by 1970, it had leapt to 2,444m tonnes; and a decade later still it had increased by a further 50 per cent to 3,632m tonnes. Its constitution was also sharply altered. In 1950, 40 per cent was accounted for by the carriage of oil and a further 10 per cent by other bulk commodities. By 1970, 50 per cent was accounted for by oil and a further 25 per cent by other bulk cargoes, and this total of three-quarters of all seaborne trade in the form of bulk cargoes remained broadly true in 1980.

Two features thus stand out very clearly. There was an enormous increase in the volume of ocean cargoes, and the traffic in bulk cargoes had grown even faster than seaborne trade as a whole. Not surprisingly, the main shift in demand took the form of increased requirement for bulk carrier ships and tankers. In 1950, bulk carriers were virtually unknown, but by 1980, the world fleet of this type of vessel stood at 189m dwt (dead-weight tonnes). In the same period the tanker fleet rocketed from 29m to 330m dwt. It was not only the aggregate tonnage of this type of vessel which increased: the size of individual vessels was also transformed. Thus the tankers, ore and other bulk carriers of the 1980s were very different ships from their counter-parts of a generation earlier. In the inter-war years, nearly all of the market for ships had fallen into one of two basic classes: dry-cargo vessels of up to 10,000 dwt and oil tankers of up to 15,000 dwt.

Ship size was the most dramatic area of change, and it was given its most spectacular expression in the production of tankers. A trend already under way was given impetus by the first Suez crisis in 1956. Tanker operators shipping oil from the Persian Gulf to Europe were forced to contemplate the alternative route around the Cape. The longer journey suggested that an increase in ship size was required if the overall cost per ton of oil was not to rise substantially. Moreover, the spectacularly increasing volume of this trade reinforced the logic of this argument. Thereafter tanker size grew by quantum leaps (Ross Belch, 1970; Corlett, 1981 gives much basic information on changing ship types).

In 1955, the common oil tanker size was 32,000 dwt, and tankers already constituted nearly 60 per cent of the world shipping tonnage launched each year. By 1959, the first 100,000 dwt tanker had been built and the combination of increasing technological capabilities and economic pressures soon led to the introduction of very large and ultra-large crude carriers (VLCCs and ULCCs). The 200,000 dwt barrier was breached in 1965, and 300,000 dwt in 1968. By the end of 1969, there were 63 vessels of over 200,000 dwt in oil service. By the mid-1970s, the largest tanker size had exceeded half a million dwt.

Similar developments occurred in the closely related field of ore and bulk carriers. In general, however, the process here was much more restrained because of the disappointing experience with larger vessels in terms of cost and safety. Indeed, so far as straightforward carriers were concerned opinion by the mid-1970s seemed to have swung against the very large vessels. Large bulk carriers of up to 150,000 dwt had been built, but these monsters were becoming uncommon. The typical bulk carrier of the 1970s was a much smaller vessel of about 36,000 dwt. In addition there had always been a considerable market in Europe for small ore carriers of around 20,000 dwt, and this demand was maintained.

The most striking development in the bulk trade, however, came in the form of a completely new ship type, the combined carrier, which emerged to meet the need to make fuller use of ships which tended otherwise to make only one leg of a voyage fully loaded. There was a succession of types. First, oil-ore carriers and then oil-bulk-ore (OBO) carriers, followed in the 1970s by the PROBOs (product-oil-bulk-ore). In 1955 the largest combined carrier was an oil-ore vessel of 55,000 dwt: by 1970, there were OBOs on order of a quarter of a million dwt. In practice, however, the gains in flexibility proved to be more elusive than expected and the average size of these combined carriers had stabilised by the mid-1970s around 100,000 dwt.

The third main shipping type was the multi-purpose cargo vessel. These ships had once dominated world shipping (and continued to dominate British shipbuilding). The growth in the demand for them was much less marked in the post-war period. The world fleet of multi-purpose cargo vessels aggregated 100m dwt in 1960 and made what was in relative terms merely a steady rise to 143m dwt in 1980.

Partly because of this, and partly because the nature of their usage did not encourage such a development, multi-purpose cargo vessels did not undergo spectacular increases in ship size. The changes that took place were subtler but, in many respects, more significant. In this product type the key innovations were determined by new methods of cargo handling. Miscellaneous dry cargo had traditionally been handled by the 'break-bulk' method: invidi- dual items were packed, crated and warehoused at the docks before being slung into a vessel's hold where they were stowed by stevedores. The system was extremely labour-intensive and also led to ships spending about half their time in ports serving as inefficient warehouses. In the post-war period, the 'break-bulk' method was increasingly superseded by the container method. Under this system, shippers now packed their goods into standard-sized containers which could be handled by mechanised equipment at the docks. Where the port facilities could be provided, the advantages of containers were substantial: in particular they required much less labour, reduced damage and cut down the time spent in port. By the late-1960s, the shipping industry was almost wholly committed to the so-called 'container revolution' (Rochdale, 1970, para. 360).

The post-war period also saw the proliferation of a variety of new specialised vessel types. These emerged from a need to adapt vessels to meet specific requirements relating to methods of loading, or to particular cargoes or purposes. Obviously, the specific need had to be of a sufficient scale to justify the development of a specialised vessel, but this criterion was met by a wide range of shipping services. The result was the emergence of roll-on/roll-off ships, barge carriers, liquefied gas carriers, LASH ships, heavy-lift ships, dynamically positionable drilling ships, pan-type cable ships, cement carriers, parcel tankers, car carriers and other ferry ships and a variety of multi-purpose vessels. Many of these were complicated, sophisticated and expensive vessels.

3 The British response

The changing patterns of the demand for ships presented shipbuilders with challenges and opportunities. In output terms, the opportunities were most marked in the case of oil tankers. World output rose from less than 5 million gross tons in 1958, when tankers accounted for just half of total world tonnage, to a peak of nearly 23m gross tons in 1975, when tankers represented two-thirds of the total. The most successful supplier in this market was Japan. Between 1958 and 1975, Japan's share of tanker output rose from 25 to 56 per cent, while that of the UK fell from 12 to 2·6 per cent, the latter percentage representing the building of 10 ships out of the 401 completed.

Big tankers were, of course, a Japanese speciality, but it is significant that British shipbuilders were less successful than many other non-Japanese producers. In 1975, seven other countries besides Japan had a higher market share of tankers than Britain and all of these had, unlike Britain, increased their absolute output since 1958. Moreover, a traditional competitor like West Germany was markedly more successful in developing the new, larger vessels. Out of 108 tankers exceeding 100,000 grt, completed in 1975, 61 were built in Japan and 10 in West Germany. The UK supplied 3, the same number as Norway, Italy and South Korea.

The other sector where large ships were developed was the market for bulk carriers. In 1975, the UK accounted for just over 6 per cent of total bulk carrier tonnage, behind Japan, Spain and Poland. In the general cargo sector, the UK share of world output fell from around 20 per cent in 1958 to 6 per cent in 1975. By that time Japan (35 per cent), the two Germanies, Spain and Poland each had a larger share of the market.

The decline in the UK share of the market for general cargo vessels was less marked than the fall in its share of the market for oil tankers. But not much consolation could be derived from this fact. Since general cargo vessels had been the traditional specialisation of British shipbuilders, the industry should have been better placed to defend its position. A more pertinent consideration was that this sector was, in any event, of declining relative importance. Only 8 per cent of total world shipbuilding output in 1975 was accounted for by traditional general cargo vessels. Finally, the UK lagged in the specialised sections of the market. Thus between 1972 and 1977, only 7 of the 233 completed container ships were built in UK yards, and of 391 liquefied gas and chemical carriers which were completed only 15 were built in the UK.

The supply response which the British shipbuilding industry made to the changed structure of demand was discouraging. It was particularly worrying that the British response was poor relative to that of nearly all her competitors, and that British builders were unsuccessful in *all* the new market sectors which were opening up.

4 Why so poor?

The changes in the types of vessel which were being demanded brought with them new production possibilities. In this new situation, success was partly determined by the ability to adapt: the countries which did well were those which resolved the technical problems involved in building the new types of vessel.

The most clear-cut opportunities for developing new production techniques were related to the emergence, as the dominant product type, of increasingly large but relatively unsophisticated vessels. The essence of the new technology was to replace the traditional 'keel-up' assembly by the method of 'block construction' which involved the prefabrication of each component construction unit at the dock-side before it was welded into position. This was a capital-intensive technology for fabricating steel plates into relatively simple structures. It was, however, developed and applied with great sophistication by the Japanese, who gained a significant cost advantage stemming from three sources. First, the optimum block size was engineered to fit a standardised mass-production system, secondly, construction proceeded in parallel, and finally, the fittings for each block were pre-installed, thus reducing outfitting time at the end of the production cycle (Shinto, 1968a; Harrison, 1980).

The new production technique carried with it two significant implications. It favoured new green-field sites and was thus best exploited by those national industries which were able, or were sufficiently flexible, to move to such sites. In this respect, it was noticeable that the Japanese, under pressure from newer shipbuilding industries in developing countries, were beginning in the 1970s to move some operations away from traditional sites in Tokyo Bay and Osaka to less industrialised parts of Japan, preferably parts with plenty of labour. The second implication was that this method of shipbuilding did not depend on traditional shipbuilding crafts. The myths about the necessity for long apprenticeships, traditional methods and inherited skills were swept aside as large purpose-built shipyards were commissioned in Spain, Singapore, Portugal, Greece, South Korea and Brazil. Large sums were spent on building new yards or green field sites to use low-wage, non-union labour (Venus, 1972; Harrison, 1980).

It was inescapable that none of these developments was favourable to Britain and that accounts for much of Britain's relative decline in this sector. It is not, however, a sufficient explanation. The new technology put all the established European shipyards at a comparative disadvantage. But some, notably in Sweden and West Germany, adopted appropriate facilities and techniques at a fairly early stage. A particularly notable development was the building, from scratch, of a 'ship factory' at Arendal in Sweden in the early 1960s, with the explicit aim of reducing building costs by combining prefabrication with cover and flow production (Stuart, 1959). There were also developments in the UK. Scott Lithgow, for example, made an ingenious attempt to circumvent the restrictions imposed by the lack of green-field sites and an inadequate launching area by developing a process of building ships in two separate parts and joining them afloat. Other developments included covered building halls at Pallion, Sunderland, and at Cammell Laird, as well as a brand new covered shipbuilding dock at Appledore in Devon. But such adjustments, being completed in the mid-1970s, were very late in Britain.

In general, however, the yards of northern Europe were unlikely to regain any sort of dominance in the building of these simpler structures. A much more promising strategy for them was to adapt to the other broad change in the demand for shipping: the demand for more specialised vessels. These were altogether more sophisticated structures and their production required high-value components and more skilled labour. They could thus be expected to remain, for a while, out of reach of the skills and technical knowledge of the newer producers. But in these areas, too, the UK yards were less successful than those of countries like West Germany, France and Norway. It was noticeable that countries like France and West Germany remained reasonably prominent in the markets for these more specialised ships and that for these West European countries the building of such specialised vessels had become a significant part of their total output. In 1977, for example, the completion of nine gas and chemical carriers represented 47 per cent of the total output of the French industry, and fourteen container vessels accounted for one-fifth of the West German tonnage.

Even our very rapid survey clearly reveals that the British industry for a long time did not participate in the building of large tankers and bulk carriers and that much of this was understandable and probably unavoidable. But it also shows the British industry's failure to maintain its position in the general cargo sector and its inability to carve a significant niche for itself in the production of specialised ships. These developments strongly indicated that the industry had not made, or had inadequately made, the necessary adjustments in production.

Technological backwardness was reflected in a lack of price competitiveness by the British industry and, when the price gap was reduced, non-price characteristics such as poor delivery performance were a problem. The problems about price competitiveness had emerged as early as the late 1950s, when it was estimated that UK prices were anything between 10 and 40 per cent higher than the lowest prices quoted by foreign shipbuilders (DSIR Report, 1960, p. 6). By the early 1970s, large ships produced in UK yards were considerably more expensive than those produced by foreign competitors. There were, for example, differentials of over 20 per cent between the price of VLCCs from UK and Japanese yards and over 10 per cent between the prices of bulk carriers of 100,000 dwt (Booz-Allen, 1973, p. 74). Where price was not a problem, other difficulties emerged. Both the Geddes report in 1966 and the Booz-Allen report in 1973 found that UK prices were largely competitive with those of European yards, but British shipbuilders failed to match their European competitors (and the Japanese) in the speed and reliability of delivery. The industry was also losing its confidence in, and its reputation for, design and technical competence, particularly with respect to new ship types.

In looking for reasons for the poor investment record, various reports repeatedly analyse a number of problems most of which can be classified into two broad groups. The first of these relates to labour and management problems such as bad working practices, poor industrial relations and inept management. The second group relates to problems of structure and organisation such as the existence of too many small yards.[1] There is no doubt that these factors contributed to a lack of investment. Equally, there is no doubt that they were themselves exacerbated by the lack of investment. These chicken and egg conundrums tend to make the analysis and recommendations in the reports go round and round in an unsatisfying manner.

More specifically, we will argue that the official reports encouraged a concentration on symptoms. It is not denied that the factors enunciated were important. The clear implication of the analyses was that it would have practically been very difficult to solve the problem of technological backwardness through more investment. Given the existing workforce, management and industrial structure, the problems were not simply technical. But accepting all that, we would argue that any effort directed towards solving the problems of technological backwardness was bound to be frustrated if the customers were not there. The most serious problem, therefore, was the slow response of British shipbuilders to the general market situation. Fundamentally, the problem was the nature of the demand linkage between British shipowners and British shipbuilders which conditioned this slow response. In the next section it will be argued that this linkage induced and maintained the technological backwardness in shipbuilding, and also left the shipbuilding industry stranded when its main customers defected.

5 The demand linkage

Historically, UK shipbuilding had been closely related to the UK registered fleet.[2] Throughout the difficult inter-war period, the industry was able to maintain its dominant world position by the servicing of a large domestic fleet with a product which remained relatively basic in type and size. The UK fleet, despite a decline in absolute size, was in 1939 still twice as large as its nearest competitor (the USA) and accounted for approaching a third (27 per cent) of total world tonnage. At the same time, UK shipbuilders produced one-third (34 per cent) of annual world output.

The close relationship persisted in the post-war period, and table 20 provides basic data on two characteristics of this relationship. The first characteristic is the proportion of UK ships which were UK built. This showed a definite but gradual decline until the mid-1960s when it fell away catastrophically: thus a period in which British shipowners gently loosened their link with home-builders was followed by a rapid shift to a situation in which the link was substantially severed. The *decline* in this proportion was disastrous for British shipbuilders. The second characteristic is the proportion of the output of British yards which was built for British owners. This remained high throughout, indicating that although British shipowners were now placing most of their orders elsewhere, the dwindling proportion which they continued to place at home still constituted the bulk of the demand for British shipbuilders. The *stability* of this proportion was disastrous for British shipbuilders, especially as behind it was a fundamental instability in the absolute level of orders (table 21).

TABLE 20   *UK output built for UK registration*

Year	As % of total UK registrations	As % of UK output
1958	78·9	75·9
1959	73·7	91·6
1960	71·8	89·0
1961	64·1	76·4
1962	61·5	84·6
1963	59·5	69·4
1964	79·3	85·7
1965	76·1	87·3
1966	61·9	71·7
1967	42·0	44·8
1968	17·4	47·1
1969	23·4	63·0
1970	38·9	85·4
1971	25·8	68·2
1972	23·4	70·0
1973	16·4	67·1
1974	25·0	79·7
1975	27·7	70·2
1976	48·2	69·1

Source: Lloyd's Register Annual Summary of Merchant Ships Launched.

TABLE 21 *Ships launched for registration in UK*

Year	Ships launched[a] in UK for registration in UK		World ships launched[a] for registration in UK	
	No.	Tons gross	No.	Tons gross
1958	229	1,064,112	266	1,349,493
1959	235	1,257,143	278	1,706,216
1960	226	1,185,596	266	1,650,577
1961	207	911,025	239	1,420,422
1962	160	907,621	190	1,476,831
1963	126	643,995	153	1,082,351
1964	144	893,539	159	1,126,409
1965	132	936,851	160	1,230,878
1966	128	777,328	152	1,256,608
1967	100	580,756	147	1,383,086
1968	94	423,089	158	2,431,876
1969	100	654,870	167	2,797,550
1970	115	1,051,580	184	2,703,133
1971	92	844,307	182	3,272,693
1972	100	863,277	219	3,696,939
1973	95	683,068	188	4,176,126
1974	87	954,428	162	3,813,362
1975	83	820,907	156	2,961,881
1976	97	1,036,067	167	2,148,320

Source: Lloyd's Register Annual Summary of Merchant Ships Launched.

[a] Figures for 1958–173 are of ships launched; for 1974–1976 of ships completed. This change does not significantly affect the continuity of the series.

The effect of these trends was softened by the fact that the absolute amount of the orders for new shipping placed by British shipowners was rising quite strongly. Total annual launchings for registration in the UK between 1958 and 1973 more than trebled from 1·3 to 4·2m grt, but the home share of these launchings fell from 1·1 to 0·7m grt, and the reduced business still constituted over two-thirds of the business of British shipbuilders. The changing composition of the home fleet partly explains why the proportion of it which was built in home yards fell so markedly. Of the overall increase in the UK fleet tonnage between 1950 and 1975, 90 per cent was accounted for by tankers. By the mid-1970s the UK had the world's largest tanker fleet and over one-third of the tonnage was made up of vessels of 110,000 grt plus which were less than five years old. Between 1966 and 1971 over 85 per cent of the UK tanker tonnage was built in foreign yards.

The position was similar in both the bulk carrier and the special-ised vessel sectors. The UK fleet had comparatively few large bulk carriers in the mid-1960s, but a decade later, just over one-quarter of total UK tonnage consisted of ore and bulk carriers. For specialised vessels, a detailed study of new ship registrations for the period from July 1974 to April 1976 indicated that 97 per cent of gas and chemical tonnage and 84 per cent of passenger and ferry boat tonnage was built overseas. It was equally significant that the same study identified Japan as being a major supplier only for bulk carriers (35 per cent) and tankers (27 per cent). The major supply source was Europe which provided 45 per cent of the tanker tonnage and all the gas and chemical carriers, and passenger and ferry ships, which were built overseas (ASB, 1977; and APEX, 1977). The one partial exception to this trend was the non-bulk dry cargo sector where the UK was traditionally strong: 63 per cent of the tonnage was still home-built.

Thus by the mid-1970s the link between shipowners and shipbuil-ders still survived but only in the form of continued dependence of British shipbuilders on British shipowners. The emergence of this one-way dependence can be largely explained by the nature of the traditional link. This had always been informal, a matter of 'custom and practice'. It was based on personal ties and conventional behaviour, rather than on the kind of organic or structural connec-tions which would have resulted from shipowners integrating back-wards into shipbuilding, or shipbuilders integrating forwards into shipowning. The implications of this informality for the two sides were, however, markedly different (Jones, 1957).

The way in which the relationship grew up customarily left the shipowner to decide upon the nature and size of his requirements for new tonnage and then to approach individual yards for quotations. British shipowners were, moreover, unusual in maintaining sizeable technical departments which tended to specify requirements in considerable detail. The system had important consequences for shipbuilders. It discouraged them from planning the development of their activities much beyond current contracts. It discouraged them from pursuing standardisation and developing a special line of ships, since their main customers exhibited a strong preference for themselves designing ships to meet their own individual needs. It tended to turn the shipbuilders into 'jobbers' for part of their activities. Shipbuilders developed a pride in their ability to meet the differing needs of particular owners. Their attachment to this bespoke trade was deepened by a fear of relying too heavily on producing a single standardised type of vessel, and by the common form of contract under which ships were constructed for the cost of labour, materials and establishment charges, plus a fixed profit margin of around 10 per cent. The process also encouraged the continuation of a large number of relatively small yards and independent companies. It also discouraged investment because any substantial changes, besides being risky, would also disrupt production schedules. It was not a system which was primarily aimed at improving efficiency and productivity.

None the less, the long survival of the system indicated that it worked reasonably well. It gave the shipowners the vessels they wanted, and the yards had close links with a major set of customers (table 22). There was, however, a fatal flaw. If the shipowners decided that they wanted a different product that builders could not provide, then they could look elsewhere. In the mid-1960s, there was just such a large, and relatively sudden, acceleration in the tendency for British shipowners to look elsewhere. This was partly because the oil companies, which owned British registered ships mostly to carry their own produce, were increasingly turning to larger ship sizes. These 'merchant operator' companies, most of which were ultimately owned by foreign multi-nationals, had always had fewer and looser links with British yards, but the effect of their 'footloose' behaviour was becoming more marked because they were a fast-growing part of the 'home' fleet. In the mid-1960s, the traditional UK shipowning sector was also suddenly conscious of the need to secure larger ships and ships suitable to perform more specialist functions. For these they went to foreign builders as British yards could not compete in price and delivery and, in many cases, in basic capability.

The inability to compete reflected lower efficiency and productivity, but it was also crucially caused by the previous links with British shipowners. For many shipbuilders the link had become so central to their enterprise calculations that it was no longer much noticed. A substantial part of their equipment, technique and practice was, indeed, specifically adapted to the needs of British

TABLE 22   *Shipbuilding orders placed in UK yards by UK owners 1963–1975*

Year	Thousand grt	As % of total orders
1963	1,271	83·5
1964	841	87·5
1965	678	38·3
1966	314	65·1
1967	971	90·2
1968	1,452	56·6
1969	1,721	81·2
1970	1,449	81·9
1971	833	81·1
1972	599	71·4
1973	3,721	85·4
1974	331	38·4
1975	43	64·2

Source: British Shipping Statistics 1973, 1975. Chamber of Shipping of the UK (from 1975, The General Council of British Shipping).

shipowners. The links had encouraged British yards to develop in ways which were not appropriate to meet the changed needs of their major customers. The links had also allowed a looser control over costs. Thus British shipbuilders were ill-equipped to meet these *new* demands by British shipowners partly because they were so committed to meeting the *old* demands of British shipowners.

What did the government do to assist the industry to negotiate this awkward corner?

6   The contribution of government

The involvement of the government effectively starts in the 1960s. Before that date there had been surprisingly little government activity. Policies like the 'scrap and build' scheme in the 1930s (which had explicitly recognised the link between shipbuilding and shipowning) did not survive the dismantling of high wartime activity, and the main relevant government scheme of the 1950s was a modest one giving some post-delivery mortgage finance for ships built in British yards. From the early 1960s, however, there was a rapid escalation. In the space of a decade and a half, there was a transformation from almost no direct government activity to the statutory nationalisation of the industry. Our contention is that a great deal of this activity was misdirected because of its neglect of the vital issue of demand linkages, both for the British industry and for its foreign competitors. We will attempt to demonstrate this contention by a brief examination of the Geddes report and of the course taken by government policies.[3] (Hogwood, 1979 is the essential source for relations between the industry and government.)

It is generally acknowledged that the 1966 Geddes report was the most influential of the various official and semi-official inquiries of these years. The pattern of its analysis was not significantly departed from, and many of its proposals were given almost immediate legislative force by the Shipbuilding Industry Act of 1967. Essentially the report identified the basic *need* to establish an industry which would be competitive in a world market which was presumed to be open to all; for Geddes, the main *obstacles* were internal to the industry. Underlying the whole approach, therefore, was the assumption that the market existed and that greater exploitation of it was prevented only by internal failings.

The problems surrounding this concept of the open world market will be returned to later. For the moment it only needs to be noticed that the committee's acceptance of this concept enabled it to reject the view that British shipbuilding should largely rely on British shipowners for orders. The rejection was further reinforced by the committee's forecast of the nature of the demand. Geddes did not consider that it was necessary for the British industry to follow the trend towards investing to build large tankers, because 'the world demand for ships below 150,000 tons deadweight would seem likely to provide ample opportunity for the industry to develop and expand' (Geddes, 1966, para. 99). Moreover, it characterised the demand for the more sophisticated, specialised vessels as being 'relatively static' and whilst reasonably asserting that such a demand would be a 'small proportion of the total market for ships' went on to forecast, less reasonably, 'that this proportion will decline' (Geddes, 1966, para. 96). The judgment was perhaps not surprising since passenger liners were the only type of specialised vessel that Geddes mentioned. Each of these forecasts reduced the urgency of the need for the industry to adjust to the changes in demand towards greater size among some types of vessels, and greater specialisation in other types. The report, moreover, reached its conclusions just as British shipowners were accelerating their moves in these directions.[4]

The prescriptions of the Geddes report concentrated on the need to restructure the industry through the grouping of yards. The larger groups would bring the British industry more into line with its international competitors and would make possible economies in the use of some resources. But grouping was also, perhaps mainly, seen as the means by which the industry could best tackle its other internal problems of poor management, weak industrial relations and inflexible working practices. The groups would be big enough to cater for a variety of jobs but allow yards within the group to specialise on a particular kind of job. It was also recognised that the industry would need financial assistance to make these changes, but the amount and direction of this was to depend on the extent and pace of the changes made by the industry (Parkinson, 1968).

These broad outlines of the Geddes analysis guided government policy-making well into the 1970s. There were modifications. Thus the Shipbuilding Industry Board (SIB, set up in 1967 in response to Geddes) corrected the Geddes view about the significance of size for tankers and steered investment by British yards into a capability to build supertankers: it was unfortunate that much of this capacity appeared in the mid-1970s, when the oil crises had induced extreme nervousness in the market for such vessels. It was more significant that what was maintained was the Geddes emphasis on the difficulties of the industry being caused almost entirely by its own internal problems.

In the event, Geddes proved an inadequate guide for dealing with these internal problems. On restructuring, the report indicated some broad criteria (geographical areas, output, size, etc.) and entered into considerable detail about the three types of specialised yards which should be contained within each group. But there was no specification of which yards should be grouped nor any attempt to quantify the gains which might be expected from various possible combinations. Inheriting this approach, the SIB seems not to have pressed or initiated mergers or takeovers which it considered desirable, but to have sought to persuade firms of the general desirability of grouping and then largely accepted what came up. In addition, no positive basis was provided for better management. It was simply hoped that with regrouping, management would reform itself. The strategy for labour improvements was similarly unspecified because although the report spent some time on examining these, no effective mechanism was suggested for implementation of its findings.

A great deal of restructuring did take place and it happened quite quickly. But the changes effected by 1969, though substantial, only loosely followed either the general (output, labour force size, area, etc.) or the particular (number and types of yards) criteria identified by Geddes. Among other effects, this increased the costs involved in regrouping, especially as the administrative problems and the disruption to production were greater than had been expected. The SIB thus found itself providing more money less discriminately than had been anticipated. The situation was further exacerbated by the misfortune that the period of the late 1960s and early 1970s saw a steady acceleration in inflation, when many builders had taken on fixed-price contracts.

Financial assistance intended to make a major reorganisation more effective was often diverted to ease severe and immediate liquidity problems. There was a sharp deterioration in the liquidity position of many shipbuilding companies from the late 1960s. A sample of nine companies had had available a positive fund of £11m for working capital in 1967; by 1971 the current liabilities of the same companies exceeded their current assets by £11m (Booz-Allen, 1973, p. 179).

Between 1967 and 1971, governments provided £160m in assistance exclusively for the shipbuilding industry, but only one-third of this was devoted to capital expenditure. Moreover, most of this capital expenditure went to just three companies – Harland and Wolff, UCS and Cammell Laird – in which the government had invested (SIB, 1972; Booz-Allen, 1973, pp. 88, 179, 182). This (together with the fact that two-thirds of the £10m paid out by the SIB as 'General Purposes' went to Harland and Wolff and UCS) suggested that the funds were being used for purposes other than restructuring (Harland and Wolff was an ungrouped yard). Government aid increasingly departed from the measured and limited course laid down by Geddes. It was also increasingly diverted to meet such needs as the protection of employment in the depressed regions where most of the shipyards were situated. Indeed, government aid continued in a steady flow for the remainder of the industry's 'private' life as what had been intended as assistance to compete became assistance to survive.

The other main financial steps taken by the government related to the provision of credit facilities for the industry and investment grants to shipowners. From the early 1960s, credit facilities were progressively extended. In 1961, an arrangement was reached under which the banks provided export credit for all goods, including ships, at a fixed rate of 5½ per cent, a rate which by the end of the decade looked very attractive. The effect was to give foreign owners buying in Britain access to credit facilities which were not available to British shipowners ordering from home yards. On the other hand, the terms were still not as generous as British shipowners could often get by buying from foreign yards. In recognition of this problem, the government, when it became concerned at the low level of home orders placed by British shipowners, announced in May 1963 that funds would be available for a short period at the government lending rate to finance new orders from British shipowners (Midland Bank Review, 1969).

In general, however, the official view was still opposed to permanent credit arrangements specifically designed to assist British shipbuilding, and the Geddes committee took the same view. Geddes recommended that a fund with a ceiling of £30m should be created to provide credit assistance to keep up order books during the transitional period of reconstruction. In this respect, the actual provision radically departed from the Geddes recommendations both in the amounts and in the timespan over which they would be available. The 1967 Act set up a permanent credit scheme with a ceiling of £200m, which was successively raised and reached £1,000m by 1972. The loans were extended to British shipowners and related to any new building orders which they placed with UK yards. This was in several ways a positive step: it offered home shipowners funds on terms comparable (or better) than they could get overseas, and it recognised and encouraged the link between home shipowners and builders.

Unfortunately, a parallel scheme of investment grants for shipowners mostly offset the inducement effect of the credit arrangements. Under this scheme, which applied to orders placed from 1966 until 1970, an investment grant of between 20 and 25 per cent of the cost of the vessel was paid to UK owners regardless of where the ships were built. It also incorporated a loose interpretation of what constituted a UK shipowner and a number of 'foreigners' registered offices in Britain, the so-called 'brass plate' companies, to take advantage of the scheme (Hogwood, 1979, pp. 126–30). Most of the funds available under this scheme went abroad: in the decade up to 1977, cash grants of £609m were made available to

UK owners for the purchase of ships and 78 per cent of this was for vessels built in foreign yards. There was, to say the least, no consistent policy of encouraging British shipowners to place more of their orders for new ships with home yards.

Such an approach was, however, broadly consistent with the basic objective of Geddes: to make British shipbuilding competitive in the world market. By competitiveness Geddes meant an ability to win orders and sustain an expanding industry without any specific reliance on orders from British shipowners. Competitiveness in this sense was a self-evident necessity in the long run, but the seeming reasonableness of this aim ignores two considerations which were fundamental in the context of the shipbuilding industry in the mid-1960s. The first, which has already been mentioned, is the extent to which British shipbuilding had been shaped by the long traditional link with British shipowners. The second consideration questions Geddes's implied assumption that the world market was readily open to efficient producers. A great deal of the market for ships was for all practical purposes closed. Not only did many countries more consistently and single-mindedly offer credit and grant facilities to their own shipowners to use their own shipbuilders,[5] but these were in some cases reinforced by more direct practices such as licensing and flag discrimination. About one-third of the demand of the non-communist world for new vessels was not open to international competition (Booz-Allen, 1973, p. 64).

The significance of this can be illustrated from the Japanese experience. The successful development of Japanese shipbuilding naturally has many roots. It was partly based upon the identification of a market for relatively simple ship types of increasing size which could be built by mass production methods. This allowed cost reductions through economies in the use of labour and materials and the development of new technological methods. These possibilities were, however, also associated with the organisation of Japanese shipbuilding firms and their relationship with other sectors of the economy. The shipbuilding firm was typically an industrial division of a major company which linked the shipbuilding enterprise to related industries like steel, to shipowners, to banking interests and to the government. By the mid-1970s, for instance, the Mitsui-Mitsubishi-Hitachi combine linked shipbuilding to a variety of suppliers of steel, machinery and electrical equipment as well as itself controlling a shipowning and managing enterprise involving nearly five hundred ships totalling 15 million tons. The linkages were not only important internally; they could also be used to arrange complicated financial deals with overseas customers. These deals developed beyond a simple provision of credit. Japanese combines were prepared to participate in infra-structure develop- ment (the provision of ports and railways) in foreign countries, and also to take payment in kind as when ships were sold in Australia in return for iron ore (Broadbridge, 1966; Venus, 1972; ASB, 1977).

It was not only the combines, but the shipbuilding groups them- selves, which were on a large scale. The depressed market for world shipping in the late-1950s led to numerous mergers in Japanese shipbuilding (Shinto, 1968b), and these groups expanded yards or built new ones. In the mid-1960s, 70 per cent of Japanese launchings were accounted for by six groups with fourteen yards, each of which launched at least a quarter of a million tons a year (Geddes, 1966, para. 314). In 1965, the Nagasaki yard of Mitsubishi Heavy Indus- tries alone launched a tonnage equal to 60 per cent of the entire British output (Broadbridge, 1966). Japanese success, therefore, rested on industrial structure as well as on complicated inter- connections between manufacturing and finance capital.

It is particularly pertinent for our purposes, however, to notice the close links between Japanese shipbuilders and shipowners and the way in which these links were fostered by government action. For example, the post-war investment programmes of the shipbuil- ders were assisted by loans from the Japanese Development Bank. From 1947 to 1951, these loans helped finance the so-called 'shipbu- ilding programmes' and constituted over 90 per cent of total domestic demand, and from 1952 to 1955 they still involved more than half the domestic demand (Shinto, 1968b). In the mid-1960s, the government was supporting orders from Japanese shipowners to domestic yards which amounted to more than the entire British output. The relationship was reinforced by flag discrimination which reserved a certain proportion of Japan's international trade carriage to ships registered in Japan and also ensured that ships registered in the country were also built there. During the 1960s and 1970s, no new shipping tonnage for home registration was built abroad. Since the Japanese fleet had shot up from being the ninth largest in the world in 1962 to the second largest by the mid-1970s, this represented an enormously powerful linkage. Its effect was, moreover, reinforced by the fact that the expansion of the Japanese fleet was mostly accounted for by the acquisition of more tankers and bulk carriers to carry Japan's huge import trade in oil and raw materials. The needs of the fleet thus generated demand for the types of ship to which the domestic shipbuilding industry had become geared.

Against this background, then, we would contend that much of UK government policy was misdirected. It ignored the significance of the link between shipowners and shipbuilders. At home the link had effectively locked-in British shipbuilders, albeit very cosily, to cater for the particular requirements of UK shipowners. When these withdrew, as they were able to, in order to secure new types and sizes of ships, British shipbuilders were bound to be stranded for a time. But government action was not addressed to that problem. It aimed at getting the industry to leap into competition in a world market. Government policy also ignored the general operation of a linkage factor abroad. The fact was that no other shipbuilding nation serviced so small a proportion of its own fleet. In 1972, 70 per cent of the additions to the West German fleet were built in West German yards and the comparable proportions for Sweden, France and Denmark were 73, 80 and 83 per cent. Moreover, despite the Geddes presumption that dependence on the home fleet would undermine the industry's competitive ability, several of the countries which competed most successfully in the genuinely open world market were countries (like Japan) which had a secure base in their own home market. It is, of course, the case that an ability to compete abroad was essential and that the internal problems of the industry needed to be tackled, but in neglecting the strategic importance of demand linkage in the market for ships, government policy was rendered largely ineffective for such purposes.

Whatever the reasons, the overall context for the shipbuilding industry was one of general decline, which from the mid-1960s provoked a great deal of government activity which failed to stem that decline. The next section will provide some case studies to show how demand and government policy conditioned the calculations of individual enterprises.

7   Enterprise calculations

(a)   *Two miscalculations*

It has already been indicated that established European shipyards
were not well placed to undertake the production of the very big,
but relatively uncomplicated, tankers and bulk-cargo carriers. It
was sensible for such yards to move towards a greater concentration
on building the more specialised and sophisticated vessels, but
British shipbuilders by and large failed to do so. Among the many
reasons for this was the fact that Geddes totally ignored this market.
None the less, various attempts were made to develop along these
lines. Roll-on/roll-off ferries were, for example, partly developed in
Britain but their main commercial exploitation took place elsewhere
(Albu, 1980). The firm of Hawthorn Leslie represents another case
where an early identification and attempt to develop a market for
a specialised ship type foundered because of lack of support.

Hawthorn Leslie Shipbuilders was a small Tyne-based firm
constructing three or four ships a year when, about 1960, it was
forced to reconsider its position. The yard was unable to build
tankers over 50,000 dwt, but it was already clear that the future
demands of some of its major customers like Shell Tankers and BP
Tanker Company would be for larger ships. To adapt itself for
the production of larger vessels was considered impractical and
undesirable. The change would certainly have disrupted the continuity of work for some time and would also have involved a general
expansion in the size of the company. But the small size of the
company was seen as a source of several advantages, especially in
labour relations. The firm had managed to sustain a steady rhythm
of work and, employing only 2,000 men, it had successfully fostered
a reasonably communal spirit among the workforce.

If the company did not follow its customers in the trend towards
larger vessels, it would have to discover a different market. A greater
concentration on the construction of more sophisticated vessels was
determined upon. In particular, the company turned towards the
very new field of liquefied gas carriers. It was initially encouraged
to do so because of an inquiry from the National Coal Board (NCB).
The NCB wanted to produce gas in the Nottinghamshire coalfield,
but the gas needed to be enriched by propane which would be
imported from the US. The imports were to be made in two fully

refrigerated liquid petroleum gas carriers (LPGs), an entirely new type of vessel (Gray and Johnson, 1971).

Hawthorn Leslie were thus drawn into the field early. The company made exhaustive technical inquiries, especially in the US where the use of liquid propane gas for urban and industrial use was growing; these investigations were behind the company's design. The first order, from a French firm, was received in 1964 and followed by an order for two more by Pemex, the Mexican State oil company, to carry ammonia gas. There was also a parallel market for liquid natural gas carriers (LNGs). Hawthorn Leslie were, however, too small a firm to move simultaneously into this market and deliberately refrained from contracting for LNGs until 1968. By that year Hawthorn Leslie had merged with other ship-yards on the Tyne to form Swan Hunter (Shipbuilders) and it became possible to enter this field. Unfortunately the new company, because of technical problems in other sectors, was not ready to bid for a major contract offered by Shell involving six 100,000 ton LNG carriers in 1969–70 as part of its LNG project for Brunei (*Economist*, 29 September 1969). Soon afterwards, a possible order from Algeria for three LNG ships in 1971 failed to materialise and in 1974, the 'gas team' was broken up.

That decision was related to the extent of the commitment made by Swan Hunter to a recently acquired £250m contract for a quite different type of ship. In the event, as we argue below, Swan Hunter's confidence in that contract was disastrously mistaken. This was especially ironic when the withdrawal from the gas carrier market was made just at a time when LPG ship tonnage was about to quadruple. If the market had been mis-judged, British involvement also suffered from the lack of support and encouragement from British shipowners or authorities. The original NCB interest had collapsed because its scheme was in direct competition with a British Gas Council scheme to bring natural gas from the Sahara. The government had in 1961 decided in favour of the Gas Council which required LNGs which Hawthorn Leslie were not then able to build. In the mid-1960s, however, the Gas Council also withdrew its interest because of the development of the North Sea gas. All of this was understandable but unfortunate, especially as the first two LNGs to go into commercial service were built by Harland and Wolff, and Vickers. In this connection it is salutary to note that the very first order for a vessel of this type was placed in a Japanese yard by a Japanese shipowner wanting to carry propane to Japan from the Persian Gulf. It was also in marked contrast to the close co-operation between Gaz de France, the French shipowner (Gasocean) and French shipyards. From the solid base that was provided, French shipyards were able to obtain all the orders for Shell's Brunei LNG project.

In 1973, there was a big increase in shipbuilding orders stimulated by the boom in oil tanker charters. One shipowning company which was very active in this essentially speculative environment was an Israeli-based firm, Maritime Fruit Carriers. This company extended its operations from the ownership of refrigerated fruit carriers into the oil transport market and placed, in 1973 alone, orders worth over £300m in the three UK yards capable of making large ships. Six 330,000 tonners were ordered from Harland and Wolff, two 250,000 ton ships from Scott Lithgow and thirteen ships from Swan Hunter, with options on a further thirteen. This last order came to the firm because of a formal link between shipbuilder and shipowner. The order was placed by Swan Maritime, a company formed to sell ships to independent owners and to own and charter ships built by Swan Hunter which held a quarter of the shares (based on ASB, 1977, pp. 25–7; Hogwood, 1979, pp. 186–8; and *Observer*, 18 March 1973).

This development seemed to illustrate the beneficial possibilities of such linkages: an order worth £¼m had been channelled to a British shipbuilder through an associated shipowning company. The ultimate order came, however, from a different shipowner, Maritime Fruit Carriers, and in the mid-1970s it was said that '30 per cent of the ships on order in British yards are for MFC' (*Economist*, 7 February 1976). The value of the order, which had led Swan Hunter to abandon the market for liquid gas carriers, thus depended on how secure Maritime Fruit was, and on how well based the expectations were, on which the orders had been placed. There were doubts on each of these counts from the outset. It had been pointed out that Maritime Fruit was short of cash, that its recent profits might have stemmed substantially from windfall sources, and that MF gave little information about who was to charter the tankers when they were built. In such circumstances 'it seemed far from wise that the future of British yards should be so dependent on orders from one group' (*Observer*, 18 March 1973). The expectations on which the orders were based were also questionable. Maritime Fruit's intention was to sell many of the ships before launch and to buy and sell charter rights. The ambitious tanker shipbuilding programme was to be financed on the basis of the prospects of future income from the ships which were being built.

Such an operation aimed to exploit a situation where high charter fees were expected. Risk was necessarily involved, though this particular case seemed especially risky because of its scale, its attachment to a single insecure shipowning company and the extent to which it involved the shipbuilding yards concerned. Even so, the extent of the decline of the charter market with the beginnings of the oil-price rises in the last quarter of 1973 could not have been foreseen. The consequences were catastrophic, especially for the shipbuilders. By the end of 1974, nine of the thirteen options to build at Swan Hunter were cancelled as were three of the Harland and Wolff tankers, and by 1976 Maritime Fruit had collapsed totally.

The whole project was substantially backed by government funds, especially in the form of construction guarantees and investment grants. As it happened, not much was actually paid out by the government which, like the shipbuilders, had its losses limited by the fact that the oil crisis came so soon after the scheme was launched and before much construction got under way. It might reasonably be said that the commitment of government funds could have been fruitful. It could have fostered the kind of series ordering which could have lent a substantial boost to big-ship building in the UK. None the less it has to be said that the choice of occasion for such government activity was inept: moreover, even if it had worked, it would have been yet another illustration of the way in which government involvement was *ad hoc* and reactive. A constructive government policy might have aimed for a more positive and formal link between shipowners and shipbuilders.

(b) Getting it right

The concept of standard vessels is an old one. Such ships have satisfied a small but significant part of market requirements for many years, but in Britain, Austin and Pickersgill (A and P) became the leading post-war supplier of standard ships. This case study analyses how and why A and P specialised, and specifically examines how the decision to specialise was conditioned by A and P's link with a shipowning company.

The company made its first move into standardisation in 1960 when it identified a gap in the single-deck bulk carrier section of the British market. A policy decision was taken to prepare a number of preliminary designs and estimated prices for a standard range of bulk carriers, from 16,000 to 46,000 dwt, suitable for the company's existing shipyard facilities. Information on the whole range, together with price indications, was tabulated and circulated to owners. Shortly afterwards, the government loan scheme gave short-term encouragement to British owners to modernise their fleets through replacement. A and P were thus well placed to take advantage of the demand, especially as much of it consisted of orders for bulk carriers. Between 1962 and 1968, nineteen vessels were delivered, totalling over half a million tons. Most of those delivered were made to one basic design together with a few modifications to meet owners' requirements (Douglas, 1967, 1979).

A and P's policy developed into one of building only dry-cargo ships of the shelter-deck or multi-deck type and single-deck bulk carriers. They did not attempt to enter the markets either for tankers or for more specialised vessels. Their philosophy was expressed by the company's managing director in 1967:

> the variety of ships now in demand is such that no single shipyard can contemplate equipping and manning to the extent that it is able to take anything that comes along. . . . It is obviously a good policy for a shipbuilder to decide what class of ship best suits his yard, and to develop along this line. By specialising in certain types of ship, a yard ensures a greater possibility of obtaining repetitive orders, with the benefits which follow, and in addition on an industry basis a more rational balance can be achieved in meeting demand (Douglas, 1967, p. 13).

The company's aim at this stage was to repeat for general cargo vessels what it had done with its single-deck bulk carriers: identifying a market and designing a ship intended for series production. The company was also prompted by a decline in orders for the standard bulk-cargo vessel in the late 1960s. But in its quest for a standard general cargo vessel, the company was able to call upon an additional factor in the form of a link with a firm of shipowners.

A and P had had a direct link with a shipowning company since 1957 when London and Overseas Freighters (LOF) had taken a half-interest in A and P (and became sole owners in 1970). But LOF seems to have played no part at all, either through design suggestions or the placing of orders, in the development of the standard range of bulk carriers. Indeed, A and P hardly figured during this period in the building up of the fleets of the LOF group, which stated that the relationship 'was entirely at arms length and the directors of that company (A and P), which included the managing director of LOF, were left to run the affairs of the company without interference' (LOF Letter, 1981). None the less in the mid-1960s, the association was responsible for what is widely acclaimed to be the success story of post-war UK merchant shipbuilding, the SD14, a series built shelter-deck freighter of 14,000 dwt.

The SD14 was simultaneously an answer to A and P's particular problem and to the general need for some replacement for the ageing standard 'Liberty' ships which had been built during the Second World War. The fact that many ships of this type were still in service indicated that their replacement represented a substantial potential market. One of the first to offer a workable design and a basic specification for this purpose was A and P, and the link with LOF was decisive in the development of the design. The fundamental concept which became the SD14 originated in the London office of LOF. B. M. Mavroleon, chairman of LOF, took the view that the appearance and growth of the giant carriers – or 'ogres' as he called them – would only marginally affect 'the traditional, orthodox, handy ship (12,000–16,000 dwt)'. The demand for these smaller ships, although inevitably less economical from the charterer's point of view, 'would continue to persist even when the orgres were on the brink of laying up'. Mavroleon did not accept that most of the vast existing tramp tonnage would be replaced by large bulk carriers and that 'on the contrary, I believe that the greatest proportion of the ageing tramp tonnage will be replaced by traditional orthodox types' (Mavroleon, 1967, p. 21). He thus 'asked A and P to design a successor to the "Liberty" ships which could be built in series production and said that it should not cost more than £800,000' (Letter from LOF, 1981). He emphasised especially the need for simplicity and reliability.

Design studies instituted by A and P seemed to confirm the notion of a ship of about 14,000 dwt and 14 knots. To keep down costs 'many of the sophisticated ideas and practices which have developed over the post-war years' were jettisoned in favour of 'a simple and functional ship without frills designed for low-cost maintenance and operation' (Douglas, 1967, p. 14). The SD14 was presented as

> the least complicated of all the Liberty-replacements on offer. . . . It demands no special shore appliances and its draught permits it to go almost anywhere. . . . There are no gimmicks of any description that may require superior technological knowledge, either on board or ashore, and there are no untried auxiliaries or gear (Mavroleon, 1967, p. 21).

Orders began to come in from mid-1966 and the first ship to be delivered, in February 1968, went to a Mavroleon family company from Greece. At the beginning of 1970, LOF ordered four ships and at the same time Welsh Ore Carriers, a subsidiary of LOF, ordered an additional couple from A and P. Although these orders were said to be placed for 'sound commercial reasons and no other' (LOF, Letter, 1981), it was acknowledged that they also served as a demonstration of 'confidence in the shipyard and the SD14' (Sedgwick and Sprake, 1977, p. 12). As demand grew, other yards at home and abroad built SD14s under licence. By the end of 1979, over 200 of the ships had been built or were on order from A and P or its licensees with over 100 coming from Sunderland itself (Douglas, 1979). Its only significant competitor was the Japanese 'Freedom' cargo vessel of 14,800 dwt, of which 120 ships were built between 1967 and 1976 at Tokyo and Singapore (Kimber and Hargroves, 1977, p. 2). The market was big enough for both ships.

In 1973, A and P needed to overhaul its yards and conducted an appraisal to gauge the prospects for the two major 'standards', the B26 and SD14. 'The evidence clearly led to the conclusion that the SD14 . . . should have many years of marketing life remaining' (Kimber and Hargroves, 1977, p. 3). As a result of this, together with the fortuitous occurrence of an opportunity to enlarge and modernise one of the yards, it was decided to go for volume orientated production in which no more than three types of ship would be offered to the market at any one time (B26, SD14 and some derivative of them). Interestingly, the financial success of such specialisation was seen to depend 'more on attaining the maximum through-put . . . than on achieving what some may regard as an unrealistically large leap forward in productivity' (Kimber and Hargroves, 1977, p. 5).

There was no doubting the essential success of A and P's operation which not only made sales but also made profits. From the late 1960s to the mid-1970s, A and P were the most consistently profitable shipbuilding company in Britain. In 1976 most yards were running short of work as orders given before the 1973 collapse were completed and were being inadequately replaced. A and P was almost unique in continuing to attract steady orders for the SD14 so that this one company secured about one-half of all new tonnage orders placed in British yards in 1976.

It would be a mistake to press too hard the 'lessons' that can be extracted from the experience of one company. But A and P does at least illustrate two aspects of the effects of demand linkages on the ability of shipbuilders to specify their particular market problems. The first is largely negative. The 1960 decision of A and P to produce its own standard ship design for a general market need, freed the company from the dependence on the informal linkages with British shipowners which held back other British shipbuilders. The second lesson is more positive. The SD14 does not simply illustrate the necessity or importance of a shipbuilder's link with national shipowners or even with a particular shipowner. LOF was not a major customer for A and P ships and the overall marketability of the SD14 owed much to A and P's general policy of 'licensing the SD14 design to Greece and Brazil, directed at getting as many ships into service, and thus known, as soon as possible' (Kimber and Hargroves, 1977, p. 25). None the less the link with LOF was crucial at a couple of vital points. Mavroleon, as chairman of LOF, did much to identify the market at which a standard design should be aimed. In addition, LOF helped with vital initial support and promotion. Although LOF could not provide the long series ordering required by standard ship production, they did order 'enough ships themselves and persuaded their Greek friends and relatives to do the same until a threshold was passed beyond which the type became well known for its characteristics in chartering terms and easily quoted on the Baltic Exchange' (Teasdale, private communication, 1981).

8   Conclusion

Shipbuilding was an industry which had, up to 1950, been dominated by Britain for a substantial period of time. It was probably unavoidable that this dominance would be lost in the following generation especially as some of the most important shifts in demand required vessels of a type and size which other countries were in a better position to produce. None the less Britain's relative decline into a minor producer in the world industry of the 1970s represented a substantial failure. It has been argued that this failure was primarily conditioned by the peculiar national relationship which existed between shipowners and shipbuilders. The nature of the informal link did, for a long time, ensure that a large proportion of the needs of the home merchant fleet was built in UK yards. But the yards had to be ready to take whatever orders came along and this largely conditioned the practices, techniques and structure of the industry. As a result, the shipbuilders were largely stranded when the shipowners in the 1960s increasingly looked abroad for the newer types and sizes of ships which they now needed.

The situation made some government activity more or less unavoidable, especially as the now very vulnerable shipbuilding industry was almost entirely located in areas of already high unemployment. The activity which emerged was, however, mostly reactive and *ad hoc*: and in so far as it was based on analysis, it adopted the basic Geddes presumption that there was a large open world market for which the industry could make itself competitive simply by resolving its internal difficulties. The need to maintain any kind of structural link between the national industries of shipowning and shipbuilding was explicitly rejected. There was thus little attempt to encourage such links: the granting of credit aid was more of an emergency reaction than a policy directed towards creating links and the effects of this policy were counteracted by the direct investment grants to shipowners which mostly went to overseas shipbuilders. The scale of overseas ordering was, indeed, large enough for a time to make imported ships a significant adverse element in Britain's balance of payments.

The three examples given of individual enterprise calculations within this context all suggest that a link between shipowners and shipbuilders could have been encouraged by government efforts. The success of A and P was partly attributable to its link with a shipowning firm, even though the link was a relatively weak one. The Hawthorn Leslie and Swan Hunter cases represented situations where the outcome could have been very different if demand had been secured. A government-induced link with home shipowners could have provided such a basis. Perhaps the same point can be made more obliquely by considering the one area, warships, where a strong link was enforced because the government was the main purchaser. One of the Geddes proposals was for naval shipbuilding to be concentrated into fewer yards and this was eventually done. In 1982 the Conservative government wanted to sell off British Shipbuilders to private industry. The only profitable (and, hence, saleable) sector were the yards engaged on building for the navy, the only yards which had an effective demand linkage with a UK shipowner.

Notes

1 In 1965, the industry profile was described by the Geddes Report as comprising 62 shipyards, 27 of which regularly built vessels of 5,000 gross tons or more, or naval vessels of equivalent value. Many shipyards also undertook shiprepairing and marine engine building. In addition, some yards were operated by private companies, some by public companies and some were subsidiaries. By the early 1970s the industry structure had changed considerably as a result of mergers prompted by Geddes, but departing from even the indecisive lines laid down in that report. The situation was compounded, moreover, because UK shipowning was also a fragmented industry.

2 The definition of the 'domestic fleet' or of a 'British' shipowner is more complicated than this brief account is able to suggest. There are at least two sets of problems which are relevant. The first relates to the difficulties presented by the 'separation which can occur between the beneficial ownership, legal ownership, management and trading of a ship' (Rochdale, 1970, para. 85). This was a complication but its dimensions were not such as to upset the general argument since 'virtually all the ships of companies and persons resident here are believed to be registered in the UK' (Rochdale, 1970, para. 90). The second relates to the emergence of the so-called 'merchant operators', that is ships belonging to companies who were primarily concerned with the carriage of their own cargoes. The 'merchant operators' were mostly oil companies whose beneficial ownership was wholly or substantially foreign. The Rochdale report estimated that just under one-fifth of the British fleet in 1968 was owned by such companies.

3 The series of inquiries began with the DSIR Report (1960) and continued

with one undertaken by the Shipbuilding Advisory Committee of the Ministry of Transport (report, March 1961). The shipbuilding industry set up its own inquiry which reported the following year (Patton, 1962). The major report was that of the Shipbuilding Inquiry Committee (Geddes, 1966), and this was followed in the early 1970s by a report undertaken by a firm of American consultants for the Department of Trade and Industry (Booz-Allen, 1973).

4 The Geddes report was also wrong in its forecast of the rate of growth of world demand, which it substantially under-estimated. This error was less significant than those on the size and nature of ships because it was inherently difficult to make; it was less strategic for an analysis of the problems of British shipbuilding; and the under-estimate would, if the rest of the Geddes analysis had been correct, have made the Geddes predictions of a growing British industry much more likely.

5 For a brief time in the early 1970s, UK subsidy and export credit arrangements compared favourably with those of most other countries (Booz-Allen, 1973, p. 59). But in response to the general difficulties of the mid-1970s there was a fresh outburst of assistance in most countries and the UK lagged behind.

References

Albu, A. (1980), 'Merchant shipbuilding and marine engineering', in Pavitt, K. (ed.), *Technical Innovation and British Economic Performance*, London, Macmillan, pp. 168–83.

Al-Timini, W. (1975), 'Innovation led expansion: the shipbuilding case', *Research Policy*, vol. 4, no. 2, pp. 160–71.

Amalgamated Society of Boilermakers (ASB) (1977), *British Shipbuilding: What Next?*, Newcastle upon Tyne, Co-operative Press Ltd.

Association of Professional, Executive, Clerical and Computer Staff (APEX) (1977), *British Shipbuilding: An APEX Initiative*, Newcastle upon Tyne, Co-operative Press Ltd.

Booz-Allen (1973), *British Shipbuilding 1972* (Booz-Allen Report) (report to the Department of Trade and Industry), London, HMSO.

British Shipbuilders (BS) (1977), *Report on Review of Affairs 1977*.

Broadbridge, S. A. (1966), 'Japan's shipbuilding example', *New Society*, 2 June, pp. 10–12.

Corlett, E. (1981), *The Ship: The Revolution in Merchant Shipping*, London, HMSO.

Department of Scientific and Industrial Research (DSIR) (1960), *Research and Development Requirements of the Shipbuilding and Marine Engineering Industries*, London, HMSO.

Douglas, K. (1967), 'Background to the design and development of the "SD 14" ', *Motor Ship*, May, pp. 13–14.

Douglas, K. (1979), 'A future based on standard design ships', *The British Shipbuilder*, no. 6, November, pp. 12–14.

Geddes (1966), *Report of the Committee of Inquiry on Shipbuilding* (Geddes Report), Cmnd 2937, London, HMSO.

Gray, R. C. and Johnson, L. (1971), 'The design and construction of liquefied gas carriers', *Transactions of the North East Coast Institution of Engineers and Shipbuilders*, vol. 87, February, pp. 69–82.

Hargroves, M. R., Teasdale, J. A. and Vaughan, R. (1975), 'The strategic development of ship production technology', *Transactions of the North East Coast Institution of Engineers and Shipbuilders*, vol. 91, July, pp. 181–94.

Harrison, R. T. (1980), 'Consequences of technological change: the case of the shipbuilding industry', paper given at the European Production Studies Group Conference, Loughborough University.

Hogwood, B. W. (1979), *Government and Shipbuilding: the politics of industrial change*, Farnborough, Saxon House.

Jones, L. (1957), *Shipbuilding in Britain: Mainly Between the Two Wars*, Cardiff, University of Wales Press.

Kimber, D. and Hargroves, M. R. (1977), 'Creating a production facility for standard ships', *Transactions of the Royal Institute of Naval Architects*, vol. 119, January, pp. 1–28.

Lloyd's Register of Shipping; Annual Summary of Merchant Ships Completed, and *Annual Summary of Merchant Ships Launched*, London.

Mavroleon, B. M. (1967), 'The "SD 14" Liberty-replacement: a shipowner's view', *Motor Ship*, May, p. 21.

Midland Bank Review (1969), 'Shipbuilding in Britain: changes in structure and financial facilities', May, pp. 6–11.

Parker, T. J. (1980), 'A profile of British shipbuilders', *Transactions of the Royal Institute of Naval Architects*, vol. 122, September, pp. 429–58.

Parkinson, J. R. (1960), *The Economics of Shipbuilding in the UK*, Cambridge, Cambridge University Press.

Parkinson, J. R. (1968), 'The financial prospects of shipbuilding after Geddes, *Journal of Industrial Economics*, vol. 17, no. 1, pp. 1–17.

Patton (1962), *Productivity and Research in Shipbuilding Organisation* (Patton Report), (Report of the Main Committee to the Joint Industry Committee).

Peat, Marwick and Mitchell (1961), *Shipbuilding Orders placed abroad by British Shipowners* (Report to the Ministry of Transport), London, HMSO.

Rochdale (1970), *Report of the Committee of Inquiry into Shipping* (Rochdale Report), Cmnd 4337, London, HMSO.

Ross Belch, A. C. (1970), 'The new decade in large ship production: forward from the cross-roads', paper given at the Symposium on Ship Technology in Transition, Newcastle-upon-Tyne.

Ross Belch, A. C. (1976), 'Construction of very large tankers in two parts', *Transactions of the Royal Institute of Naval Architects*, vol. 117, July, pp. 245–66.

Sedgwick, S. and Sprake, R. F. (1977), *London and Overseas Freighters Limited 1949–1977*, Kendal, World Ship Society.

Shinto, H. (1968a), 'Big ships', *Science and Technology*, vol. 75, pp. 56–66.

Shinto, H. (1968b), 'Shipbuilding industry in Japan after world war II', *Ishikawajima Heavy Industries Engineering Review*, Japan.

Shipbuilding Advisory Committee (1961), *Report of the Sub-Committee on Prospects*, London, HMSO.

Shipbuilding Industry Board (1972), *Report and Accounts for the period 1 April to 31 December 1971*, London, HMSO.

Sloan, N. A. (1973), 'British shipbuilding in today's world', *Transactions of the Royal Institute of Naval Architects*, vol. 115, January, pp. 1–18.

Stopford, R. M. (1979), 'The shipbuilding market', paper given at the Conference on Port and Shipping Industries, Liverpool University.

Stuart, D. (1959), 'Change in shipbuilding techniques', *Time and Motion Study*, vol. 8, no. 8, August, pp. 10–14.

Venus, J. (1972), 'The economics of shipbuilding', *Transactions of the North East Coast Institution of Engineers and Shipbuilders*, vol. 88, March, pp. 131–42.

Unpublished reports and correspondence from British Shipbuilders.

The Economist
Guardian
Financial Times
Fairplay International Shipping Weekly
Motor Ship
The Observer

3 BMC/BLMC/BL – A misunderstood failure

Karel Williams

The present British Leyland (BL) enterprise is the result of past mergers and company failures. The British Motor Corporation (BMC) was formed in 1952 by the merger of the two major independent British-owned car producers – Austin and Nuffield alias Morris. Leyland was a Lancashire heavy truck and bus manufacturer which in 1961 bought the virtually bankrupt Standard-Triumph car company and subsequently bought Rover. British Leyland Motor Corporation (BLMC) was formed in 1968 when Leyland took over British Motor Holdings, as BMC had been renamed after its merger with Jaguar. BMH was in difficulty and losing money at the time of the 1968 takeover. Seven years later, BLMC was losing very large sums of money; the 1975 accounts show a pre-tax loss of £75 million. In this situation, in 1975, the company was effectively nationalised as British Leyland (BL). This did not resolve the enterprise's problems because losses mounted again after 1978; in both 1980 and 1981, the accounts show pre-tax losses of more than £300 million.

The identifying initials may change, but the core of the business has always been a British-based volume-car (Austin-Morris) manufacturing operation. BMC and BLMC never ran a multi-national production operation. When BLMC was formed in 1968, it inherited car manufacture or assembly operations in Australia, Belgium, Italy and Spain, but British factories accounted for 80–85 per cent of all sales through the early 1970s. Foreign markets were generally served through direct export of built-up vehicles or 'knocked-down' kits; exports averaged nearly 40 per cent of total British factory sales in the first half of the 1970s. Since the 1968 merger BMC's old volume-car operation (Austin-Morris) has been combined with a specialist car operation (Jaguar-Rover-Triumph) and a quality heavy truck business (Leyland). Trucks and buses, however, were always a sideshow since cars as a whole accounted for four-fifths of British factory sales in the early 1970s. The car business itself was dominated by Austin-Morris which consistently accounted for around half of all British factory sales in the 1970s.

In this essay we aim to answer the central question about the BMC/BLMC/BL failure: why have successive managements over the past twenty years been completely unable to make a success of the Austin-Morris volume car operation? The volume car operation has never made decent profits and since the mid-1960s has recorded recurrent ever larger losses, while its share of the UK car market has slipped from nearly 40 per cent to well under 20 per cent. Problems in volume cars have largely accounted for the biggest single company failure in post-war British manufacturing. When BLMC was formed in 1968, the company consistently sold 1 million vehicles per annum and had some claim to being the fourth or fifth largest motor vehicle manufacturer in the world; in 1981, BL was a minor league producer which sold just 525,000 vehicles. In British terms, BLMC, with a workforce of around 200,000 employees in 1968, was Britain's largest single employer and Britain's largest single exporter; at the end of 1981, BL's workforce was 117,000 and still falling.

The question of what had gone wrong was first raised in the mid-1970s when there were major public autopsies into the collapse of BLMC and the more general decline of the British motor industry. There were three major inquiries and reports: the Ryder Report (1975) specifically on BLMC; the report of the Commons Expenditure Committee (1975); and the Central Policy Review Staff (1975) report. The last two were more concerned with the British motor industry in general. The CPRS blamed bad work practices which obstructed efficient capital utilisation in the factories of BLMC and other British car producers: process comparisons showed that British firms needed more labour to make the same product using the same capital equipment. Ryder and the Commons Expenditure Committee emphasised the inferiority and age of BLMC's capital stock; on a fixed assets per employee basis, BL trailed a long way behind every major European manufacturer and more than half of BL's machinery and equipment was more than fifteen years old.

Using our general framework about the national conditions of enterprise calculation, we would analyse the problems of BLMC and BL rather differently. On our analysis, both the capital utilisation and capital stock explanations of this company failure are inadequate and unsatisfactory; the company's failure was determined by BLMC and BL's inability to identify and solve problems about market limitations. The other problems were real but of secondary importance. On our interpretation therefore, the company's failure has been recognised but also misunderstood.

We would not, of course, deny the existence of bad work practices or the adverse effects of strikes in BMC or BLMC. Nevertheless, there was not a complete failure of control over the labour process and these struggling companies were increasingly disabled by problems about the character and composition of demand. Paradoxically, indeed, by the mid-1970s, restriction of output through bad work practices and losses of output through strikes were beneficial in the short run because they prevented the company's accumulation of stocks of unsaleable cars. As for the low investment thesis, that has been disproved by the experience of the company since 1975 when large sums of government money have been injected into the company; increased investment (even with a co-operative workforce) is not sufficient to guarantee success in the marketplace. More generally, we would argue that the problem of 'under-investment' has to be seen in context as the legacy of BMC's pre-1968 strategy of low-capital-intensity output expansion. This strategy not only left BMC ill-equipped but also compromised profitability so that the company was vulnerable to an opportunist takeover.

1   BMC's output expansion and its results, 1952–68

After the 1952 merger of Austin and Morris, BMC boldly went for increased output. Capacity was deliberately doubled to approximately 1 million vehicles per annum, while vehicles actually produced trebled from under 300,000 in 1951–2 to a peak of 886,000 in 1964–5 (table 23). The strategy was a success in that it allowed the company to maintain its market leadership in the rapidly expanding British car market; BMC held a steady 38 per cent of the British car market in the years from 1953 to 1966. But the technical and financial results of this expansion, in terms of productivity and profit, were disappointing. In this section we will argue that the pattern of BMC's expansion necessarily compromised the possibility of higher productivity and profits. The underlying problem was BMC's commitment to low-capital-intensity expansion of its output of small cars.

To begin with the issue of the capital intensity of expansion, the key point here is that BMC spent very little to obtain the extra production capacity to build 1 million vehicles. The chairman's annual statement and the company accounts enable us to estimate how much it spent. BMC's chairman claimed that capital expenditure incurred or planned (before government grants) amounted to some £78 million in the eight years 1954–5 to 1961–2 (BMC *Annual Report*, 1959). On the evidence of the company accounts, this seems to be about right: over these eight years, depreciation (£34·9 million) plus retained earnings (£29·6 million) plus share issue (£4·0 million) plus investment allowances (£4·8 million) provided the company with £73·3 million for capital investment. A significant part of this £78 million must have gone on development and tooling expenses for new models; in these years, the company introduced five new body shells (A40, A55, A99, Mini and 1100) and one new front-drive power train (Mini and 1100). Substantially less than £78 million must, therefore, have been left to buy the production facilities which doubled capacity from 450,000 vehicles to some 900,000 vehicles.

It seems like a miracle that BMC got so much extra capacity for so little money except that this miracle can be explained if we look at the production facilities which BMC developed. BMC did not build any new factory for car production, but instead reorganised and re-equipped its existing factories: the first all-new BMC factory for vehicle production was the Bathgate truck and tractor plant which opened in 1962. Wherever possible, capacity was expanded by the duplication and replication of existing machines and lines. Adding a second machine or line was always cheap because the original machine or line could be kept in production. In some cases the duplicate lines were not even in the same factories; the 1100 was always assembled at Cowley as well as at Longbridge and so was the Mini up to 1969.

In the 1950s, BMC did have the management capability to plan and run modern production facilities. This point is established by the rationalisation of engine production at Longbridge shortly after the merger. BMC was one of the two European pioneers in adapting American automatic transfer machine technology to lower volume European engine production. The result was a substantial increase in profit and productivity; transfer machines at Longbridge saved 85 per cent of the direct labour costs in engine block production (Maxcy and Silbertson, 1959). The constraints on innovation were financial rather than managerial; because of BMC's commitment to a large expansion of output for a small outlay of money, the company could not afford to buy much in the way of new high-quality production facilities. It is not surprising, therefore, that the productivity figures show BMC failed to secure technical economies of scale from output expansion.

As table 23 (cols iv, vii) shows, from the early 1950s to the mid-1960s, vehicle output trebled to nearly 900,000, but the number of vehicles produced per employee never rose much above the early 1950s level of around 7; the company's best-ever performance was in fact around 9 vehicles per employee in the years 1963 to 1965. By contemporary standards, this was a very poor achievement. Inter-company productivity comparisons in terms of vehicles per employee are difficult to interpret mainly because the output mix of cars and commercial vehicles varies between companies. Nevertheless, it is significant that, while BMC's output was more or less constant, other European majors, who started from lower levels, managed to double the number of vehicles produced per employee as they expanded output (Central Policy Review Staff, 1975). Furthermore, the available comparisons show that, by the late 1960s, BMC not only lagged behind the other European major producers, it also lagged behind its direct competitors like Ford and Vauxhall who could produce ten to twelve vehicles per employee in their UK factories (Rhys, 1972).

Given the technical nature of the production facilities which BMC was rebuilding, it is perhaps not surprising that the number of vehicles produced per employee did not rise. The production facilities do not, however, directly explain why the financial results of expansion were so disappointing. Why could the company not make more profit from making more cars, especially as it did make individual models in higher volume? The answer is that the strategy of output expansion locked BMC into the mass production of small cars with low profit margins.

Expansion of small car production was dictated by the composi-

TABLE 23   *BMC production and profit*

	Employees (000)	Home vehicles produced (000)	Export vehicles produced (000)	Total vehicles produced (000)	Net pre-tax profit (£m)	Pre-tax profit per vehicle (£)	No. of vehicles per employee
	(i)	(ii)	(iii)	(iv)	(v)	(vi)	(vii)
1951–2	40	97	180est	277	–	–	6·9
1952–3	–	–	–	279	12·3	44·1	–
1953–4	–	184	170	354	10·4	29·4	–
1954–5	–	–	–	419	14·2	33·9	–
1955–6	60	252	187	440	11·7	26·6	7·3
1956–7	60	174	179	363	8·3	23·5	5·9
1957–8	65	292	213	505	21·0	41·6	7·8
1958–9	69	287	199	486	16·3	33·5	7·0
1959–60	76	383	286	669	26·9	40·2	8·8
1960–1	79	402	199	601	10·2	17·0	7·6
1961–2	80	377	224	600	4·1	6·8	7·5
1962–3	87	478	270	748	15·1	20·2	8·6
1963–4	93	539	320	859	21·2	24·7	9·2
1964–5	100	560	326	886	22·8	25·7	8·9
1965–6	120	531	314	846	20·5	24·2	7·1
1966–7	114	372	322	694	(3·2)	(4·6)	6·1

Source: BMC, *Annual Report and Accounts*, various years.

tion of demand; BMC could only get mass sales with small cars. In late 1950s Europe, car manufacturers could only get 100,000–400,000 per annum production of one model by selling in the 'people's car' market. The people's car offered basic transport for four people and their luggage; cars like the Beetle, Citroen 2CV, Renault 4CV, Fiat 500 and the Morris Minor were all variants on this theme. The BMC 850cc Mini of 1959 was a second try at this market, like the Renault Dauphine or the Fiat 600. BMC then managed to upsize and retain volume with the 1962 Austin-Morris 1100 which offered a larger full four-seat body and was the antecedent of the later 1970s 'super-minis' like the Renault 5 and the VW Golf. But BMC, like other European majors in the 1960s, could not find mass sales with its larger front-wheel-drive cars in the 1500 to 1800cc class. The company's production figures show that the Austin/Morris 1800, which was introduced in 1964, only twice topped 50,000 per annum production levels; the 1500/1750cc Austin Maxi, which was introduced in 1969, again only topped 50,000 per annum twice (appendix B, tables 4, 5).

'Small car, small profit' was one of the motor industry clichés of the 1950s and 1960s when small cars were basic boxes sold at a cheap price. BMC aggravated the problems of inherently narrow margins by keen pricing and rudimentary cost control on its technically innovative front-wheel-drive cars. The 1100 of 1962 was conventionally priced at just over £600 but, when the Mini was introduced in 1959, it was priced at £496 which was £100 below the cost of other small cars like the Ford Anglia or Triumph Herald. Most industry observers always believed that the Mini, which accounted for one-quarter of BMC's vehicle output, was being sold at or near the cost of production. The later larger front-wheel-drive cars (1100, 1800 and Maxi) might have offered fair margins if they had not been so expensive to make. Their designer Alec Issigonis was obsessed with providing the roomiest passenger cabins and he insisted on the expense of transverse front-wheel-drive power trains and long wheelbases; the latter necessarily required high body weight and pushed up manufacturing cost as surely as the engineering under the bonnet.

BMC, nevertheless, did obtain the benefit of long production runs and high-model volume with the Mini and 1100. In 1959, no British car was being made in a volume of much over 100,000 per annum; BMC's own long-standing bestseller was the Morris Minor which was produced at an average rate of some 70,000 per annum over its first fifteen years of model life after 1947. But, after 1959, BMC's two new front-wheel-drive small cars (the Mini and the 1100) were produced in much larger volume for long periods. The company's production figures show that BMC, and its successor BLMC, produced more than 200,000 Minis in every year from 1962 to 1977 inclusive; the 1100 managed to achieve production volume of more than 200,000 in every year except one between 1963–4 and 1970–1 (appendix B, tables 2, 3). The Mini and 1100 were not only long-lived bestselling motor cars, they were also joint products because they shared a common engine and power train which the company was producing at a rate of 500,000 per annum by the mid-1960s.

With a given production technology, however, long production runs would only translate into big profits if there were substantial fixed costs of development and tooling which could be spread over a large volume of output. BMC was not so lucky because, in the era before safety and emission regulations, development and tooling costs were relatively low. Maxcy and Silbertson (1959) are the most authoritative sources on the economics of the car business in the late 1950s; they claimed that fixed costs probably accounted for only 15 per cent of total costs of car production and in one of their 'typical examples', fixed costs were actually under 10 per cent of total costs. There could be significant economies of scale in car manufacture; Maxcy and Silbertson (1959) were confident that there were worthwhile economies of scale in production of up to 500,000 identical units per annum. But these economies could only be obtained by firms, like VW, which invested heavily in capital-intensive efficient mass production. The economics of the business were such that volume in itself would not generate profit for a firm like BMC where there was under-investment.

The financial results of output expansion in BMC were therefore mediocre; vehicle output rose dramatically but company profits did not. In absolute terms, pre-tax profits never rose far above the £20 million level which the company achieved in 1957–8 and never significantly improved upon later in its best years from 1963 to 1966 (table 23, col. v). Furthermore, profits were not always maintained at this level because BMC was prone to cyclical profit collapse. Wherever the British car market turned down, BMC's slim profit margins tended to vanish altogether; pre-tax profits were reduced to £8 million in 1956–7 and to £4·1 million in 1961–2, while a loss of £3·2 million was recorded in 1966-7. In relative terms, BMC's profit performance looks even worse. Since output was being dramatically expanded, profit per vehicle is a highly pertinent measure of company performance. After the great expansion in the good years from 1962–3 to 1965–6, profit per vehicle was in the range of £20 to £25. During the good years in the 1950s, like 1952–3, 1957–8 and 1959–60, the company had been able to earn nearly twice as much profit per vehicle (table 23, col. vi).

BMC paid a high price for expanding in such a way as to compromise profitability; the emphasis on short-run profitability in the merger boom was such that BMC became vulnerable to takeover by the smaller and more aggressive firm of Leyland.

2   The 1968 merger and saving the company with new models, 1968–74

The Leyland takeover of BMH (*née* BMC) was sponsored by the British government whose enthusiasm for the merger was part of a naive industrial policy which was aptly caricatured as 'find the most efficient company in Britain and merge all the rest into it'. The Industrial Reorganisation Corporation and the Ministry of Technology, therefore, supported a merger of all the independent British-owned car manufacturers into a new combine which would be run by the management of a Lancashire heavy truck company. The government helped Leyland management in many ways; it provided an informal assurance that any merger would not be referred to the Monopolies Commission and Harold Wilson himself hosted a dinner party at Chequers for the BMH and Leyland chairmen. Significantly, however, the government did not provide large-scale financial assistance for the new BLMC; the only financial assistance offered was a £25 million loan on favourable terms from the IRC.

In any case, the merger would probably have gone ahead without active government encouragement; Leyland wanted BMH and could easily afford to buy BMH under the share exchange arrangements which were commonplace during the merger boom. Furthermore, there was no doubt about the Leyland management's financial aptitude. Leyland's competence at the British merger game was demonstrated in the 1961 purchase of Standard-Triumph which took Leyland into cars with a deal that was a carbon copy of the

later 1968 BMH deal. In 1961 and 1968, Leyland paid in shares –
not cash. Shareholders in the acquired company were offered an
exchange at the rate of eight Standard shares for one Leyland share
and one BMH share for one Leyland share. Leyland prepared for
the BMH takeover by a 1967 're-structuring' of its own equity;
Leyland split its own shares into smaller five-shilling denominations
and made a scrip issue which brought the nominal capitalisation of
Leyland and BMH to rough equality.

Share exchange deals were always advantageous to Leyland since
Leyland paper was highly rated on the stock market. Leyland shares
were rated as a growth stock and in 1964, before BMC was in
difficulty, were priced so as to yield only 3 per cent when BMC
shares yielded 8 per cent. Leyland moved decisively to exploit this
advantage when the target company was in trouble. Both Standard
Triumph and BMH were taken over when they were losing money
and embarrassed by a large overdraft. The long-standing difference
of market value plus temporary embarrassment in late 1967 brought
BMH and Leyland shares to the same nominal value of thirteen
shillings and allowed Leyland to make a one-for-one offer to a much
larger company. BMH was bought at a price which was probably
below the break-up value of its assets.

The rise of Leyland provides us with a classic merger boom
example of how the ability to pay in paper allowed a small company
to buy its way into the big time. In this, as in other cases, neither
government nor stock market carefully scrutinised the small firm's
past record of achievement or its present capability. Universal opti-
mism about the ability of Leyland management was based on Leyland's record of increased profits. In fact, these profits had been
opportunistically obtained by buying out Leyland's main competitor (ACV) on the home market and by selling trucks and buses
into soft third-world markets. Furthermore, by 1967, Leyland's old
management triumvirate had broken up and Leyland *was* Donald
Stokes (Turner, 1971). Leyland's immediate problem was that it
did not have a professional management team which was capable
of running a company as large as the new BLMC. The company
was therefore forced to recruit senior management from the British
Ford company. Significantly, Leyland was unable to recruit anyone
who had high-level production or product-planning experience in
Ford; the most senior of the new recruits (John Barber) had been
a finance specialist.

It is not surprising that, when Ford's junior team transferred to Leyland in 1968, they began to introduce an early 1960s Ford strategy; measured day-work was to be introduced in the factories and a Cortina-type car was to be developed and sold through a pruned dealer network. They undoubtedly neglected the situational element; the strategy which had worked for Ford against BMC would not necessarily work for BLMC against Ford and the importers. At the same time, it would be wrong to be too critical of the ex-Ford executives since they had a very limited choice of strategic options. Their chief executive, Donald Stokes, personally decided against any large-scale rationalisation of BLMC's production facilities; he did not want to sack workers and incur the odium which Weinstock brought upon himself with the Woolwich closure (Turner, 1971). With this decision taken, the choice of strategy was largely determined by the company's chronic shortage of investment funds.

Investment could be internally financed from depreciation plus unappropriated profit. But, as table 24 shows, BLMC's internal investment fund was relatively small because, after modest depreciation allowances had been taken, unappropriated profit was virtually non-existent. In the seven years 1967–8 to 1973–4 this internal fund totalled £312 million and averaged just £45 million per annum. The mediocre profitability which limited internal resources also limited the availability of external funds which (under the British rules of the game) could only be obtained on the stock market. The company obtained some £50 million through a rights issue in 1972 (Ryder, 1975), but that represented the once-and-for-all limits of the company's borrowing power.

Investment funds (internal plus external) available to the firm therefore totalled some £360 million over the seven years after 1967. This kind of money could not and did not build many new production facilities because the development and tooling costs for new models were rising rapidly with the coming of crash safety and exhaust emissions regulations in the early 1970s; by 1974, it was estimated that development and tooling for a new body would cost £75 million, and for a new engine it would cost £150 million (CPRS, 1975). Both new factories and new models were desirable but the available funds would finance only one of these strategic objectives. In this situation, because the car business was a fashion business, there really was never any choice: new models had to have first priority.

TABLE 24   *BLMC's internal investment fund (£m)*

	Depreciation[a]	Unappropriated Profit (loss)[b]	Internal Investment
	(i)	(ii)	(iii)
1967–8	40	4	44
1968–9	40	3	43
1969–70	42	(11)	31
1970–1	47	5	52
1971–2	43	12	55
1972–3	44	18	72
1973–4	42	(27)	15
	298	4	312

Source: BLMC, *Annual Reports and Accounts*.
[a] Depreciation = total depreciation on properties and plant plus tooling amortisation.
[b] Unappropriated profit = post-tax profit minus minority interest minus 'extraordinary items' (mainly closure costs) minus dividends.

BLMC, therefore, staked everything on developing a few new models or, more exactly, new body-shells which would carry existing BMC mechanicals. *If* the new models sold, the whole workforce would be employed, the factories would be fully loaded and the profit must surely come through. The new models were:

(i)   The Marina introduced in 1971 which was intended as a competitor for conventional rear-wheel drive '3 box' saloons like Ford's Cortina and Escort.
(ii)   The Allegro introduced in 1973 which was a re-skin of the front-wheel-drive 1100/1300 which had long been Britain's bestselling car.
(iii)   The Princess introduced in 1975 which was a re-skin of the old BMC 1800 'land-crab'.

BLMC's strategic aim was to capture greater market share with the new models; as Turnbull the managing director of Austin-Morris put it, 'we concentrated on trying to take market share from our competitors' (Turner, 1971). The priority accorded to the

Marina shows that this strategy was primarily designed to take market share from Ford on the home market. Academic and journalistic conventional wisdom of the time endorsed this order of priorities; one of BLMC's problems in the late 1960s was its product range and the absence of a 'medium sized saloon to compete with the products of Ford' (Rhys, 1972; see also Ensor, 1971). This argument appeared plausible, but market share strategy was never sensible because it neglected the BLMC's increasingly pressing problems about market limitations at home and abroad.

3 Market limitations at home

The question of market limitations arises in particular form in most of Britain's problem industries. In the case of British cars and more especially in the case of BLMC, market problems were acute and failure to resolve them led to collapse. If BLMC's strategy was to save the company with new models, the question of markets was crucial. The issue was: where were the new models to be sold or, more exactly, in what segments of which national markets could BLMC find profitable sales in sufficient volume? Although BMC had dramatically expanded production before 1968, it had never properly resolved this problem. Furthermore, when in 1969 and 1970, BLMC management planned a programme of new model introductions, the company faced intensifying problems about the limits of the market and the composition of demand. We will begin to analyse these problems in this section by examining the home market.

In the 1950s and 1960s, BMC's increased output was largely sold at home. In the 1950s, indeed, vehicle exports were on a plateau and the company simply diverted increased production on to the home market (table 23, col. iii). In the longer term, from 1951–2 up to the record year of 1964–5, home sales increased nearly six times from 97,000 vehicles to 560,000 vehicles; in the same period, export sales less than doubled, increasing relatively modestly from 180,000 vehicles to 326,000 vehicles (table 23, cols ii, iii). BMC's home sales grew rapidly because car ownership and use was rapidly growing in Britain at that time. In 1951, when BMC was formed, 138,000 new cars were registered; just thirteen years later in 1964, 1,216,000 new cars were registered (appendix C, table 1). The number of new registrations on the home market doubled from 1951 to 1953, doubled again from 1953 to 1958 and then doubled yet again from 1958 to 1964. In this period, car use and ownership was growing equally rapidly in other West European countries. But, for BMC, home sales were particularly attractive because the British market was chauvinist in its tastes and sheltered by 20 to 30 per cent tariffs right through the 1950s and 1960s; margins were, therefore, almost certainly higher on home sales and this was a major consideration for a company with profit problems.

Existing discussions of BMC's home market problems have been narrowly preoccupied with the one issue of cyclical fluctuations in the home demand for new cars which were induced by the stop/go policy cycle in the era of fiscal Keynesianism. We would not deny that there were switchback fluctuations in the demand for new cars. The rapid increase in new registrations periodically faltered. After the Suez fiasco in 1956, new registrations declined by some 20 per cent, as they did during the oil crisis around 1974 (appendix C, table 1). In three lesser fluctuations in the 1960s, smaller declines of 7 to 12 per cent in new registrations were recorded; the peak to trough decline was 7·3 per cent in 1961 versus 1960, 10·3 per cent in 1966 versus 1964 and 11·5 per cent in 1969 versus 1968 (appendix C, table 1). Furthermore, although the situation was more complicated in 1956 and 1974, government policy changes on purchase-tax levels and hire-purchase repayments clearly did precipitate all three downturns in the car market of the 1960s. Nevertheless, we would argue that authors like Dunnett (1980) have placed too much emphasis on the damaging effects of such policy-led fluctuations.

In the period of BMC's existence, from 1952 to 1968, there was only one really severe downturn in the market after the Suez crisis. Furthermore, policy changes were probably the occasion rather than the cause of the three lesser downturns in the 1960s. The demand for new cars is inherently volatile since the purchase of a new car can usually be postponed; car market fluctuations in other advanced capitalist countries, such as West Germany, were quite as severe as they were in Britain. The real question, therefore, is: how and why was BMC damaged by cyclical fluctuations which other major car manufacturers survived? As we have already noted, BMC's particular problem was that profits increasingly collapsed whenever the car market turned down. Profit collapse had two enterprise-specific causes: first, BMC had not properly developed its export business and, therefore, could not switch to alternative markets when the home market turned down; second, as we have already argued, BMC's margins were poor and deteriorating even in the good years, because under-investment in expanded production facilities had compromised profitability.

The emphasis on fluctuations in the quantity of home demand is also misplaced because BMC had equally serious problems about the quality or composition of home demand. On the British car market, a taste for diversity had been nurtured by a fragmented industry which included five indigenous volume-car manufacturers in the 1950s and 1960s. In Germany, VW's Beetle took one-third or more of new car registrations. But no British manufacturer has ever produced one model which takes more than 15 per cent of new car registrations; this feat was achieved by the BMC 1100 in 1965 and 1966 and by the Cortina in 1967 (appendix C, table 3). A British bestseller usually claims just over 10 per cent of the market. This national taste for diversity was a particular problem for BMC because, as market leaders in cars, BMC was trying to defend a normal market share of nearly 40 per cent.

BMC always had to make *two* small cars to take 20 per cent of the market; the Mini and 1100 which together took over 20 per cent of new registrations after 1962 were successors to the Austin A30/A35 and the Morris Minor of the 1950s. The company could not develop a bestselling larger car. Therefore, to defend its 40 per cent market share, BMC had to introduce, or keep in production, a variety of other models which sold in smaller quantities. Some of these models, such as the Farina A55, offered decent volume and fair margins; the A55/A60 was produced at a rate of 60,000 to 90,000 per annum in its heyday from 1959 to 1966 (appendix B, table 1) and these cars sold at a premium price. Other models, including the increasingly geriatric Morris Minor of the 1960s, were more dubious propositions. In this way, the composition of market demand compelled BLMC to produce 'stocking filler' models which further compromised already slim margins.

When BLMC was formed at the end of the 1960s, the market problems facing the company were intensifying. The most obvious change was the end of rapid secular growth in new car registrations since the British car market was maturing and approaching saturation at the European level of one car per four persons. Through the 1970s, new car registrations in the UK fluctuated erratically between just over 1 million and a peak of 1¾ million which was reached in 1972 just before the oil crisis and then reached again in 1979. Some neo-Marxist commentators, such as Friedman (1977), have placed much emphasis on the limits imposed by overall home market size and growth. We would argue, however, that there was a more fundamental problem: BLMC was pinned down in particular sectors of the home market.

The old BMC achieved volume by selling smaller cars to private buyers. By the early 1970s, the private buyer's sector was shrinking in size and fiercely contested by importers. As this market sector became increasingly difficult, BLMC found it was impossible to sell larger cars in volume to business users because the medium car sector of the market was limited in size and dominated by Ford. The disaggregated market analysis which follows, demonstrates that BLMC's problem was not the limited size and slow growth of the British car market as a whole; the company's problem was the contraction of the particular market sector which BMC had traditionally dominated.

To begin with, it is necessary to understand the limited size of the market for larger cars in the UK. This point has never been properly appreciated. It is usually argued that BMC's larger front-wheel-drive cars (the 1800 of 1964 and the 1500/1750 Maxi of 1969) failed to sell in volume because they were too big and expensive. The essential problem was not that these cars were too big, but that the market above 1300cc was too small. Small cars have always dominated the British car market; in every year since 1960 around half the cars sold in Britain have been under 1300cc in capacity (appendix C, table 4). Within this sector, the main change has been a switch away from small cars of under 1100cc which consistently sold 40–45 per cent of the market up to 1966. Subsequently, the largest single market sector was the 1100-1300cc class which consistently accounted for around one-third of new registrations between 1968 and 1978 (appendix C, table 4). Above this sector there was a market for medium cars, but showroom 1500 and 1600s (in the 1400–1600cc displacement class) accounted for less than one-fifth of new registrations in every year from 1968 to 1976 inclusive (appendix C, table 4). The difference between 33 per cent for 1100–1300cc cars and 18 per cent for 1500–1600cc cars was quite crucial. The 1100–1300 sector, where BMC had been the market leader, was large enough to support a couple of bestsellers or several volume sellers; in the late 1960s it sustained the BLMC 1100/1300, the Ford Escort and the Vauxhall Viva HB. But the 1500–1600cc sector was only big enough to support one best-seller which takes 10–12 per cent of the market; ever since the Cortina was moved up-market when the Escort was introduced in the late 1960s, that car was always the Ford Cortina.

To understand the Cortina's success in the medium car sector, it is necessary to understand the institutional peculiarity of the British market for new cars; in the 1960s and 1970s, the company car sector, which was effectively served by Ford, was rapidly growing in importance. In most European countries, business users bought their cars and claimed a mileage allowance for company use. In Britain in the 1960s and 1970s, as a way of avoiding income tax and pay-policy restrictions, business employees were increasingly given a company car as a perk, even if they did not use a car on company business. According to Inbucon consultants, in 1981, 85 per cent of company executives earning over £10,000 a year had a company car. The really dramatic change came in the decade between 1964 and 1974. In 1964, the Economist Intelligence Unit estimated that only 7 per cent of 'household cars' were owned by a firm and a further 10 per cent were subsidised by an employer (*Motor Business*, July 1964). By 1973, one-third of new UK registrations were in company names (Commons Expenditure Committee, 1975b) and, in the following year, the Central Policy Review Staff (1975) estimated that 40 per cent of new car registrations were company sponsored. By the early 1970s, individual purchases by private unsubsidised buyers had declined in relative importance and only accounted for something like 50 per cent of new car sales.

Ford had developed a distribution network to serve the growing company sector; a few large retailers were geared-up to make volume sales and, in particular, to make the company 'fleet' sales in lots of twenty or more cars which accounted for 20 per cent of UK new registrations by the early 1970s. What made the Cortina unbeatable was not so much the product itself as the fact that it was sold by Ford's specialised dealer networks. BLMC's inherited distribution network was adapted to BMC's traditional business; many small retailers were geared-up to make individual sales to private customers. As late as 1974, Austin/Morris had twice as many retailers each selling half as many cars as Ford's retail dealers (Commons Expenditure Committee, 1975a). Such a distribution network is well suited to the private sale business; this point is proved by Renault (UK)'s efforts in the early 1980s to develop a dense British network of small service shops and dealers for its private customers. BLMC's failure to recognise this point and its ill-conceived attempts to rationalise its dealer network in the early 1970s simply compounded its distribution problems. A programme of axeing small Austin-Morris dealers did not increase the capability of those which were left to make company sales. At the same time, it released dealers who took franchises for imported cars which sold into the private buyer sector against BLMC; a Chrysler survey of the early 1970s showed that more than one-third of the dealers who were dropped by a British manufacturer took out a foreign franchise (Central Policy Review Staff, 1975).

If Ford's distribution network prevented BLMC from selling medium and larger cars to company customers, at the same time, the available private customer sector was being increasingly fiercely contested by the importers. Imports of foreign manufactured cars accounted for 10 per cent of new registrations in 1969 and by 1979 had reached 56 per cent of new registrations; in BLMC's last years (1973 and 1974), imports already sold more than one-quarter of the market (appendix C, table 5). Since about 1977, overall car import levels have been higher in Britain than in other West European countries because of a flood of tied imports (principally Fords and Vauxhalls) which are manufactured abroad and sold under British badges. Interestingly enough, identifiably foreign-built and badged motor cars (principally VW, Renault, Datsun and Fiat) in the later 1970s held a steady one-third of the British market for new cars as they did in West Germany or Italy. This 'normal' level of import penetration in Britain and elsewhere in Europe is underpinned by the European private car buyer's taste for the marginal packaging differences which distinguish different small cars.

Rising import penetration in the British car market may have been 'normal' in European terms, but it was a major threat to BLMC in the early 1970s. As we have already noted, the British private buyer's taste for diversity had been nurtured by five indigenous manufacturers in the 1960s. In the 1970s, this taste was served by importers; by 1974, when imports had a mere 4 per cent of the fleet market, 45 per cent of private buyers bought a foreign car (Central Policy Review Staff, 1975). By this date, BLMC was thus attempting to sell its volume cars on the home market to private buyers who now accounted for, at most, 60 per cent of the market, and half these private buyers were already buying foreign cars. In the early 1970s, the home market effectively available to BLMC was rapidly shrinking in size. The company desperately needed export sales, but here again it encountered market limitations.

4 Market limitations abroad

BMC and BLMC were never really multi-national manufacturing companies; as we have already noted, British factories accounted for 80 per cent or more of BLMC's sales in the first half of the 1970s. To load its British plants, the company always needed foreign markets which would take built-up cars or knocked-down kits for final assembly. The problem was that from the late 1950s, many world markets were reluctant to take built-up cars or kits; in areas like Latin America or Australasia, indigenous manufacture with significant local content was required. By the 1960s, only North America and Western Europe offered large markets which were open to imports of built-up Austin-Morris cars; by the late 1960s, 8 million new cars per annum were being sold in each of these markets.

The North American and West European markets may have been large but they were also highly competitive. In this situation, both BMC and BLMC had difficulty in finding and holding export markets where cars could be sold in volume. The slow overall growth of company car exports is an index of these difficulties. In the first half of the 1950s, BMC exported approximately 180,000 vehicles per annum and most of these vehicles were Austin-Morris cars; twenty years later, in the first half of the 1970s, BLMC's British factories exported just 250,000–300,000 Austin-Morris cars per annum. A disaggregated market-by-market analysis is even more instructive, and the rest of this section provides this kind of analysis. It shows that BMC, before 1968, was a company which was opportunistically switching markets in an attempt to take short-run advantage of volume export sales wherever it could find an opening. It also shows that BLMC after 1968 failed to develop the European export business which it had inherited. Given BLMC's increasing difficulties on the home market, the failure to develop export markets sealed the company's fate.

In the early and mid-1950s, BMC (like the rest of the British car industry) took most of its export sales in the Commonwealth. In 1950, more than two-thirds of British car exports went to Commonwealth countries (Commons Expenditure Committee, 1975a); Australia and New Zealand together were far and away BMC's largest export markets and in 1955–6 accounted for 31 per cent of BMC's overseas unit sales (*Motor Business*, January 1967). However, Commonwealth markets like Australia were increasingly spoiled by regulations insisting on manufacture with substantial local content; BMC could still take profits by manufacturing there, but it could not dispose of British factory output in these markets. BMC's next gambit was to develop the North American market which had traditionally taken sports cars in small volume; as late as 1954–5, the USA and Canada together took 19,000 cars or just 12 per cent of BMC's total vehicle exports (BMC, *Annual Report*, 1956).

In the short run, the market switch to North America was an outstanding success; by 1959–60, Canada and the United States took 110,000 cars or 39 per cent of BMC's vehicle exports (BMC, *Annual Report*, 1960). At this time, the big three American manufacturers (GM, Ford and Chrysler) all had huge volume, high productivity and low prices. BMC and a variety of other European manufacturers were successful only as long as the American manufacturers did not produce smaller European type cars. In 1960, when the American manufacturers introduced their compact lines, BMC, like all the other European importers except VW, was overwhelmed because the big three native manufacturers could offer more car for less money: in 1962, the North American market would take only 40,000 BMC cars (BMC, *Annual Report*, 1961).

Subsequently, the company staged a limited recovery in the American market, although it was in something of a dilemma about product lines; the small front-wheel-drive cars, like the Mini and 1100, which had been developed for European tastes and driving conditions, were unsaleable in America. Austin-Morris saloons like the 1300-based Austin America (and the later Austin Marina) failed dismally in the American market. BMC and BLMC were therefore pinned down in the company's traditional niche in the American market as a supplier of specialist sports cars like the MGB. BLMC's record in this market sector was mediocre; the company's new sports model, the TR7, was no match in the market-place for the Datsun 240/260. In any case, sports cars were an irrelevance because 50,000 or so specialist sales in the USA could not solve the company's problems about getting volume on Austin-Morris saloons.

After its reverses in the American market in 1960 and 1961, BMC again switched markets and deliberately concentrated on West European markets. Again, in the short run, things went well. From a small base, production for Europe built up so that, by 1964, European markets took 130,000 units or 41 per cent of BMC's world exports (BMC, *Annual Report*, 1964). To get around tariff barriers, the company developed European assembly of British knocked-down kits in Italy, Belgium and Spain; by 1967, these European assembly plants were producing nearly 100,000 cars per annum (BMC, *Annual Report*, 1967). This strategy had certain inherent weaknesses, BMC had sub-contracted much of this work and the company did not own or control the operations of its two major assemblers – Innocenti in Italy and NMQ (alias Authi) in Spain. Nevertheless, in 1968, BLMC inherited a promising European export business which it subsequently failed to develop.

It must be admitted that the European car market of the 1960s and 1970s was never an easy one because volume cars, like Austin-Morris saloons, were sold under conditions of intense competition. In BLMC's period from 1968 to 1974, no fewer than eight 'majors' each sold more than 500,000 cars per annum; BLMC, Chrysler, Fiat, Ford, Peugeot, General Motors, Renault and VW could all claim this status. A further six or more independent European companies also made cars and, by the end of this period, Japanese importers were a reality or a threat in many West European markets. With the possible exception of VW, all the major European car manufacturers specialised in exporting to nearby West European countries; in 1975, two-thirds of West German car exports and four-fifths of Italian and French car exports went to neighbouring West European countries (Bhaskar, 1980).

In these conditions, no European manufacturer found it easy to make profits out of exporting to other West European countries; export business helped plant loading, but profit margins on export sales were often low or non-existent. British manufacturers, however, were a special case because they could not, or would not, make volume sales to near West European countries; in 1977, for example, the British car industry as a whole sold less than 200,000 cars to near West European countries when France and West Germany each sold 1,250,000 (Bhaskar, 1980). The general failure of the British industry can largely be attributed to the sourcing decisions of American multi-nationals who by 1977 manufactured in Britain and imported cars from Europe to Britain but exported virtually no cars from Britain to Europe; by this date, almost all the British cars sold in Europe were BL cars. This line of argument, however, does not explain why BLMC could only achieve European sales of around 100,000 Austin-Morris cars when other European major manufacturers of volume cars could sell three or four times that number in near West European markets.

The immediate condition of BLMC's low sales was poor distribution. BLMC and BMC had reasonable distribution and volume sales in Belgium and Italy where Austin-Morris cars were locally assembled and had the status of semi-indigenous products: in 1975, when official figures became available (SMMT, 1976), they show that BL sold 25,000 cars in Italy and 50,000 cars in Belgium. Elsewhere in Europe, the dealer network was patchy or non-existent except in some small peripheral markets like Denmark and Eire. The extraordinary fact is that BLMC, like its predecessor BMC, never had a dealer network in France or Germany, two of the big three national markets on mainland Europe. Consequently, in 1975, when 3½ million new cars were sold in France and Germany, BLMC managed to sell just 7,204 cars in these two markets (SMMT, 1976).

In the 1970s, Japanese car-makers have shown that, if the imported product is right for the private buyer, it is possible to build a European distribution network from scratch. But BLMC's problems about distribution, in this same decade, were increasingly insoluble because the company did not develop a range of models which was attractive to the European buyer. When BLMC was formed in 1968, it inherited a one-model European operation where the Mini accounted for 70 per cent of European sales (Turner, 1971). The company's later attempts to save the company with new models were geared to the struggle with Ford on the home market rather than to the requirements of the European market. Thus, the company's first priority was to develop the Marina which was the wrong product for Europe where the 'conventional' three-box, rear-wheel-drive car never enjoyed the pre-eminence that it achieved in Britain in the early 1970s. The product range not only limited distribution but also ensured that the local assembly operations in Italy and Spain would get into difficulty; in the event, these operations collapsed at the worst possible time, in 1974 and 1975 when BLMC management was distracted by massive problems at home.

In summary, the long-standing problems about market limitations at home and abroad were getting much worse in the late 1960s and early 1970s; BLMC was staking its future on new models which were unlikely to sell in large volume. The next section will show that they did not do so and the result was a product-led failure.

5 Product-led decline 1971–9

New models could and did save VW when sales of the Beetle flagged in the early 1970s. But VW had up-to-date factories and an outstandingly good service and distribution network in Europe and North America. The only thing VW needed was a modern product range which sold in high volume. BLMC was in a very different position when it had a legacy of under-investment in its factories and was beset by market limitations at home and abroad. It is clear, however, that the last thing BLMC needed was a modern product range which sold in low volume. This section will demonstrate that low model volume was the outcome of the programme of new model introductions in the early 1970s and that, furthermore, the resulting loss of volume completely undermined profitability.

New models could have helped BLMC if they had been outstandingly attractive to private buyers in Britain and Europe over a long life of ten years. Cars like the Fiat 127, Renault 5 and VW Golf had the qualities which made them into long-life European bestsellers; they offered clever packaging which maximised usable interior space along with a measure of dynamic refinement which the 'first generation' BMC front-wheel-drive cars had lacked. BLMC's two key new models lacked these qualities. The Marina, which was designed to beat the Cortina, aimed at, and missed, a different market target; it failed in the British company car market partly because it was a mechanically compromised 'bitsa job' knocked up by a front-wheel-drive manufacturer which lacked the basic product building blocks for a rear-wheel-drive 1500/1600cc car. The Allegro did compete in the 'super-mini' class but failed dismally because it was a mechanically uncouth styling disaster; this piggy little saloon could never sell against chic and functional hatchbacks like the Renault 5 and VW Golf.

BLMC's mediocre new models were the result of a corporate product planning process which was preoccupied with the design of 'high style' motor cars which were cost engineered so that they were cheap to manufacture (Turner, 1971). In setting these objectives, Leyland management mis-read the European car market and misunderstood the significance of cost engineering which could improve margins in the volume car business, but could not produce profits if individual models did not sell in volume. Furthermore, when mediocre products were sold in BLMC's limited markets, low model volume was the almost inevitable result. We will now demonstrate that the inevitable did happen: our disaggregated analysis of model sales in home and export markets will establish the extent and nature of the new products' failure.

We can first examine the home market sales of the Morris Marina in relation to home sales of the Ford Escort and Cortina, the two models which the Marina was planned to beat. There is no sign that the Marina ever took sales from the Ford Cortina; table 25 shows that the Marina's best years in 1972 and 1973 were also very good years for the Cortina. Ironically, the Marina seems to have taken sales from another BLMC car; home sales of the 1100/1300cc fell by nearly one-third to 100,000 in 1972 (appendix C, table 3). This outcome strongly corroborates our earlier general arguments about BLMC's market problems at home. The Marina, therefore, could never challenge the Cortina's status as number one bestseller; the bestselling Cortina sold up to 11·5 per cent of the market in a good year, while the Marina never reached 7 per cent and sagged towards 5 per cent by the later 1970s (table 25). The Marina was no more successful against the Ford Escort which, as table 25 shows, easily outsold the Marina in the years after 1973 when Marina sales tailed off rapidly; in 1976, and subsequent years, Marina home sales averaged a modest 70,000 units, despite increasingly desperate special promotions and a face lift which turned the Marina into the Ital. After a production life of just four years, BLMC's 'high-style' motor car was out of style and uncompetitive against re-skins like the Cortina IV and Escort II.

TABLE 25 *Marina home market sales versus Escort and Cortina*

	Marina		Cortina		Escort	
	No. (000)	% market	No. (000)	% market	No. (000)	% market
1971	41	3·2	102	8·0	89	6·9
1972	105	6·4	187	11·4	141	8·6
1973	115	6·9	182	11·0	114	6·9
1974	81	6·4	131	10·3	92	7·2
1975	79	6·6	107	9·0	104	8·7
1976	71	5·5	126	9·8	134	10·4
1977	66	5·0	121	9·1	103	7·8
1978	83	5·2	138	8·7	114	7·2
1979	62	3·6	194	11·3	132	7·7

Source: SMMT, *Motor Industry of Great Britain*, various years.

We can next examine home market sales of the Austin Allegro relative to sales of the Austin-Morris 1100/1300, the BLMC model which the Allegro replaced. Through the 1960s the 1100 had consistently been Britain's bestselling motor car. In its heyday in the mid-1960s, the 1100 had managed home sales of more than 150,000 and taken more than 14 per cent of the market. The Allegro was a sales flop; from 1974 to 1979, this model could only sell 55,000 to 65,000 on the home market and its market share averaged 4·3 per cent in the years 1974–9 inclusive. The volume prospects for any 1100

TABLE 26 *Austin Allegro home sales versus 1100/1300*

	1100/1300			Allegro	
Year	No. (000)	% market	Year	No. (000)	% market
1965	158	14·4	1973	29	1·7
1966	152	14·5	1974	61	4·8
1967	131	11·8	1975	63	5·3
1968	151	13·7	1976	55	4·3
1969	133	13·8	1977	56	4·2
1970	133	12·3	1978	62	3·9
1971	134	10·4	1979	60	3·5
1972	102	6·2			

Source: SMMT, *Motor Industry of Great Britain*, various years.

replacement were always poor when market limitations ensured that the 1100 replacement would have to compete against the Marina for those private customers who remained loyal to Austin-Morris. It is notable however that the failure of the Austin Allegro did not ensure the success of the Morris Marina; as private customers defected to importers, the main beneficiaries of the Allegro's failure were the importers of small front-wheel-drive hatchbacks (VW Golf, Renault 5, Fiat 127, Datsun Cherry, etc.) who divided amongst themselves the 'super mini' market which had been created and dominated by the 1100.

Good export sales did not compensate for poor home sales of the Marina and Allegro. The new models, especially the Marina, turned out to be less exportable than the old Mini. In the three years 1975–7 inclusive, 57 per cent of Mini production was sold abroad, but in the same period, only 49 per cent of Allegro and 21 per cent of Marina production was exported (Bhaskar, 1979). As a result, by 1973–4, after the introduction of both new models, the company still did not have a range of models to offer European buyers; it continued to run a one-model operation because in 1973–4 the Mini continued to account for two-thirds of BLMC's European car sales (Ryder, 1975).

Largely thanks to its export sales, the old Mini survived as the only model which BLMC was producing in decent volume; in seven years, from 1968 to 1974 inclusive, the Mini was being produced at an average rate of 297,000 vehicles per annum (appendix B, table 2). BLMC planned to produce its two new models in this kind of volume; the Marina at a rate of 300,000 per annum (Turner, 1971) and the Allegro at a rate of 200,000 per annum (Daniels, 1980). Newly released production statistics from BL show that each model was produced at around half the projected rate. In its first five years of full production from 1971–2 to 1975–6, Marina production averaged 157,000 vehicles per annum (appendix B, table 6). In its first five years of full-volume production, from 1973–4 to 1978, Allegro production averaged around 102,000 cars per annum (appendix B, table 7).

The failure to attain planned volume on the new models had serious repercussions for BLMC because, in the early 1970s, the economics of the car business were changing so that low-volume production of mass market saloons was inherently unprofitable.

With the market failure of the Marina and Allegro, there was an automatic doubling of development and tooling costs per unit sold; by 1973, BLMC had developed and tooled up two saloons (Marina and Allegro) which together achieved the 250,000 per annum production volume which BMC had achieved with one saloon (1100/1300). In fact, the problem was much more acute because, in the era of emissions regulations and safety legislation, the real costs of developing individual new models were rising rapidly. Fixed costs were consequently accounting for an increased proportion of the total costs: as we have already noted, in the late 1950s, Maxcy and Silbertson estimated that fixed costs accounted for 15 per cent of total costs; by the mid-1970s, the Central Policy Review Staff (1975) estimated that fixed costs accounted for just over 30 per cent of total costs. High-model volume became crucial in the 1970s because it allowed fixed costs in general, and development charges in particular, to be spread over a large number of units so that profit per unit was maintained. Ironically, BMC had gained model volume in the 1950s and 1960s, when high model volume did not translate into fat profits; BLMC then lost model volume in the 1970s, when low model volume did translate into no profit.

It is possible to quantify these arguments about low model volume using contemporary BLMC estimates of developing costs. Company estimates of the Marina's direct development costs varied between £16·7 million (Turner, 1971) and £30 million (Ensor, 1971); both estimates explicitly exclude the £35 million cost of modernising Cowley to build the Marina on a gate-line production system. If the Marina were made at a volume of 300,000 per annum and the model had a life of four years, then each car would have carried a development charge of £15–£25. Halve the volume to obtain the 150,000 per annum levels of production actually achieved by the Marina and each car then bore a development charge of £30–£50. The same estimation procedures suggest that each Allegro carried a development charge which was at the upper end of this range. The company claimed that development, plant and tooling for the Allegro had cost £21 million (BLMC, *Annual Report*, 1973). This charge was actually carried on an annual volume of around 100,000; over a four-year write-off period, each Allegro would then bear a development charge of just over £50.

The Marina and Allegro were both keenly priced mass market saloons; the base model Marina cost £996 when it was introduced in 1971 and the base model Allegro cost £1000 when it was introduced in 1973. At these retail prices, a development charge of around £50 per car would have probably killed most of the unit profit. This argument about profit per unit is indirect and the conclusion must be tentative; the company has never disclosed any direct information on costs of production or on receipts from sales net of rebates which were given, for example, to encourage export business. However, even if BLMC did manage to make a moderate unit profit on the two new models, it is clear that the failure to achieve projected model volume on the Marina and Allegro must in itself have undermined profitability because of its effect on capacity utilisation and the break-even point.

Low model volume on the Marina and Allegro affected capacity utilisation and the break-even point in the Austin-Morris car business because BLMC did not have any other volume models which sold in quantity and made a decent profit. Old models like the Morris Minor and Morris Oxford had been phased out before the new model introductions, leaving only the Maxi and the Mini in production. The Maxi cannot have made large profits because it only achieved sales of more than 50,000 units in the boom years of 1972 and 1973 (appendix B, table 5). The Mini did sell at the rate of over 250,000 per annum, but the Mini never gave the company a good margin because it was sold very cheaply although it was relatively expensive to make. In 1970, the standard ex-works price of the Mini gave the company a margin of £15 on each car (Turner, 1971); in 1977, the BL management information service discovered that, after rebates on the ex-works price of the Mini were taken into account, the company was making a small loss on each Mini sold (Golding, 1979). Even if the new models (Marina and Allegro) did make a moderate profit per unit, the old Austin-Morris models had a low, or negative, profit per unit. The company must, therefore, have had a high break-even point; BLMC needed to achieve high levels of capacity utilisation before it would show any kind of profit. However, the company could not achieve high levels of capacity utilisation because the newly introduced BLMC models did not sell well.

The arithmetic of capacity utilisation is fairly straightforward. In 1974, the Austin-Morris volume car operation had a standard two-shift capacity of around 850,000 cars; after the limited modernisation of Cowley in 1971, both Longbridge and Cowley could separately build around 400,000 cars per annum (Commons Expenditure Committee, 1975a). But, even in the boom years of 1972 and 1973, Cowley was operating at around three-quarters of capacity and, in 1974 and subsequent years, Longbridge and Cowley did not manage better than two-thirds of capacity utilised (Bhaskar, 1979). Arithmetically, this under-utilisation is almost entirely the result of the company's failure to produce Marinas and Allegros in the volume that was originally projected. If planned model volume had been achieved, this would have loaded Longbridge and Cowley with an extra 250,000 volume cars per annum and, over the four-year period 1974 to 1977 inclusive, this would have ensured 94 per cent capacity utilisation in the two major assembly points.

This arithmetic does not, of course, prove that the inherent unsaleability of the Marina and Allegro models directly caused the company's over-capacity problem. In 1972 and 1973, poor industrial relations and an unco-operative workforce limited Cowley production. Then with the oil crisis in 1974, the market for new cars in Britain and elsewhere dropped 25 per cent from its boom levels of 1972 and 1973. The generally depressed state of the home market, with around 1,250,000 new car registrations per annum from 1974 to 1977, clearly did not help capacity utilisation. Nevertheless, it is arguable that, after the introduction of the Marina and the Allegro, BLMC lacked the right models to generate sufficient demand under almost any conceivable market circumstances. This argument is supported by the observation that, when the British new car market revived towards 1,750,000 new registrations in 1978 and 1979, BL could not take more sales and lost market share badly.

With the sales failure of the Allegro in 1973, BLMC's collapse inside three or four years became more or less inevitable. In the short run, with the new BLMC models paid for, the company could carry on doing what it was already doing. But with the new models selling in low volume, the Austin-Morris volume car operation was not generating the profits which would allow the company to replace models, leave alone to modernise production facilities. The company did not have any strategic options left.

6   Accounting practices delay a profits crisis, 1971–4

If BLMC was inherently unprofitable, paradoxically it did manage
to declare a profit in every year up to and including 1974; if we
except the profit collapse in 1970, the company regularly made
£30–£50 million in pre-tax profit, and this represented a return on
sales of between 2·5 and 4·2 per cent (table 27, cols iii and iv). The
BLMC merger, like so many others, was a 'disappointing merger'
because BLMC's profits were lower than those of the separate
constituent companies before merger; BLMC's record profit of £51
million in 1973 was less than the 1964 total for its constituent
companies. Nevertheless, by the standards of profit achieved by
other European car companies in the 1970s, BLMC's profit
performance was quite respectable. Even before the oil crisis, most
manufacturers found it difficult to get a decent rate of return. In
the boom year of 1973, only GM (Europe), Ford (Europe) and VW
managed a post-tax return on sales of 2·5 per cent or better; at 1·8
per cent, BLMC's 1973 post-tax return was substantially better
than Fiat's 0·6 per cent and Renault's 0·2 per cent (Bhaskar, 1980).

The explanation for this paradox is that BLMC's profits were
more apparent than real; declared profits were obtained by accounting procedures which were used to support the failing company.
BLMC's accounting practices were trenchantly criticised in the
Ryder Report (1975), and these points have been elaborated by left
wing critics of the company (Friedman, 1977; Harrison and
Sutcliffe, 1975). On this basis, we can analyse the expedients which
were used to find profit when the company was inherently unprofitable as a going concern.

Practice 1
Profit was inflated by taking low depreciation allowances. Unrealistically low historic cost allowances on depreciating capital equipment did not allow for replacing that equipment at inflated current
prices. Profit could only be found as long as the company took low
historic cost allowances: the depreciation and amortisation charge
averaged £42·4 million in the seven years 1968–74 (table 27, col.
ii); the residual pre-tax profit in those years averaged £28·6 million
and would have been wiped out by replacement cost depreciation
provision.

Much of the company's capital equipment was in fact so old that

TABLE 27 *BLMC/BL sales and profit, 1968–81*

Year	Sales	Annual depreciation + amortisation	Net pre-tax profit	% on	Net post-tax profit	% on	Extraordinary items	Dividends paid
	£m (i)	£m (ii)	£m (iii)	sales (iv)	£m (v)	sales (vi)	£m (vii)	£m (viii)
1968	907	40	38	4·2	20	2·2	–	15
1969	970	40	40	4·2	21	2·1	(2)	15
1970	1,021	42	4	0·4	2	0·2	(6)	5
1971	1,177	47	32	2·8	18	1·6	(1)	11
1972	1,281	43	32	2·5	21	1·7	(1)	12
1973	1,564	44	51	3·3	28	1·8	(1)	9
1974	1,595	42	2	0·1	(7)	(0·4)	(16)	3
1975	1,868	50	(76)	(4·1)	(63)	(3·3)	(60)	–
1976	2,892	72	71	2·4	45	1·5	–	–
1977	2,602	62	3	0·1	(5)	(0·2)	(44)	–
1978	3,073	76	2	0·1	3	0·1	(38)	–
1979	2,990	84	(112)	(3·8)	(119)	(4·0)	(23)	–
1980	2,877	108	(388)	(13·5)	(391)	(13·6)	(139)	–
1981	2,869	134	(333)	(11·6)	(339)	(11·8)	(152)	–

Source: **BLMC/BL,** *Annual Report and Accounts,* 1968–81.

Note: Figures in brackets denote losses and deductions from profits or earnings. Results for 1976 are for the 15 months ended 31 December 1976.

it was fully depreciated; approximately half the company's capital equipment (in historic cost terms) was fully depreciated pre-1966 equipment (Ryder, 1975). BLMC never made *any* allowance for replacing this depreciated capital equipment. The 1975 company report disclosed that fixed assets costing £222 million were fully depreciated and still in service on 31 October 1974 and estimated that depreciation at normal (historic cost) rates on these assets would have amounted to £34 million. This item was again large enough on its own to wipe out the declared pre-tax profit.

Practice 2
Profit was inflated by making no allowance for stock depreciation on stocks and materials and finished goods. Stock appreciation was a large and growing part of declared profit as inflation rates escalated in the early 1970s. Harrison and Sutcliffe (1975) estimated that stock appreciation should have been entered at £19 million in 1972 and £70 million in 1974. In the latter years of BLMC, stock appreciation was growing rapidly until this item again was large enough to wipe out profits.

Practice 3
Profit was inflated by taking closure costs as a special 'extraordinary item' after profit had been declared. Extraordinary items of £6 and £16 million in 1970 and 1974 were of some importance because they allowed the company to declare a small pre-tax profit rather than a small pre-tax loss.

The remarkable transformation produced by these accounting practices is calculated in the table below which re-works BLMC's declared profits for the years 1972–4 inclusive. Table 28 suggests even in the boom years of 1972 and 1973, BLMC could not turn in a genuine profit; the company was making substantial losses of £35 million or more. When the car market turned down in 1974, after the oil crisis, the company was in a desperate position.

To cap it all, in an attempt to keep the shareholders happy, a large proportion was distributed in the form of dividends. In the seven years from 1968 to 1974 inclusive, net profits after charges (including extraordinary items) amounted to £74 million, of which no less than £70 million was paid out by way of dividend (table 27, col. vii). When genuine accounting profits were not being earned,

TABLE 28   *BLMC estimated pre-tax loss, 1972–4 (£ million)*

		1972	1973	1974
	BLMC *declared pre-tax profit*	31·9	51·3	2·3
less				
(a)	current cost depreciation allowance	13·0	17·5	20·0
(b)	depreciation allowance on fully depreciated equipment	34·0	34·0	34·0
(c)	stock appreciation	18·8	35·0	70·0
(d)	extraordinary items	0·9	0·6	15·7
	BLMC *estimated pre-tax loss*	(34·8)	(35·8)	(137·4)

Sources:
(a)   Harrison and Sutcliffe (1975) estimate.
(b)   BLMC, *Annual Report* (1975) estimate (on historic cost basis).
(c)   Harrison and Sutcliffe (1975).
(d)   BLMC, *Annual Report* (1972–4).

the directors of BLMC were, in effect, distributing the fixed and working capital of the business to the shareholders; this is a practice which all elementary accounting textbooks warn against. Of course, BLMC's directors may have done this inadvertently. All three of the accounting practices which inflated profitability were normal under British accounting conventions of the early 1970s; on depreciation and stock appreciation, BLMC could be represented as the unwitting victim of historic cost conventions which were increasingly inappropriate in an inflationary age. This interpretation is not entirely plausible, however, because BLMC showed some sophistication in other accounting matters. Like any other unprofitable company, BLMC could only survive in the short run by looking after its cash flow, which was indeed attended to in a deliberate and careful manner.

The company looked after cash flow in the classic way by getting prompt payment for goods despatched from its factories while suppliers were kept waiting for their money. Thus, from 1968 to 1974, 'debtors and bills receivable' increased by only 38 per cent to £181 million (table 29, col. i), but in the same period of seven years, 'creditors and bills payable' increased by 138 per cent to £479 million (table 29, col. ii). BLMC also got cash by borrowing from the banks. The company was a net short-term borrower in most years; net short-term borrowings averaged nearly £70 million in the three years 1970–2, and, by 1974, these borrowings were back up to £35 million and rising fast to an astronomical £250 million by 1975 (table 29, col. iii).

TABLE 29   *BLMC/BL indebtedness and operating assets, 1968–81 (£m)*

Year	Current debtors + bills receivable	Current creditors + bills payable	Net short-term borrowing	Net interest charge	Net operating assets	NOA as % of sales
	(i)	(ii)	(iii)	(iv)	(v)	(vi)
1968	131	201	–	8	98	10·8
1969	148	223	–	5	125	12·9
1970	167	245	79	10	176	17·2
1971	165	239	90	14	221	18·8
1972	160	262	39	9	151	11·8
1973	189	363	21	7	122	7·8
1974	181	479	35	17	139	8·7
1975	254	576	248	38	185	9·9
1976	311	715	230	47	382	13·2
1977	356	781	328	54	525	20·2
1978	398	741	117	56	623	20·3
1979	448	759	228	66	651	21·8
1980	434	916	296	94	390	13·6
1981	341	924	144	88	264	9·2

Source: BLMC/BL, *Annual Report and Accounts*, 1968–81.

None of these expedients generated adequate amounts of cash, so the company finally kept going by running down its working capital. Ryder (1975) argued, and the company accounts suggest, that the company needed to maintain an operating assets-to-sales ratio of at least 15 per cent. In its early years, the company did not have this kind of ratio, and, by 1973 and 1974, the ratio of operating assets to sales had been run down to 8 per cent (table 29, col. vi). The operating assets necessary for day-to-day trading were run down to a critical level at which continuous uninterrupted production was difficult because the company could not finance stocks of components or finished products.

All this suggests one obvious conclusion: creative accounting could only deal with the problems of inherent unprofitability to a limited extent over a short time period. The company's nemesis came in 1975 when, with all its accounting practices and expedients, it could not avoid declaring a large pre-tax loss of some £76 million.

7 The workforce as scapegoats

Our introductory essay argued generally that the importance of labour control problems in British manufacturing has been exaggerated. We must now consider whether this general conclusion holds in the particular case of BLMC, which could be simply the exception that proves the rule. The media presentation of BLMC/BL through the 1970s has encouraged popular pre-conceptions about the importance of the company's labour problems. On television news and in the tabloids BLMC/BL was strikes. Even in quality newspapers, like *The Times* and the *Guardian*, a few features, which analysed the company's problems, were swamped by news stories about strikes; in the crisis year of 1975 when BLMC collapsed, *The Times* carried 523 separate items on the British car industry and almost exactly three-quarters of these items were about labour disputes. There is a media stereotype of BLMC/BL which implies that the unreasonable behaviour of the workforce has been the central problem of the company in the 1970s. In this section, it will be argued that this stereotype is a misrepresentation.

To begin with, it is necessary to understand the problems which BMC created for itself before 1968 by its reliance on a primitive form of direct control over the labour process. Workers were motivated by a complicated system of piece-rate payments to individuals and gangs (*Motor Business*, October 1960), where the key agent of control was the foreman who put effort into rate-busting and speed-up. The practice can be illustrated by considering Mini final assembly in 1960 (Golding, 1979). The first Minis were built on Longbridge car assembly building line four which had 57 work stations; at every station on the line, an operative had just two minutes and twenty-four seconds in which to complete one assembly operation. In this system, the time allowance was crucial and the foreman's job was to control padded time allowances without compromising build quality. The company did not use work study, but relied on the line foreman's ability to do any job at least as fast as the operative.

BLMC's problem was that informal control was met by informal resistance. Unofficial shop steward organisation was important in all British car factories because of the peculiar national system of two-tier (national and plant level) wage bargaining; in BMC's major plants unofficial organisation was unusually well-developed because endless disputes about complicated piece-rate structures provided the stewards with a real *raison d'être*. As table 30 shows, through the 1950s and 1960s, BMC was increasingly plagued by small unofficial strikes about wage structure and work norms, under a regime where collective bargaining by 'downer' became the recognised way of settling grievances. BMC management made no constructive response. It institutionalised the role of the senior steward, or convener, who increasingly acted as a full-time negotiator in settling disputes; but that did not solve the strike problem because the senior stewards were always arsonists as much as firemen.

TABLE 30   *Annual average strike liability, 1946–64*

	1946–52		1953–9		1960–4	
	No. of strikes	Days lost (000)*	No. of strikes	Days lost (000)*	No. of strikes	Days lost (000)*
BMC	3	18	12	84	39	106
Ford	3	51	3	21	8	52
British car industry	10	87	29	153	76	257

Source: Turner et al. (1966).
*days lost = days directly lost, excluding consequential day-offs.

None of this proves that BMC before 1968 was seriously damaged by its labour control problems. There is no evidence that BMC's control of the labour process failed catastrophically; bad work practices which restricted output must have been contained because, as the company expanded by replication, a more or less constant 7–9 vehicles per man-year were produced (table 23). The workforce did resist tight informal control by striking early and often, but the extent of this strike problem should not be exaggerated. In 1963, even when consequential lay-offs are included, each hourly paid BMC manual worker lost less than five working days due to strikes. It is true that strikes did cause output loss. Nevertheless, by the early 1960s, the company's immediate problem was not lost volume but low profitability, which was determined by management decisions about low-capital-intensity expansion of small car production.

When BLMC was formed in 1968, it inherited an 'industrial relations' problem. However, the company also inherited other more serious problems which were themselves sufficient to account for the company's failure over the next seven years; the pre-1968 expansion strategy had compromised profitability in a company which was increasingly beset by market limitations. Furthermore, as we have already argued, the fate of BLMC was then sealed by the inept execution of the new model strategy. The failure of that strategy was determined at the product planning and development stage where management was clearly and unequivocally in charge. If BLMC was killed by massive managerial miscalculation, it is unnecessary to blame the workers. Indeed, our question must be: why were the workers blamed?

The answer is that, in the early 1970s as BLMC's problems deepened, strikes and bad work practices were not so much a real injury as an ideological opportunity since they allowed management to scapegoat the workers for the company's deteriorating performance. Management argued that the company's dealers could sell cars which the factories were unable to produce because the strikes lost output and bad work practices restricted output (BLMC, *Annual Report*, 1974). The company's chief executive, Donald Stokes, claimed that lack of product availability caused a variety of problems including increased import penetration.

> What they (the importers) have had is something that we have lacked and that is availability. We have lost 150,000 cars a year due to industrial disputes and so on. . . . There is no doubt that people will not wait for a motor car for a year or eighteen months if there is another car available (Commons Expenditure Committee, 1975b).

The management's analysis may have been made in good faith but it is hardly convincing.

The relative unavailability of Austin-Morris cars has been greatly exaggerated. Even at the height of the Barber boom, in 1972 and 1973, the waiting lists were nowhere near as long as one year. In the depressed car markets of 1974 and subsequent years, the estimates published in *What Car* show that the customer usually had to wait three months or less for delivery of an Allegro or Marina. The impact of such waiting lists on sales should have been limited since at this time, many other British and foreign cars were not freely available. According to *What Car* in 1974, for example, customers would have to wait seven weeks for a Ford Escort or Cortina and, from summer 1977 to summer 1979, customers for the bestselling

Escort and Cortina were waiting twelve to thirty-two weeks. As Ford's marketplace performance shows, with differentiated products like motor cars, customers are prepared to wait when the product is sufficiently attractive. If waiting lists of a few months lost volume sales for BLMC, that was mostly because the perceived quality of Austin-Morris cars was low.

The company did, of course, lose large amounts of output because of interruptions to scheduled production; in 1973–4, BLMC lost 36 per cent of its scheduled product. But up to one half of the output loss was caused by management's poor co-ordination of complex and inter-related production processes which were often interrupted by poor scheduling, component unavailability and line breakdowns. Even the unsympathetic Central Policy Review Staff in the strike-prone early 1970s had to concede that industrial disputes generally accounted for only two-thirds of lost output in the British car industry (CPRS, 1975). On the company's own evidence, BLMC's record was often in line with the industry norm; there was a 37 per cent loss of scheduled production in October-November 1974 and about half the loss was due to quality faults, plant failure, build-programme changes and absenteeism rather than labour disputes. Over a longer period, management's responsibility for output loss may have been much greater; as we have argued, when the company was in difficulty, working capital was cut down so that, from 1972 to 1975, the company almost certainly did not have the working capital to finance uninterrupted production.

Furthermore, if management had been able to finance uninterrupted production with full co-operation from the workforce, this might have cleared the waiting lists and left the company with large stocks of unsaleable cars. In the boom years of 1972 and 1974, the company could probably have sold the 100,000 or more cars per annum which were lost at its two major assembly plants, Long-bridge and Cowley. But from the autumn of 1973 onwards, when the car market turned down, the situation was very different. From 1974 through to 1977 Longbridge and Cowley could have built 300,000 cars per annum more than the 500,000 they did build (Bhaskar, 1979). This would have been disastrous because there was nowhere an extra 300,000 cars per annum could have been sold. When lost output was not readily saleable, production interruptions did not simply represent lost revenue and profit. Indeed, by 1974, the company needed the production interruptions caused by management and workforce; 'beneficial strikes' were one means by which the company avoided piling up stocks of unsaleable Marinas and Allegros.

If strikes were very much less important and less harmful than management alibis and media stereotypes would lead us to believe, we are left with the broader question as to whether and how bad work practices harmed BLMC after 1968. The general issue of bad work practices in the British car industry was discussed in our introductory essay where it was admitted that more man-hours were required to build cars in British factories of the 1970s. At the same time it was argued that, in cost terms, lower British wages partly compensated for the greater man-hour requirement, while other, more serious, cost problems were created by the low volume production of individual models. We could now add the point that the famous Central Policy Review Staff labour process comparisons were invalid and unfair in so far as they were based on data supplied by BLMC; the output expansion strategy of earlier decades had ensured that by the mid-1970s BLMC's production methods were necessarily labour intensive. With this point made, however, it is worth examining the systematic evidence on physical productivity levels in Austin-Morris; a deterioration in productivity performance in the 1970s might indicate the spread of bad work practices as control over the labour process weakened.

TABLE 31   *Austin-Morris division productivity performance, 1969–75*

	Employees (000) (i)	UK car prodn (000) (ii)	Cars per employee–year (iii)
1969	81	634	7·8
1970	88	588	6·7
1971	81	666	8·2
1972	80	698	8·7
1973	85	672	7·9
1974	81	561	6·9
1975	81*	450	5·5

Source: BLMC, *Annual Reports*, 1969–75.
*1975 employee total estimated.

It is often argued that the abolition of piece-rates and the introduction of measured daywork between 1971 and 1974 was a management-sponsored disaster whereby the company paid out higher wages, while it lost control of manning levels and work norms in the labour process. The physical productivity evidence suggests that this interpretation is too melodramatic. Over the period in which measured day-work was introduced, there was no increase in the workforce or decline in output per man-year; Austin-Morris produced nearly seven vehicles per man-year in both 1970 and 1974 (table 31, col. iii). The impact of measured day-work on production costs is more uncertain. However, the ratio of BLMC wages and salaries to sales does provide indirect evidence on this point. The ratio barely changed; from its normal level of 27 per cent in the late 1960s, the ratio rose to just over 30 per cent in 1973–4. Hourly wage costs in Austin-Morris cannot have been completely out of control.

If BLMC management did not lose control over the labour process in the short run, it is clear that, in the long run, physical productivity levels were consistently lower in the Austin-Morris division in the early 1970s than they had been ten or twenty years previously in the old BMC. In physical terms, both the Austin-Morris division and the old BMC achieved similar ratios of between 7 and 9 vehicles per man year (table 23, col. vii, table 31, col. iii). The Austin-Morris division however produced only cars and light vans. It had a more favourable product mix from the productivity point of view than the old BMC whose output had included medium-weight commercial vehicles which were counted as part of BLMC's truck and bus division output after 1968, and are therefore excluded from the calculations in the table. The maintenance of a similar ratio in the 1970s therefore represents a real deterioration in long-run productivity performance.

If neither BMC nor BLMC had the wherewithal for ambitious plant modernisation, the quality of the company's capital equipment was probably much the same in the early 1960s or the early 1970s. It is, therefore, tempting to attribute the secular deterioration in physical productivity to long-run changes in work practices. The evidence, however, does not support this inference. As table 31 shows, in BLMC, the number of vehicles produced per man-year varied because the number of vehicles sold changed, while the number of employees remained more or less the same at just over 80,000 (table 31, col. i). Bad work practices and strikes are not the primary cause of fluctuations in vehicles sold; the company produced 698,000 Austin-Morris cars in 1972 because the car market was booming, but sales fell back to 561,000 and 450,000 in 1974 and 1975 because the company was selling relatively unattractive new models in a depressed and limited market (table 31, col. ii).

By 1982 the press was carrying features on a 'productivity miracle' (*Sunday Times*, 21 March 1982) in the volume-car operation at Longbridge and Cowley, now designated 'Austin Rover Group'; BL has claimed that Austin Rover in 1981 achieved a 40 per cent improvement in productivity (BL, *Annual Report*, 1981) and that Longbridge is now running at 'European levels of efficiency'. These claims are rather dubious because the 'miracle' has been largely achieved by sacking nearly half the divisional workforce to bring employment in line with reduced output; by the end of 1981, the volume-car operation employed just over 43,000 workers (BL, *Annual Report*, 1981).

Furthermore, despite large-scale redundancy in other divisions, the labour productivity performance of the BL company as a whole remains overshadowed by market failure and cumulative loss of volume. In 1981, the company as a whole produced 5·1 vehicles per man-year and this represented a very modest recovery from the nadir of about 4·5 vehicles per man-year reached in the 1977–80 period (table 32, col. viii). The current level of performance is, however, significantly below the best results achieved by the BLMC company in the years 1968–75; the newly formed BLMC achieved 6·3 and 6·2 vehicles per man year in 1968 and 1969 (table 32, col. viii). As we have already argued, differences in output mix prevent any exact comparison with the performance of the old BMC. Nevertheless, it must be significant that the newly formed BMC achieved 6·9 vehicles per man year in 1951–2 (table 23, col. vii).

The real productivity 'miracle' is that BMC/BLMC/BL's labour productivity has been static for the past thirty years, and it should by now be clear that BMC and BLMC's management must bear the responsibility for these dismal results. The workers are not the villains of the piece and could more plausibly be described as the victims because they have suffered the consequences of management miscalculation in the form of mass redundancy; in its heyday, in the early 1970s, BLMC employed 184,000 workers in the UK, but by December 1981, BL employed only 94,000 workers in the UK (BL, *Annual Report*, 1981).

TABLE 32   *BLMC/BL cars, UK production and productivity, 1968–81*

	Austin-Morris production (000)	Total UK car production[a] (000)	Total car export allocation (000)	Total car home sales (000)	Company share of car market (%)	Total vehicle sales (000)	Total UK employees (000)	Vehicles per man-year
	(i)	(ii)	(iii)	(iv)	(v)	(vi)	(vii)	(viii)
1968	609	818	398	420	41	1050	168	6·3
1969	634	831	409	422	41	1083	175	6·2
1970	588	789	368	421	38	984	176	5·6
1971	666	887	386	501	41	1057	169	6·3
1972	698	917	348	569	35	1127	184	6·1
1973	672	875	348	527	31	1161	171	6·8
1974	561	739	323	416	32	1020	173	5·9
1975	450	605	256	349	30	845	164	5·2
1976	–	688	321	367	27	981	162	6·1
1977	–	561	293	358	25	785	172	4·6
1978	466	611	248	363	23	797	169	4·7
1979	355	504	200	304	23	693	155	4·5
1980						587	135	4·4
1981						525	104	5·1

Sources: cols (i) – (v) SMMT, *Motor Industry of Great Britain*, various years.
cols (vi) – (viii) BLMC/BL, *Annual Report and Accounts*, 1968–81.
[a] includes Jaguar, Rover and Triumph cars plus Austin-Morris.

8 Profits crises after 1974

Market failure has been the dynamic force which caused BLMC's collapse in 1975 and BL's subsequent chronic difficulties. In six of the eight years since 1974, vehicle sales have declined so that the company which sold 1,020,000 vehicles in 1974 sold only 525,000 in 1981. The plight of BLMC/BL was dramatised by the monthly publication of statistics on the company's share of the domestic car market. If Jaguar-Rover-Triumph sales are added to Austin-Morris, BLMC's home market share was 40 per cent in 1968 (table 32, col. v); by 1975, after BLMC's new model introductions, the company's share was down to 30 per cent and it has since declined further to under 20 per cent (table 32, col. v). The company's situation was equally bad in export markets which had taken 400,000 cars per annum at the end of the 1960s but were only taking 200,000 cars at the end of the 1970s (table 32, col. iii). BMC's successful defence of market share up to the mid-1960s had produced few financial benefits for the company; it was ironic, therefore, that BLMC and BL were completely undermined by their loss of market share. Since 1974, management's primary problem has been that market failure, through its effect on capacity utilisation, has produced huge financial losses.

The company reports show that the first acute financial crisis came in the year 1975 when the company lost £76 million before tax (table 33, col. iv). By 1975, BLMC's problem was that it was losing a large sum on each vehicle sold; it lost £90 per vehicle before tax and, if closure costs are added on, then the company lost £160 per vehicle. Cash was haemorrhaging out at a phenomenal rate, and the company could only survive in the short run by borrowing from the banks to finance everything from new investment to the weekly wage bill; net short-term borrowings increased from £35 million in 1974 to almost £250 million in 1975 (table 33, col. iii). Through 1974, short-term borrowing was growing well beyond the company's capacity to service the loans, leave alone repay the principal and, by the summer of 1974, the clearing banks were increasingly nervous and unwilling to lend.

In our general introductory essay we argued that British financial institutions have, in a variety of ways, conditioned British manufacturing into the pursuit of short-run profit. Conversely, we would argue that under British institutional conditions, there is no 'free-

TABLE 33   *BLMC/BL profit and loss, 1968–81 (£ million)*

	Total sales	Net interest charges	Net short-term borrowing	Pre-tax profit (loss)	Post-tax profit (loss)	Closure costs ('extraordinary items')	Pre-tax profit (loss) £ per vehicle
	(i)	(ii)	(iii)	(iv)	(v)	(vi)	(vii)
1968	907	7·6	–	37·9	20·3	(0·3)	36·1
1969	970	5·3	1·1	40·4	20·8	(1·9)	37·3
1970	1021	10·3	(79·3)	3·9	2·3	(6·4)	4·0
1971	1177	14·3	(90·2)	32·4	18·4	(1·0)	30·7
1972	1281	9·1	(38·9)	31·9	21·1	0·9	28·3
1973	1564	6·9	(21·3)	51·3	27·9	0·6	44·2
1974	1595	17·1	(35·2)	2·3	(6·7)	(15·7)	2·3
1975	1868	38·0	(248·3)	(76·1)	(63·2)	(59·6)	(90·1)
1976	2892	47·2	(230·1)	70·5	44·6	–	71·9
1977	2602	53·6	(327·7)	3·1	(5·0)	(43·9)	4·0
1978	3073	56·0	(117·3)	1·7	2·7	(38·3)	19·2
1979	2990	66·0	(227·9)	(112·2)	(118·5)	(23·0)	(161·9)
1980	2877	93·6	(295·9)	(387·5)	(390·7)	(139·0)	(660·1)
1981	2869	88·3	(144·0)	(332·9)	(339·2)	(152·0)	(634·1)

Source: BLMC/BL *Annual Report*, 1968–81.

market' mechanism for supporting short-run operating losses; the situation is obviously different in Japan or Germany where there are strong ownership links between finance capital and manufacturing. Under British rules of the game, there are only two solutions for short-run losses – liquidation or state ownership. The 1975 solution for BLMC was state ownership. In December 1974, the British government guaranteed a further £50 million loan from the banks to the company, subject to investigation of the company's affairs by a team under Don Ryder. Ryder proposed, and government endorsed, a new strategy. A new nationalised company, BL, was to be formed and large sums of public money (matched pound for pound from BL's future profits) were to be injected into this company over an eight-year period; a total of £2,090 million in inflated price terms was to be applied to the renovation of production facilities, the development of new models and the topping up of working capital.

Public investment was made in the expectation of profit, but these expectations were disappointed; in 1979, 1980 and 1981, the BL company recorded losses of £112, £388 and £333 million before tax (table 33, col. iv). In this second profits crisis, all the elements of the first were repeated in more dramatic form. Again the company's immediate problem was a cash haemorrhage; in 1979, the company lost £160 per vehicle before tax and, by 1980 and 1981, the loss had mounted to more than £600 per vehicle (table 33, col. vii). After 1979, the position was even worse because, as major closures took place, so 'extraordinary items' rose towards £150 million per annum. When closure costs are added on the company was losing a stupendous £900 per vehicle sold in 1980 and 1981. Again the company survived in the short run by borrowing; in 1979, net short-term borrowings were over £225 million and in 1980, nearly £300 million (table 33, col. iii).

These operating losses and the consequent short-term borrowings were a massive problem for BL. The losses were so large that they defeated the government's worthy aim of providing long-term equity finance for the strategic development of the company; from 1975 onwards, much of what the government injected appears to have been applied to servicing or re-paying short-term debt. The problem of operating losses caused by capacity under-utilisation could not therefore be avoided. There are, in principle, two broad ways in which problems of this type can be resolved: the enterprise can respond offensively by aggressively marketing new or developed products to win the sales volume which will load the plants; or the company can respond defensively by taking lower demand as a given, and reducing capacity to meet demand. Given the national conditions of enterprise calculation, British firms usually respond in a defensive way and, in the case of BL, state ownership only delayed and qualified this response. In 1974 and 1975, BLMC closed only peripheral loss-making assembly operations in Australia, Spain and Italy. In the 'false dawn' period in 1976 and 1977, the company was actually hiring workers for the car division; by autumn 1977, the number of employees in the car division had increased by more than 10,000 (Bhaskar, 1979).

From 1976 onwards, however, BL management did respond defensively and pushed through large-scale plant closure and redundancy. Major British plant closures began with the 1978 closure of Triumph's Speke (Liverpool) plant which reduced capacity by some 100,000 cars. In 1980, this was followed by the abandonment of final assembly at Triumph's Canley (Coventry) plant and the decision to close the Austin-Morris assembly plant at Seneffe in Belgium. The next major development was the 1981 closure of Rover's recently built Solihull (Birmingham) car plant, which reduced capacity by a further 150,000 cars. If we exclude Jaguar's specialist operation at Brown's Lane (Coventry), all car final assembly has now been concentrated in the company's two central plants, the old BMC factories at Longbridge (Birmingham) and Cowley (Oxford). This was symbolised by the transfer of Rover (SDI) car production from Solihull to Cowley.

The company's most recent report (for 1981) claims BL will break even in 1984, but the accompanying accounts suggest that closures have not solved the problems of high operating losses. In 1981, the accounts show the company made an operating loss of more than £300 million (before tax), paid out £150 million in closure costs and paid back £150 million of short-term bank borrowing; these burdens must have absorbed most of the £620 million of state equity finance injected in the year to March 1982. Operating losses remain high – and short-term debt is a constant problem because the company still has excess capacity. Longbridge and Cowley have a two-shift capacity of more than 800,000 cars but, by 1980, the company was only making 500,000 cars and fast approaching the point where it needed only one of its two major assembly plants. Over-capacity, despite previous closures, explains the company's increasingly aggressive use of the closure threat to discipline a workforce which in 1981 was persuaded to take a wage increase well below the rate of inflation for the fourth year running. Over-capacity also explains the rapid run-down of employment in the central plants at Longbridge and Cowley; in mid-1982, Longbridge employed 9,500 workers, or less than half the 19,400 of 1977 (*Financial Times*, 17 June 1982).

Much now depends on the sales success of the new Maestro saloon (LC10) which is due to be launched in 1983 and may win the company desperately needed extra volume. If the medium saloon fails in the marketplace, management will probably be caught in a vicious downward spiral, where it will attempt to control operating losses by contracting the business to the point where it ceases to be a volume car manufacturer. From this perspective in 1982, Ryder in 1975 stands out as the company's last chance to stay in the European major league of volume car producers. Our final question must therefore be: why did Ryder fail?

9 Why did Ryder fail?

Ryder's strategy was a 'massive programme to modernise plant and equipment at BL', whereby £2,000 million was to be invested in the company over eight years. It was accepted that, in the early years of the programme, government would supply most of the investment funds and nationalisation therefore represented a removal of the secular financial constraints established by low private profitability. The result was disastrous, because the Ryder team took a naive productionist view of the company's problems and committed the company to investments which were wasted when market limitations constrained the saleability of the company's existing product lines. As our introductory essay argued, similar strategic mistakes were made in steel.

In principle, the availability of large amounts of long-term funds represented a strategic opportunity; for the first time, for example, the company could contemplate building modern, integrated volume-car production facilities. At the same time, increased investment was also a problem because, for reasons explained in the introductory essay, new investment was likely to lower a rate of return which was already negative in BL's case. In volume cars the dilemma was that, if development costs had killed the profit on the Marina and Allegro, their replacements would have to carry an extra charge for new build facilities. In the company as a whole, the problem was simply that the depreciation charges on the better part of £2,000 million would inevitably be swingeing. An investment of £2,000 million was therefore large enough to be embarrassing, but it was never large enough to let the company do everything at once; the sum actually available for new build facilities, for example, was very modest when Ryder calculated £400 million was required for new models and £750 million was required to remedy the company's chronic shortage of working capital (Ryder, 1975). The question of where and how £2,000 million could be spent for the best long-run results was therefore absolutely crucial.

The question of where investment should be concentrated could not be posed in the Ryder Report because, as the Commons Expenditure Committee (1975a) observed, Ryder assumed that the company should continue all its activities in their present or expanded form. Ryder would not even accept that the new strategy of massive investment logically required large-scale redundancy. If all went well, investment in new facilities would raise productivity to the European level of between 9 and 14 cars per man-year. In this case, as Bhaskar (1979) argued, the cars division would have to reduce its workforce from 130,000 to between 60,000 and 90,000. Within a broad framework where everything was to stay the same, Ryder decided where the £2,000 million should be spent by endorsing a BLMC management shopping list of investment projects which would be desirable, given 'relatively free availability of cash' (Commons Expenditure Committee, 1975b, question 2158). As Donald Stokes admitted, this shopping list already existed *before* Ryder's investigation in the form of an internal BLMC 'concept study' (Commons Expenditure Committee, 1975b, question 2150). There never was a distinctive government strategy for the firm, because Ryder simply allowed the existing management team to determine how the money was spent.

The inconsistencies and illogicalities of the Ryder report were covered up by projecting a large increase in car output from 'depressed' 1975 levels; Ryder assumed that the company would sell 843,000 cars by 1980 and 961,000 by 1985. Although volume was absolutely crucial to obtaining a decent rate of return on the new state investment, Ryder never seriously inquired whether government could sell the large output from modernised plants. On this issue Ryder uncritically endorsed the sales forecasts of the existing BLMC management; as John Barber admitted, 'these are effectively our figures' (Commons Expenditure Committee, 1975b, question 2158). The crucial assumptions in these sales forecasts concerned BLMC's share of the car market in future years; it was assumed that BLMC could maintain its home market share at 33 per cent and increase its European share from 1·7 to 4·0 per cent (Bhaskar, 1979). In a company where volume was being lost and market share had fallen because of market limitations, these assumptions were at best optimistic and at worst unrealistic. They certainly demanded close scrutiny.

Ryder made the sales projections appear plausible by defining market objectives in percentage terms and by making a highly aggregative market analysis. In percentage market share terms, BL's objective appeared to be modest; the company's share of the European market would only have to be raised from 2 to 4 per cent. In absolute terms, the objectives would have looked very different; Ryder was projecting an increase in BL's European car sales from 125,000 in 1975 to 400,000 in 1985. At the same time, an aggregative analysis of trends in the British and European markets was crucial because it allowed Ryder to avoid facing the specific issue of which models would be sold in what segments of particular national markets. A disaggregated market analysis would have shown that, until the company had a new product range for the home market after 1980 and, unless the company completely overhauled its distribution facilities, BL's home and export market objectives were completely unattainable.

When Ryder avoided the issue of whether increased output was saleable, it is not surprising that the report did not examine what would happen if the increased output was not saleable. This was nevertheless a remarkable omission when BL's profits were being undermined by low volume in 1975, and any analysis would have shown that the enterprise's profits were highly sensitive to volume. Bhaskar's (1979) sensitivity analysis traced the change in BL profits in a variety of different scenarios. On the basis of plausible assumptions about, for example, size of workforce, Bhaskar showed that 1982 vehicle sales of 1,200,000 would produce profits of £400 million; at sales of 850,000, the company would break even and, at sales of 600,000 the company would make a loss of £400 million.

The lower band estimates of losses at low volume originally made by Bhaskar in the late 1970s appear to have subsequently been vindicated by experience.

It is now a matter of record that Ryder's predictions of overall market share were hopelessly optimistic. By 1981, the company was having difficulty in holding 20 per cent of the home market and was selling nearer 1 per cent than 4 per cent of the European market; BL sold 80,000 cars in Europe in 1981 when Ryder had projected it would sell more than 300,000 (*Financial Times*, 21 April 1982). If Ryder ignored market limitations and never considered the profit implications of failure to meet market objectives, the management team under Edwardes in the 1977–82 period had to deal with the consequences.

10   BL under Edwardes 1977–82

The failure of Ryder, on profit and market-share yardsticks, was obvious before the profits crisis of 1979–80. In November 1977, Michael Edwardes was brought in to head the company for a five-year period and Ryder was abandoned in favour of a more modest corporate plan of February 1978 which was to be supported by the issue of £450 million in government equity. The new management's strategy was defensive in that it relied upon a programme of plant closures which we have already discussed. At the same time, state financing allowed that new management to make offensive plans for a 'product-led recovery'. New models like the super-mini LC8 (Metro) and the medium saloon LC10 (Austin Maestro) would pull back some of the lost market share and, for the first time, new models were to be built in modern facilities; Metro was built in a new robotised body-shop at Longbridge. At the time of writing (1982), this offensive strategy has not yet succeeded.

Profit was depressed and market share necessarily remained low until the new models could be launched. The offensive strategy burdened the company with higher model development and depreciation charges in an interim period when the strategy could not improve sales because new models took time to develop. The first of the new BL volume models was the Metro which was launched in the autumn of 1980 and the new medium saloon was not to be launched until 1983. The strategy appeared to be partly vindicated when the Metro became a sales success; one year after its British launch and just after its European introduction, Metro was being produced at a rate of 4,600 cars a week (*Autocar*, 17 October 1981). For the first time in more than fifteen years, the company had succeeded in developing a new model which was sufficiently attractive to sell at a rate of over 200,000 units per annum.

The introduction of the Metro did not however solve BL's problems about low volume because market limitations continued to operate. Metro did not win greater share for the company against its competitors; in a familiar pattern, Metro took sales from older models in BL's own range. As the Marina had damaged 1100 sales in 1971, so Metro killed Mini sales in 1981: Mini production was already declining from the 200,000 per annum level sustained in the years from 1975 to 1978, but in 1981 BL made just 70,000 Minis (appendix B, table 2). To obtain a stopgap new model, BL decided to assemble a variant of the Honda Civic which was launched as the Triumph Acclaim in October 1981. This simply aggravated the poaching problem because Metro and Acclaim together finally killed off the old Allegro; the company produced 42,000 Allegros in 1980 and just 23,000 in 1981 (appendix B, table 7).

In this situation, with continuing high operating losses and low volume, the new Maestro saloon (LC10) which will be launched in 1983 is crucial to the survival of the company in its present form. This new model must not only sell in volume at over 200,000 units per annum, it must also take sales from other companies. The company has never in the past succeeded in doing this and its task is clearly not going to be easy on the home market where LC10 will compete against the strong model offerings of Ford (Escort/Sierra) and General Motors (Astra/Cavalier). BL may succeed because the team which designed the Metro is clearly capable of developing models which are technically class-competitive in any European market. However, if the company's British and European market share does not improve after the launch of LC10, low volume and capacity utilisation will probably trap the company in the down spiral which we have already analysed and continuing operating losses will have to be met by further contraction of the business. In this situation only massive capital-asset write-offs could produce a profit.

If LC10 succeeds in 1983 and 1984, BL can probably make a genuine accounting profit on its assets, or at least break even at production levels of 500,000 to 600,000 cars per annum. There are two reasons for being optimistic on this point. First, BL can as a junior partner share the development costs of new models in co-operative deals with other manufacturers. It is significant here that BL has already announced it will collaborate with Honda in developing a large saloon which BL will sell as a Rover. Second, if the current productivity gains are as remarkable as the company claims, there is no reason why assembly using major mechanical components bought in from other manufacturers should not be profitable at model volumes as low as 100,000 to 200,000 cars per annum. It is significant here that BL has already announced that it will buy in the gearbox for the new LC10 from VW. Further large reductions in the workforce will, of course, be necessary if the company moves towards assembly rather than manufacture of motor cars.

Government policy is the other condition which crucially influences BL's prospects of survival. The company will not survive into the mid-1980s unless government continues to support operating losses with the aim of preserving a modest and viable British-owned car manufacturing capability. If LC10 succeeds, this aim is realistic and the government's attitude to continuing operating losses will then show whether government has learnt that enterprise calculation in the private or public sector should not be determined by the consideration of short-run accounting profit and loss. More fundamentally, government is involved because, with overcapacity in the European car industry and with European car prices currently much lower than British prices, BL's new models will not profitably find their own way to market. By the mid-1980s, BL's market success will have to be politically sponsored and defended. If we leave the Common Market, the home market will have to be protected. If, as seems more likely, we stay inside the Common Market, the British government will have to negotiate favourable production quota arrangements for BL cars in an era when the European production of most kinds of consumer goods is likely to be cartelised. The problems of BL are increasingly ceasing to be problems which can be resolved by management at the enterprise level; these problems now require the exercise of political power. In this respect, BL's current problems are a paradigm of the broader problems of British manufacturing as a whole in the 1980s.

Appendix B, Production totals for selected BMC/BLMC models, 1958–81

TABLE 1   *Production totals^a for Austin A55/60 Farina and variants^c*

Financial^b year	Vehicles produced
1958–9	43,673
1959–60	88,674
1960–1	67,295
1961–2	68,756
1962–3	74,442
1963–4	62,089
1964–5	80,946
1965–6	76,895
1966–7	42,883
1967–8	62,250
1968–9	31,297
1969–70	22,988
1970–1	21,923
1971–2	6,535
1958–72	787,246^d

TABLE 2   *Production totals^a for Austin-Morris Mini and variants^c*

Calendar^b year	Vehicles produced	Calendar year	Milestones
1959	19,749	1959–65	1 million
1960	116,677	1959–69	2 million
1961	157,059	1959–72	3 million
1962	216,087	1959–76	4 million
1963	236,713		
1964	244,359		
1965	221,974		
1966	213,694		
1967	237,227		
1968	246,066		
1969	254,957		
1970	278,950		
1971	318,475		
1972	306,937		
1973	295,186		
1974	255,336		
1975	200,293		
1976	203,575		
1977	212,323		
1978	196,799		
1979	165,502		
1980	150,067		
1981	69,986		

TABLE 3 *Production totals[a] for Austin-Morris 1100/1300 and variants[f]*

Financial[b] year	Vehicles produced
1961–2	2,904
1962–3	97,649
1963–4	241,381
1964–5	279,599
1965–6	269,081
1966–7	185,191
1967–8	291,598
1968–9	268,280
1969–70	202,688
1970–1	220,685
1971–2	145,644
1972–3	117,162
1973–4	23,747
1961–74	2,345,609

TABLE 4 *Production totals[a] for Austin-Morris 'land-crab' 1800 and variants[g]*

Financial[b] year	Vehicles produced
1963–4	50
1964–5	25,395
1965–6	56,876
1966–7	33,828
1967–8	45,009
1968–9	42,766
1969–70	42,351
1970–1	53,739
1971–2	34,003
1972–3	37,831
1973–4	27,251
1974–5	8,548
1963–75	407,647

TABLE 5 *Production totals for Austin Maxi[h]*

Financial[b]/ calendar year	Vehicles produced
1968–9	23,294
1969–70	27,618
1970–1	39,210
1971–2	65,903
1972–3	64,057
1973–4	47,873
1974–5	41,745
1975–6	48,218
1977	34,085
1978	38,567
1979	27,490
1980	15,778
1981	12,435
1968–81	486,273

TABLE 6 *Production totals for Morris Marina[i]*

Financial[b]/ calendar year	Vehicles produced
1970–1	36,039
1971–2	155,817
1972–3	201,724
1973–4	155,071
1974–5	134,989
1975–6	137,913
1977	111,636
1978	105,667
1979	96,487
1980	24,959
1970–80	1,160,302

TABLE 7   *Production totals for Austin Allegro*[j]

Financial[b]/ calendar year	Vehicles produced
1971–2	1
1972–3	27,528
1973–4	106,256
1974–5	95,173
1975–6	125,420
1977	95,460
1978	86,177
1979	61,415
1980	42,443
1981	22,908
1971–81	662,781

TABLE 8   *Production totals for Princess*[k]

Financial[b]/ calendar year	Vehicles produced
1973–4	288
1974–5	20,476
1975–6	55,031
1977	47,955
1978	33,951
1979	37,128
1980	14,732
1981	15,381
1973–81	224,942

Notes to appendix B

[a] Totals are of world-wide production and include knocked-down kits originating in Britain which were assembled abroad. All production totals, except those for the Mini, were supplied by British Leyland in February 1982. I would like to thank Mr Clive Richardson (BL product affairs manager) who agreed to release these figures and Mr Ray Taylor (BL production planning and control) who abstracted the relevant totals from the Longbridge records. The series on Mini production totals reproduces figures which BL released to Rob Golding and which were originally published in Golding's 1979 book *Mini*.

[b] Most annual totals are of production in a company financial year. BMC's financial year ran from August to July up to and including 1966–7. BLMC's financial year ran from October to September for the years 1968–9 to 1974–5. BL production totals for 1977 and subsequent years cover a calendar year, January to December, as does the series on Mini production from 1959 onwards. The changes in the definition of the production year produce two long years of approximately 15 months. 1967–8 runs from July 1967 to September 1968 while 1975–6 runs from October 1975 to December 1976.

[c] The Farina styled Austin A55 was designated ADO 9 for design and development purposes. This model represents the zenith of BMC badge engineering. The Austin A55/60 was also sold in variant saloon (and sometimes estate) form under Morris, MG, Wolseley and Riley badges. Production totals for the A55/60 include the A55 van and pick-up commercial vehicles. These were not re-styled by Farina but shared major mechanicals with the saloon. From 1958 to 1972, the company produced 44,217 vans and 89,982 pick-ups.

^d Annual totals do not exactly add up to give the cumulative grand total because the annual totals exclude MG Magnettes which are included in the grand total. This discrepancy is not of great significance because the MG was a low volume variant; a grand total of 36,600 Farina Magnettes was produced.

^e The Mini was designated ADO 15 for design and development purposes. Total production figures include all badge engineered variants of the saloon and estate such as the Wolseley and Riley 'big boot' versions. The Mini was the first, and last, of BMC's new generation front-wheel drive cars to have a commercial vehicle variant. Production totals here include the Mini van and pick-up.

^f The 1100/1300 was designated ADO 16 for design and development purposes. Totals again include Austin and Morris saloons and estates along with the other variants badge engineered as MG, Wolseley, Riley and Vanden Plas.

^g The 1800 was designated ADO 17 for design and development purposes. Variants include not only all badge engineered 1800s such as the Wolseley 18/85 but also all 2200 six-cylinder cars which shared the ADO 17 bodyshell.

^h The Maxi was designated ADO 14 for design and development purposes. The Maxi was only sold with an Austin badge. Under BLMC's half-executed plan to differentiate the Austin and Morris Marques, Austin dealers were to sell front-wheel-drive cars while Morris dealers sold 'conventional' rear-wheel-drive cars.

ⁱ The Marina was designated ADO 28 for design and development purposes. On the British and European markets this car was sold under the Morris badge. In the United States the car was briefly and unsuccessfully marketed as the Austin Marina. Production totals for the Marina include the Marina van and pick-up commercial vehicles which shared many panels and all mechanicals with the saloon.

^j The Austin Allegro was designated ADO 67 for design and development purposes. The Allegro was a development of, and replacement for, the old 1100/1300 which had long been BMC's bestselling model.

^k The Princess was designated ADO 71 for design and development purposes. This car was effectively a rebodied 'land crab' 1800 which replaced the latter model. This new model was originally launched as the 18/22 in Austin, Morris and Wolseley badge engineered versions. After corporate reorganisation, from September 1975 the car was simply sold as the Princess.

Appendix C
The UK market for new cars, 1945–80

TABLE 1   *New car registrations in the UK and cars in use, 1946–79 (000)*

	New car registrations	Cars in use
	(i)	(ii)
1946	121·7	1807·1
1947	147·8	1983·5
1948	112·7	2002·2
1949	154·7	2178·4
1950	134·4	2307·4
1951	138·4	2433·2
1952	191·0	2564·7
1953	301·4	2824·8
1954	394·4	3172·9
1955	511·4	3609·4
1956	407·3	3980·5
1957	433·2	4282·4
1958	566·3	4651·0
1959	657·3	5080·5
1960	820·1	5650·5
1961	756·1	6113·8
1962	800·2	6706·2
1963	1030·7	7546·7
1964	1215·9	8436·2
1965	1148·7	9131·1
1966	1091·2	9746·9
1967	1143·0	10554·2
1968	1144·8	11078·0
1969	1012·8	11504·3
1970	1126·8	11801·8
1971	1334·7	12357·9
1972	1702·2	13022·8
1973	1688·3	13815·0
1974	1273·8	13947·9
1975	1211·7	14061·0
1976	1307·9	14372·8
1977	1335·3	n.a.
1978	1618·2	14417·0
1979	1731·9	14926·6

Source: SMMT, *Motor Industry of Great Britain*, 1980.

TABLE 2a   *Company shares of UK new car production, 1946-70 (%)*

	Ford	A-Nuffield BMC A-Morris	Standard	Rootes	Vauxhall	Others
	(i)	(ii)	(iii)	(iv)	(v)	(vi)
1946	14·4	43·4	11·6	10·7	9·0	11·0
1947	14·8	39·3				
1948	19·8	40·2				
1949	18·7	39·4				
1950	19·2	39·4				
1951	18·9	40·3				
1952	21·1	39·4				
1953	27·0	35·2				
1954	26·5	37·9				
1955	27·0	38·9	9·8	11·4	8·5	4·4
1960	26·8	39·5	11·2	10·0	9·1	3·4
1961	32·8	38·3	6·5	10·5	8·5	
1962	29·7	38·0	6·4	10·8	11·7	
1963	31·4	38·4	6·6	10·6	10·3	
1964	28·0	38·5	6·5	11·7	12·6	
1965	29·5	38·2	6·5	10·6	12·8	
1966	29·0	37·6	7·6	10·7	10·7	
1967	28·4	34·7	7·9	11·7	12·7	
1968	30·5	33·6	7·6	10·4	13·5	
1969	29·4	37·7	7·5	10·5	11·0	4·7
1970	27·3	35·8		13·3	10·5	

Sources: Maxcy and Silbertson (1959); Rhys (1972).

TABLE 2b   *Company shares of UK new car registrations, 1968–79 (%)*

	BL	Ford
1968	41	27
1969	41	27
1970	38	27
1971	41	18
1972	35	24
1973	31	22
1974	32	22
1975	30	21
1976	27	26
1977	25	27
1978	23	26
1979	23	28

Source: SMMT, *Motor Industry of Great Britain*, various years.

TABLE 3 *UK new registrations of selected models (total number and as per cent of all registrations)*

	1965	1966	1967	1968	1969	1970	1971	1972	1973	1974	1975	1976	1977	1978	1979
BMC Mini	104,000 9·5%	92,000 8·8%	82,000 7·4%	86,000 7·8%	68,000 7·0%	81,000 7·5%	104,000 8·1%	96,000 5·9%	96,000 9·8%	90,000 7·1%	85,000 7·1%	81,000 6·3%	60,000 4·5%	73,000 4·6%	83,000 4·8%
BMC 1100/1300	158,000 14·4%	152,000 14·5%	131,000 11·8%	151,000 13·7%	133,000 13·8%	133,000 12·3%	134,000 10·4%	102,000 6·2%	59,000 3·6%	8,000 0·6%	–	–	–	–	–
BMC 1800	22,000 2·0%	28,000 2·7%	27,000 2·4%	24,000 2·2%	29,000 3·0%	33,000 3·0%	39,000 3·0%	34,000 2·1%	32,000 1·9%	25,000 2·0%	29,000 2·4%	32,000 2·5%	(Princess) 30,000 2·3%	(Princess) 37,000 2·3%	–
BMC Maxi	53,000 4·8%	48,000 4·6%	34,000 3·1%	30,000 2·7%	31,000 3·2%	37,000 3·4%	43,000 3·3%	54,000 3·3%	53,000 3·2%	36,000 2·8%	27,000 2·2%	33,000 2·6%	26,000 2·0%	32,000 2·0%	–
BL Marina							41,000 3·2%	105,000 6·4%	115,000 6·9%	81,000 6·4%	79,000 6·6%	71,000 5·5%	66,000 5·0%	83,000 5·2%	62,000 3·6%
BL Allegro									29,000 1·1%	61,000 5·3%	63,000 5·3%	55,000 4·3%	56,000 4·2%	62,000 3·9%	60,000 3·5%
Ford Cortina	117,000 10·6%	127,000 12·1%	165,000 14·9%	138,000 12·5%	116,000 12·0%	123,000 11·4%	102,000 8·0%	187,000 11·4%	182,000 11·0%	131,000 10·3%	107,000 9·0%	126,000 9·8%	121,000 9·1%	194,000 11·3%	–
Ford Escort				98,000 8·9%	85,000 8·8%	96,000 8·9%	89,000 6·9%	141,000 8·6%	114,000 6·9%	92,000 7·2%	104,000 8·7%	134,000 10·4%	103,000 7·8%	114,000 7·2%	132,000 7·7%

Source: SMMT, *Motor Industry of Great Britain*, various years.

TABLE 4   UK new registrations by cubic capacity, 1960–79

	1960	1961	1962	1963	1964	1965	1966	1967	1968	1969
under 1100cc	362,000 45%	328,000 44%	324,000 41%	416,000 41%	538,000 45%	504,000 45%	444,000 42%	366,000 33%	357,000 32%	253,000 26%
1100–1300cc	71,000 9%	83,000 11%	84,000 11%	156,000 15%	168,000 14%	158,000 14%	173,000 16%	292,000 26%	330,000 30%	318,000 32%
1300–1400cc	6,000 ·8%	22,000 3%	27,000 3%	3,000 ·3%	3,000 ·3%	2,000 ·2%	2,000 ·1%	1,000 ·06%	1,000 ·06%	1,000 ·08%
1400–1600cc	214,000 27%	170,000 23%	174,000 22%	233,000 23%	264,000 22%	230,000 20%	128,000 12%	244,000 22%	153,000 14%	178,000 18%
1600–2000cc	48,000 6%	52,000 7%	94,000 12%	102,000 10%	125,000 10%	145,000 13%	245,000 23%	222,000 20%	208,000 19%	167,000 17%
2000–2500cc	39,000 5%	19,000 3%	16,000 2%	15,000 1%	14,000 1%	12,000 1%	18,000 2%	18,000 2%	19,000 2%	19,000 2%
TOTAL: all cc classes	805,000	743,000	785,000	1,009,000	1,191,000	1,122,000	1,065,000	1,117,000	1,117,000	987,000

	1970	1971	1972	1973	1974	1975	1976	1977	1978	1979
under 1100cc	261,000 24%	273,000 21%	301,000 18%	269,000 16%	240,000 19%	258,000 21%	250,000 19%	218,000 16%	253,000 16%	250,000 14%
1100–1300cc	365,000 33%	425,000 33%	520,000 31%	526,000 31%	396,000 31%	396,000 32%	432,000 33%	450,000 34%	541,000 33%	504,000 29%
1300–1400cc	1,000 ·09%	1,000 ·08%	1,000 ·06%	1,000 ·04%	1,000 ·08%	1,000 ·08%	1,000 ·08%	3,000 ·2%	13,000 ·8%	56,000 3%
1400–1600cc	132,000 12%	240,000 18%	317,000 19%	318,000 19%	230,000 18%	212,000 17%	247,000 19%	269,000 20%	342,000 21%	381,000 22%
1600–2000cc	185,000 17%	274,000 21%	388,000 23%	421,000 25%	281,000 22%	229,000 19%	263,000 20%	262,000 20%	299,000 18%	341,000 20%
2000–2500cc	21,000 2%	26,000 2%	64,000 4%	75,000 4%	62,000 5%	65,000 5%	57,000 4%	62,000 5%	80,000 5%	94,000 5%
TOTAL: all cc classes	1,097,000	1,302,000	1,663,000	1,688,000	1,274,000	1,223,000	1,321,000	1,335,000	1,618,000	1,732,000

Source: SMMT, *Motor Industry of Great Britain*, various years.

TABLE 5   *Import share of new car registrations, 1965–79*

	Total registrations (000)	Registrations of British manufactured cars (000)	Registrations of imported cars (000)	Import share of all registrations (%)	Import share minus tied imports (%)
	(i)	(ii)	(iii)	(iv)	(v)
1965	1,099	1,042	57	5·2	
1966	1,048	980	68	6·5	
1967	1,110	1,018	92	8·3	
1968	1,104	1,012	92	8·3	
1969	965	865	100	10·4	
1970	1,077	923	154	14·3	
1971	1,286	1,038	248	19·3	
1972	1,638	1,253	285	23·5	
1973	1,661	1,206	455	27·4	
1974	1,269	915	354	27·9	
1975	1,194	797	397	33·2	30·0
1976	1,286	798	388	37·9	31·0
1977	1,324	723	601	45·4	33·0
1978	1,592	807	785	49·3	35·0
1979	1,716	750	966	56·3	

Source: SMMT, *Motor Industry of Great Britain*, various years.

References

Bhaskar, K. N. (1979), The *Future of the UK Motor Industry*, London, Kogan Page.

Bhaskar, K. N. (1980), *The Future of the World Motor Industry*, London, Kogan Page.

Central Policy Review Staff (1975), *The Future of the British Car Industry*, London, HMSO.

Commons Expenditure Committee (1975a), (14th Report), *The Motor Vehicle Industry*, London, HMSO.

Commons Expenditure Committee (1975b), *The Motor Vehicle Industry, Evidence*, vol. I, London, HMSO.

Commons Expenditure Committee (1976), *Appendices to Minutes of Evidence*, Friedman, A. L. and Bhaskar, K., 'The Central Policy Review Staff Report on the Motor Industry: a critique', London, HMSO.

Daniels, J. (1980), *British Leyland: The Truth about the Cars*, London, Osprey.

Dunnett, P. J. S. (1980), *The Decline of the British Motor Industry: The Effects of Government Policy, 1945–1979*, London, Croom Helm.

Ensor, J. (1971), *The Motor Industry*, Harlow, Longman.

Friedman, A. L. (1977), *Industry and Labour: Class Struggle at Work and Monopoly Capitalism*, London, Macmillan.

Golding, R. (1979), *Mini*, London, Osprey.

Harrison, J. and Sutcliffe, B. (1975), 'Autopsy on British Leyland', *Bulletin of the Conference of Socialist Economists*, vol. 4, no. 1, February.

Maxcy, G. and Silbertson, A. (1959), *The Motor Industry*, London, Allen & Unwin.

Rhys, D. G. (1972), *The Motor Industry: An Economic Survey*, London, Butterworths.

Ryder, D. (1975), *British Leyland: The Next Decade* (abridged version of a report to the Secretary of State for Industry), London, HMSO.

SMMT (1976), *The Motor Industry of Great Britain*, London, Society of Motor Manufacturers and Traders.

Turner, G. (1971), *The Leyland Papers*, London, Eyre & Spottiswoode.

Turner, H. A. et al. (1967), *Labour Relations in the Motor Industry: A Study of Industrial Unrest and an International Comparison*, London, Allen & Unwin.

Index

Aaronovich, S., 78, 84, 87
acquisition of companies: by GEC, 155;
  Avery, 155, 156; overseas, 155–6;
  Shreiber furniture, 155, 156
AEG, 134, 156
AEI, 89, 133, 137, 138, 139, 140, 141,
  152, 154, 158, 160
America, 22, 23, 24, 56, 70, 134, 150,
  156
Appledore, 189
applied economics, 2–3, 16–18, 92–3
audio cassettes and video recorders,
  165, 166
Austin-Morris volume cars: dealer
  network, 233–4; home and export
  sales, 55, 229–38, 240–4, 256–7,
  164–6; plant closure, 262; plant
  utilisation, 244–5, 254–5, 262–3;
  productivity, 221–2, 254–8
Austin and Pickersgill, 51, 52, 207, 211,
  212
Australia, 15, 16, 56, 149, 150, 155,
  202, 217, 235, 236, 262
Avery, 155, 156, 171, 172

Bacon, R., 2, 3
balance of trade in manufactures:
  British, 6–7; general repercussion of
  adverse, 5–6
banks: importance relative to stock
  exchange lending, 59–61; loan
  practices in Britain and abroad,
  69–70, 72–4
Barber, J., 162, 226, 253, 265
Belgium, 46, 56, 182, 217, 237, 238,
  262
Bhaskar, K. N., 237, 238, 242, 245,
  246, 254, 262, 264, 265, 266
BICC, 138
big business: as segment of

manufacturing capital, xi; effect of
  merger boom on, 85–91; plant size
  in, 91; relation to banks and stock
  exchange, 73–6; size and growth of
  in Britain, 18, 31–3, 82–5, 88–9, 91
Blackaby, F. T., 16, 17
BL (1975–82): xii, 43, 57, 104, 107,
  109, 165, 179, 217–219, 259–68; car
  sales, 264–6; Edwardes's strategy,
  266–8; financial losses, 259–63;
  labour productivity, 257–8; Ryder's
  strategy, 263–6
BLMC (1968–75): xii, 54–7, 78, 105,
  217–68 passim; export demand
  problems 56–7, 237–9; home demand
  problems, 55–6, 231–5, 240; labour
  process control, 251–8; market
  failure, 239–45, 259; new model
  strategy, 225–9, profits and
  accounting practices, 246–50
BMC (1951–67): xii, 54–7, 217–25;
  export market problems, 56–7,
  230–1; home demand problems, 54–
  5, 229–35; labour process control,
  251–2; labour productivity, 221, 256;
  output expansion, 54, 219–21;
  production techniques, 220–4;
  profitability problems, 221–5
Board of Trade, 93, 139
Bolton Report (1971), 73, 74, 75
Bond, K., 167
Booz-Allen Report, 190, 199, 201, 214
Brazil, 182, 183, 189, 211
British Gas Council, 205
British Telecom, 161
British Thompson Houston, 134, 137
Brittan, S., 97, 183, 187
Brown, C. J. F., 17
Brunei, 205, 206
Bryer, R., 108

BSC, 107, 109

Cammell Laird, 189, 199
Canada, 12, 31, 56, 149, 155, 236
capacity utilisation: car industry, 218,
  219, 244–5, 257, 259, 261, 262, 267
capitalist economy in general: as object
  in theory of firm, 20–3; as object in
  theory of profit, 65, 66–7; in
  explanations of mergers, 77
capital investment: 2, 82; cost of
  capital, 67–8, 72; quality of capital
  equipment, 41–2; *see also* investment
cash flow: BLMC, 249–50, 259, 261
cash reserves, GEC: 153; contributions
  to earnings, 154; debts of AEI and
  EE, 154; sales of assets, 154;
  strategic importance of, 157
CBI, 75, 76
CEGB, 139, 148, 149, 173
Central Policy Review Staff, 42, 46,
  218, 221, 227, 233, 234, 243, 254,
  255
Chandler, A. D., 23, 24, 25, 90
Channon, D. F., 11, 32, 88, 89, 90
Common Market, 4, 5, 9, 30, 94, 101,
  107, 150, 183, 268
Commonwealth, 15, 56, 135, 150, 155,
  236
conditions of enterprise calculation,
  x-xi, 28–30; *see also* labour process,
  market structure, financial
  institutions, government
consumer products, GEC: audio-
  cassettes and video recorders, 165,
  166; complete kitchens, 163; failure
  to export, 164; relative failure in
  1970s, 162–3; television, 162, 164,
  165, 166; washing machines, 163–4,
  166
cost-competitiveness, 12–15
costs, of car production, 223, 224, 227,
  240, 243–4, 255, 256, 264, 281
crossbar telephone system, 160
Cutler, A. J., x, 20, 21

de-industrialisation, 1, 2–3
demand fluctuations, in Britain, 47,
  97–8
demand linkage: in shipbuilding, 179,
  191–6
Denmark, 56, 182, 183, 203
Department of Economic Affairs, 93

Department of Scientific and Industrial
  Research, 182, 190, 213
Department of Trade and Industry, 93,
  214
devaluation, 6, 13
dividends: BLMC, 248; GEC, 142
Douglas, K., 208, 210
Dow, J. C. R., 97

economic planning, in Britain, 93
economic theory, x, 18–22, 77
Edwardes, M., 266
EEC, *see* Common Market
efficiency indicators: car industry, 218,
  251–8; GEC, 141; shipbuilding, 195–
  6
electrical engineering: early history and
  American capital 134, 135; effects of
  Second World War, 135; importance
  of change, 157; import penetration,
  149–50; international cartel, 134,
  135, 138; Monopolies Commission
  and government policy, 135, 139,
  172; Research and Development
  expenditure, 162
Eltis, W. A., 2, 3
employment: in manufacturing sector,
  6; in nationalised industry, 109; in
  specific labour processes, 42–3; *see
  also* labour
English Electric, 81, 133, 137, 138, 139,
  140, 141, 152, 154, 158
enterprise strategy: 25–8; and
  investment appraisal, techniques,
  25–7, 67, 101–9; BMC strategy of
  expansion, 219–21; BLMC new
  model strategy, 227–9, 245, 252–3;
  BL post-nationalisation strategy, 262,
  263, 264, 266; GEC, 166–8, 175–6;
  shipbuilding enterprise strategies,
  204–13
enterprise structure: in Chandler, 23–5
enterprise v. industry: in labour
  process, 43; in little Neddies, 100
Ericsson, 161
explanatory frameworks for
  manufacturing performance: 16–34;
  conditions of enterprise calculation,
  29–34; macro-economic, 16–18;
  management theory, 23–8; micro-
  economic, 18–22
Europe, 32, 51, 56, 57, 149, 150, 155,
  156, 182, 183, 185, 189, 190, 194,

204, 223, 234, 235, 237, 238, 239; *see also* Common Market

exports
car exports: 54–7, 217, 218, 229; declining export sales, 237–9, 259; new models, 242; Ryder forecasts, 265, 266; shifting overseas markets, 235–9
GEC: by product division, 148–9; growth of, 141, 147–8, 150; markets for, 150; of telephone systems, 161 manufacturers: British, 3–5, 9–16, 47–9; other countries, 9–14

factorial explanation, 17, 36
Fairchild, 159, 165
Fetherston, M., 14, 45
financial calculation, in merger boom, 79–82
financial institutions; as condition of enterprise calculation, xi, 1, 30, 46, 57, 58–9; contractual savings, 70–1; links with car manufacturing, 259–61; *see also* banks, stock exchange
financial losses: BL, 217, 218, 250, 259, 260, 261, 262, 265–6, 268; BLMC, 217; BMH, 217
financial management, in GEC: 157, 160, 161, 165, 166–7; and labour process, 169, 171; relation to enterprise strategy, 166–8, 175–6; right to fire, 169–70; wage bargaining, 169
Ford, 31, 43, 55, 221, 226, 227, 229, 232, 233, 234, 236, 237, 246, 267
France, 5, 9, 12, 15, 32, 37, 38, 51, 57, 60, 70, 88, 100, 149, 162, 182, 183, 190, 203, 205, 206, 237, 238
Friedman, M., 232, 246

Gale, B. T., 67, 108
GEC, xii, 27, 78, 81, 86, 90, 93, 94, 103, 133–78, 179
GEC, formation of, 134
Geddes Report (1966), 190, 197, 198, 199, 200, 201, 202, 203, 204, 212, 213, 214
General Motors, 23, 44, 236, 237, 246, 267
government policies (as condition of enterprise calculation): xi, 57, 130; British economic policies, 92–5;

corporation tax, 101–4; in other countries, 100; macro policy, 95–9; micro policy, 99–100; middle-range policies, 100–1; mergers, 77–9; nationalised industries, 104–9
government
and car industry: effect on demand fluctuations, 230; encouraged 1968 merger, 225; official inquiries, 218, 261, 263–6; nationalised, 261, 263; provision of funds, 261, 262, 263–5, 266, 268
and GEC: 171, defence expenditure, 174–5; effects of government policies, 172–3; effects on demand, 173; encouraged major British enterprise, 172
and shipbuilding: early links, 196; failure to identify problems, 180, 197–9, 201, 203, 207, 212, 213; financial assistance for, 199–201, 207, 208, 212, 214n; Geddes Report analysis, 197–8, 201; official inquiries, 180, 191, 213n
Greece, 189, 210, 211
growth of firm as theoretical object, 21–2, 77; *see also* mergers
Grundig, 165

Hannah, L., 84, 85
Harland and Wolff, 199, 205, 206, 207
Hawthorn Leslie, 204, 205, 212, 213
Hayes, R. H., 25, 27
heavy electrical plant, UK exports of and markets for, 149
Hitachi, 165, 201
Hogwood, B. W., 197, 200, 206
home car market: composition of, 231, 232–5; failure of new models, 240–2, 259; import penetration, 234–5, 241, 280; increase and fluctuations in, 229–30; limitations of 219, 229–39, 263, 265, 267; market share of, 218, 219, 258, 259, 265–7, 276; rate of growth of, 230–1, 245
Honda, 28, 73
Hong Kong, 149, 155
Hood, N., 31, 32, 33
Hu, Y. S., 58, 59, 70

Imberg, D., 100
imports: electrical engineering, 149–50; of cars, 234–5, 241, 280; of manufacturers, 3–5, 6, 7–9, 98

Inbucon, 55, 233
industrial production, in Britain, 7
industrial relations, *see* labour
Industrial Reorganisation Corporation
   99, 138
innovation: in car industry, 221, 223; in
   GEC, semi-conductors and telephone
   exchanges, 160–1; in shipbuilding,
   186, 188, 191
investment
   in car industry 218, 219, 220, 224; of
   public money, 261, 262, 263–5; post-
   merger shortage of funds, 227, 228,
   231, 239
   in shipbuilding: lack of, 179, 191,
   195; government encouragement,
   197, 198, 200; *see also* capital
   investment
Italy, 10, 56, 187, 217, 234, 237, 238,
   239, 262

Japan, 4, 9, 12, 26, 30, 52, 60, 61, 70,
   100, 135, 149, 162, 182, 187, 189,
   194, 202, 203, 205, 261

Kanter, R. M., 24
Kay, J. A., 84, 103
Kilpatrick, A., 35, 36
King, M. A., 102, 103
Kodak, 26, 27

labour
   in car industry: bad working
   practices, 218, 219; exaggerated
   effects of, 253–4, 255–6, 257;
   methods of labour control, 227,
   251–4, 256; poor industrial relations,
   245, 251; redundancies, 262, 263,
   264; size of workforce; 218, 222, 256,
   257, 258, 263
   in GEC: employee remuneration,
   141, 151; methods of labour control,
   168–71; redundancies, 152, 170, 171;
   size of workforce, 151–2, 153;
   turnover, 141, 168; union structure,
   169, 170; working practices, 168
   in shipbuilding: 179, 189, 191, 198,
   204
labour costs: international, 38–9; effect
   on tradeshare, 45
labour process (as condition of
   enterprise calculation): xi, 1, 29; and
   demand management, 95–9; and size

of plant, 91; in Britain, 34–47;
   output comparisons, 42–4; strikes,
   34; work practices and their effects,
   34–46, *see also* labour
labour productivity: 2, 65; in advanced
   countries, 7, 37–8; in Britain, 7,
   37–42; *see also* productivity
Leyland Motors, 225–7
Liberty Ships, 209, 210
London and Overseas Freighters, 51,
   52, 209, 210, 211

management
   in car industry: 218, 220, 221; of
   Leyland motors, 225–6; post-merger,
   252, 253, 254–5, 257, 265, 266, 268
   in GEC: 136, 140; EE and AEI, 137,
   140
   in shipbuilding; 179, 191, 198
manufacturing sector: in Britain, 3–5;
   growth rates, Britain and EEC, 40;
   market place performance, 2–16
Marconi, 174
Maritime Fruit Carriers, 206, 207
marketing function: 46, 47; in cars,
   55–7; *see also* exports and home car
   market
market, for cars, *see* home car market
   and exports
market structure (as condition of
   enterprise calculation): xi, 1, 29,
   47–58, 98; as problem for
   nationalised industries, 107;
   differentiated national demand, 48,
   49–55; problems of international
   distribution, 53–7
Marriott, O., 133, 152
Mavroleon, B., 51, 209, 210
Maxcy, G., 221, 224, 243
Meeks, G., 60, 61, 72, 81, 82, 86, 87,
   140
mergers: 22, 46; and government
   policies, 77, 78–9, 99; as cause of
   increasing concentration, 82–5;
   explanations of, 76–81; in car
   industry, 217, 218, 219, 220, 225–6,
   246; in shipbuilding, 198, 205, 213n;
   in Japan, 202; of GEC, 134, 135,
   137–8, 139, 141, 155, 170; results of
   merger boom, 85–91
Metropolitan Vickers, 134, 137
Ministry of Technology, 139, 225
Mitsubishi Heavy Industries, 201, 202

models, of new cars, 228, 239–42, 245, 263, 265, 266, 267, 270–2, 277
Monopolies Commission, 135, 139, 172, 225
monopoly, 85
Morris, 217, 218, 219, 228, 233, 234, 235, 245
motor bike industry, British and Japanese, 27–9, 73
motor car industry, 42–6, 54–7, 98, 109, 217–81
multi-divisional organisation: in management theory, 23–25; adoption in Britain, 89–90
multi-national companies: xi, 30, 31: British, 11, 31, 32, 88–9; American, 31, 32, 43, 44–5

National Coal Board, 204, 205
National Economic Development Council, 14, 99, 100, 106
National Enterprise Board, 105
nationalised industries: xi, 67; nationalisation of manufactures in 1970s, 104; control and direction of, 104–9; *see also* government
Nelson, Lord, 135, 172
new car registrations, 275, 277–8
New Zealand, 15, 16, 155, 236
non-price characteristics of manufacturing goods, 13–5, 46–7, 97, 190, 195
North America, 56, 235, 236, 239
North Sea Gas, 205
Norway, 182, 183, 187, 190

oil crisis, 198, 207, 230, 231, 245
output
    car industry: 218, 219, 220, 221, 222, 223–4, 241, 242, 262, 270–3; causes of output loss, 253–5; Ryder Report forecasts and after, 264–5, 268
    GEC: difficulties of measurement, 143–4; value of, by division, 146–7; value of, total, 144–5

Pallion, 189
Parsons, C. A., 149, 154
Philips, 158, 159, 161, 165
Plessey, 81, 138, 160, 161, 165
Post Office, 173
Prais, S. J., 31, 34, 42, 79, 82, 91
Pratten, C. F., 31, 39

price competitiveness: of shipbuilding, 190, 195, 201, 203; non-price factors, 190, 195
pricing of cars, 223, 231, 236, 244, 268
product specialisation, British, 11–12, 13–14
productivity, car industry, 219–20, 221, 222, 255–8, 264, 268
profit
    car industry: achieved by accounting practices, 246–9; 1950s and 1960s, 220, 221, 222, 223, 224–5; small post-merger, 227, 239, 240, 243, 244, 246, 247, 249, 260, 265–6, 267, 268
    GEC: 133, 136, 137, 139, 140–3, 168, 169
    shipbuilding: 195, 199, 211, 213
profits: accounting profit in Britain, 61–4; in other advanced countries, 63–4; interpretations of declining, 64–7; maximisation, 19–22, 142, 176; variably defined, 21–2

rate of return on capital: car industry, 246, 263, 264; GEC, 154
redundancies, *see* labour
return on investment (appraisal technique), 25–7, 67, 107–9
Reyrolle-Parsons, 138, 149
Rochdale Report, 186, 213
Rowthorn, R. E., 108
Ryder, D., 57, 107, 218, 227, 242, 246, 248, 250, 261, 263, 264, 265, 266

sale of cars, 217, 218, 229, 230, 240–3, 244–5, 248, 250, 253, 257, 259, 265, 266, 267
Schreiber, 156, 163
Scott Lithgow, 189, 206
segments of manufacturing capital: xii; *see also* big business, multi-national companies, nationalised industries, small business
Shell, 204–6
shipbuilding industry: xii, 49–53, 179–216; decline of, 180–2, 183–4, 187–8, 193, 203, 212; output of, 180–1, 182, 183, 187–8, 192–4, 208, 210; policies of other countries, 201–3; production in other countries, 182–3, 187, 189, 190, 194, 210; reason for decline of, 179, 184; relation to UK shipowners, 179–80, 191–6, 200, 201,

203, 206, 209–11, 212; structure of,
179, 191, 194, 195, 198, 213n; world
output of, 181, 187, 188
Shipbuilding Industry Board (SIB),
198, 199
ships: demand for, 179–80, 184–8, 189,
191–6, 201–2, 204, 208–11, 213;
design of, 190, 194, 205, 208, 209–10;
size of, 184–8, 190, 191, 197, 201,
204, 205, 206, 208, 209, 210
ship types: bulk carriers, 184, 185, 187,
190, 194, 203, 204, 208, 209; cargo
vessels, 184, 186, 187, 190, 194,
208–11; chemical carriers, 188, 190,
194; combined carriers, 185, 186;
container ships, 186, 188, 190; ferry
boats, 187, 194; liquefied gas
carriers, 186, 188, 190, 194, 204–6;
ore carriers, 184, 185, 194; passenger
ships, 194, 197; roll on/roll off ships,
186, 204; specialised, 186–7, 189,
190, 194, 197, 204, 206, 208;
standard, 207–11; tankers, 184, 185,
187, 190, 193, 194, 197, 198, 203,
204, 206, 207, 208
Siemens, 134, 137, 159
Singh, A., 2, 3, 17
Slater, J., 81, 86
small business: xi, 33–4, 74;
constrained by bank lending
practices, 73–6
Sobell, 136, 164
social factors, ix–x, 17, 142, 175
Sony, 26, 27
South Africa, 16, 149, 155
South Korea, 182, 183, 187, 189
Spain, 56, 183, 187, 189, 217, 237, 239,
262
Standard-Triumph, 217, 218, 225, 226
steel industry, 108, 109
STC, 160, 161, 165
stock exchange: importance to
manufacturing, 59–61; new issue
market, 71–2; secondary market and
merger boom, 76–91
Stokes, D., 226, 227, 253, 264
strikes: in British manufacturing, 34; in
car industry, 219, 251, 252, 256; *see
also* labour
Strowger, 160, 173
success indicators: for firm (GEC),
140–3; for society as whole, 142, 175
Sunderland, 52, 189, 210

Swan Hunter, 205, 206, 207, 213
Swan Maritime, 206–7
Sweden, 182, 183, 189, 203

television, 162, 164, 165, 166
Texas Instruments, 158
Thatcher, M., 109, 142, 170
Thirlwall, A. P., 6, 17
Tomlinson, J., 95
Treasury, 66, 93, 105
Turner, G., 226, 227, 228, 240, 242,
243, 244
turnover, GEC in 1970s, 141

UCS, 199
UK, 31, 32, 33, 37, 38, 39, 42, 45, 50,
59, 60, 65, 70, 71, 141, 146, 147, 148,
149, 150, 151, 152, 155, 158, 159,
164, 168, 174, 175, 179, 180, 181,
182, 183, 187, 188, 189, 190, 191,
192, 193, 194, 195, 200, 203, 206,
207, 212, 213, 214, 218, 221, 231,
232, 233
USA, 12, 15, 22, 31, 32, 39, 41, 45, 60,
64, 66, 77, 83, 135, 149, 150, 155,
159, 182, 191, 204, 236, 237

Volkswagen, 54, 55, 224, 231, 236, 237,
239, 246, 268
volume car production, 217, 218, 221,
223, 224, 231, 234, 235, 237, 238,
239, 240, 241, 242, 243, 244, 245,
252, 254, 255, 257, 262, 263, 264,
265, 266, 267

washing machines, 163–4, 166
Weinstock, A., 90, 93, 133, 136, 138,
139, 152, 154, 164, 166, 167, 168,
169, 170, 171, 173, 174, 227
Welsh Ore Carriers, 210
West Germany, 5, 9, 12, 15, 30, 31, 32,
33, 37, 38, 41, 45, 46, 51, 54, 57, 60,
61, 64, 70, 88, 95, 98, 135, 149, 162,
182, 183, 187, 189, 190, 203, 230,
231, 234, 237, 238, 261
Williamson, O. E., 18, 20, 22
Wilson, H., 59, 66, 69, 71, 73, 75, 76,
225
Winter, S. G., 20
Wood, A., 66
Woolwich, 152, 170, 171, 227
work practices, *see* labour
world trade: size of, 184; constitution
of, 184